Recovering the Frontier State

Recovering the Frontier State

War, Ethnicity, and State in Afghanistan

Rasul (Bakhsh) Rais

LEXINGTON BOOKS

A division of
ROWMAN & LITTLEFIELD PUBLISHERS, INC.
Lanham • Boulder • New York • Toronto • Plymouth, UK

LEXINGTON BOOKS

A division of Rowman & Littlefield Publishers, Inc.
A wholly owned subsidary of The Rowman & Littlefield Publishing Group, Inc.
4501 Forbes Boulevard, Suite 200
Lanham, MD 20706

Estover Road
Plymouth PL6 7PY
United Kingdom

British Library Cataloguing in Publication Information Available

Library of Congress Cataloging-in-Publication Data

Rais, Rasul Bukhsh.
  Recovering the frontier stage : war, ethnicity, and state in Afghanistan / Rasul
Bakhsh Rais.
     p. cm.
  Includes bibliographical references.
  ISBN-13: 978-0-7391-0956-4 (cloth : alk. paper)
  ISBN-10: 0-7391-0956-1 (cloth : alk. paper)
  1. Afghanistan—Politics and government—2001– 2. Ethnicity—Afghanistan. 3.
Afghanistan—Ethnic relations. I. Title.
  DS371.4.R34 2008
  958.104'7—dc22   2007046975

Printed in the United States of America

∞™ The paper used in this publication meets the minimum requirements of
American National Standard for Information Sciences—Permanence of Paper
for Printed Library Materials, ANSI/NISO Z39.48-1992.

This book is dedicated to the peoples of
Afghanistan, who have struggled endlessly
with all the power they had and the sacrifices
they could make to establish peace,
rebuild their homeland, and make it
worth living and dreaming for.

Contents

Preface

Ravaged by wars over the last three decades, Afghanistan has struggled to find peace and stability in the face of serious internal and external challenges, including its history, demography, geography, and global power politics. This book examines the effect of a continuous state of war on Afghanistan from various angles. Placing particular emphasis on how multiple conflicts shaped the question of ethnic identity, quest for empowerment, and political fragmentation, the book seeks to explain the structural impediments in reviving the Afghan state.

It is argued that the state of war has added to the complexity of problems in the context of rebuilding state and nationhood in a fractured multiethnic society of Afghanistan. The increased polarity between various ethnicities and power groups has also reduced the likelihood of restoring the old social balance that provided stability to the country for generations. Moreover, one cannot be too sanguine about the prospects of a fresh social contract among Afghanistan's diverse, and often competitive, social groups on the fundamental questions of power, legitimacy, state and institution building, without long-term positive engagement of international community.

This book places Afghanistan's political and security issues in a global and historical framework, analyzing its position as a "frontier state" and how that position has determined its tragic path from an isolated kingdom to a battleground of the deadliest conflicts of our time. Although many diverse forces—internal groups and external actors—have contributed to this dismal transformation, we should not forget that the last and the most disastrous episode of the cold war took place in the deserts and mountains of Afghanistan.

The conflict in Afghanistan has generated a considerable amount of global academic interest and scholarship. One of the most absorbing questions that the community of Afghan scholars, regardless of their fields of inquiry, has tended to focus on is how a country that was historically on the margins of the world system came to occupy a central position in the cold war rivalry between the two superpowers leading to its occupation by one, and fomenting of resistance against that occupation by the other. Another equally interesting area of inquiry is the issue of motivations and interests of the United States, which was compelled to invade Afghanistan to remove the Taliban regime under a set of completely different circumstances. Equally important for the historians, sociologists, and students of politics and security studies are the troublesome legacies of turning a tribal, agrarian country into a battleground of the two most modern armies. These legacies not only have gravely affected the Afghan state, state-society relations, and ethnic dynamics but have greatly made the country vulnerable to foreign intrusion and manipulation.

Afghanistan continues to be in the middle of a new war on terrorism that defines the American security framework in this part of the world. This has pushed the country into a new phase of dialectic politics of reconstruction under the foreign security umbrella and consequent Pashtun-based Taliban resistance to foreign intrusion. There is a genuine interest among the international community to rehabilitate Afghanistan as a normal conflict-free society. Afghanistan has never received the amount of international attention as it does today, because there is a primary concern that its troubles and weaknesses are not confined to its borders. There is a great deal of evidence to substantiate this assumption from the ruins of the World Trade Center to the simmering conflict in the western borderlands of Pakistan and beyond. It is in the self-interest of regional states, the United States, and the world community to facilitate the process of rebuilding state and nationhood in Afghanistan. Otherwise, the consequences of letting Afghanistan's state and society lay wasted on the wayside of history would be horrendous for the entire region.

This study endeavors to make a modest contribution to the global policy debate and academic discourse on what went wrong in Afghanistan and on how this country can be reconstructed in the interest of its people, regional states, and the world community at large. In doing so, it raises questions about how the war has affected the ethnic balance among various contending social groups and their capacity to recover their social energies and rebuild the new Afghanistan. There is no pretension of offering definitive answers to any of the troubling questions about the country; it is merely an effort to share a perspective and a view, in hopes that it will generate some interest about Afghanistan among scholars and policy makers around the world.

In writing this book, I have greatly benefitted from so many scholars, colleagues, students, and friends. It is my privilege to acknowledge their unfailing support and assistance without which I might have failed in completing this work. I would like to offer my thanks to a great number of Afghans and Pakistanis without mentioning all of them who have been involved in the Afghan conflict for the larger part of their careers or have watched and reported it to the media. Their insights greatly helped me understand Afghanistan better than perhaps I could have done on my own. I would especially like to thank Professor Rasul Amin, Haji Din Mohammad, Commander Hazrat Ali, Afrasiyab Khattak, Ajmal Khattak, Rahimullhah Yusufzai, Ismail Khan, Rustom Shah Mohmand, Abdullah Sahib, former director generals of Pakistan's Inter-Services Intelligence generals (retired) Assad Durrani, Ziauddin Butt, and Colonel Imam for the generosity of their time and frank comments. Mavara Inayat and Irfan Ashraf extended a great deal of assistance as well.

A number of students at the Lahore University of Management Sciences (LUMS) have offered their assistance without expecting any material reward. Prominent among these volunteers were Qasim Nauman, Usman Ahmad, and Zainab Saeed. Zainab has done a great job on cleaning the text of the book page by page. I cannot thank her enough. I am highly indebted to my research assistants, Mehreen Zaidi, Khawaja Zain, and Nasreen Akhtar. All of them have worked with a great sense of commitment researching material, making notes, and going through my rough drafts. Nasreen was the last research assistant in a row and did a great deal of work on the final version of the book.

I also gratefully acknowledge the continuing support of LUMS to this work and other research projects. And finally, let me thank Joseph Parry, Lynda Phung, and others at Lexington Books for their interest in this work and for bringing it out sooner than I had expected. I cannot leave this page without acknowledging the support and encouragement of my wife Khalida and my children, Faiza, Shan, and Sana; all of them have been deeply involved in my career in one way or the other.

Rasul Bakhsh Rais
Department of Social Sciences,
LUMS, Lahore
November 13, 2007

1

Introduction

The fall of the Taliban regime through the intervention of an international coalition of forces, authorized by the United Nations and led by the United States, has ended one of the most tragic episodes of Afghan history—an era during which some of the most abhorring atrocities were committed both by the religious militia as well as its adversaries from the Northern Front.[1] Since the launch of "Operation Enduring Freedom" in October 2001, the western countries have undertaken a difficult and complex task of nation and state building in a tribal, Islamic society that has been and remains on the periphery of world order. The intervention in Afghanistan to revive the state and its institutions and help the Afghans to rebuild their lives and economy was motivated by self interest, mainly the national security concerns of the intervening coalition. Anger and retribution over the tragic events of 9/11, and some reflective realization, though late, that Afghanistan in turmoil presented grave danger to the world peace with transnational terrorist organizations finding a safe sanctuary under the Taliban rule, influenced the American decision to invade the country.[2]

The American and Western involvement in Afghanistan is not unprecedented. The United States was a major player in the Mujahideen resistance against the former Soviet Union in the 1980s during the second wave of the Cold War that ended with the defeat of the Soviet Union in Afghanistan, and later the Soviet Union's disintegration. Having achieved remarkable triumph against its strategic and ideological rival, the United States and other countries that had supported Afghanistan's liberation war quit the scene rather too quickly. Frustration with the warring Mujahideen factions, shifting strategic priorities, and a fresh assessment of future threats in which Islamic fundamentalism and militancy, one of the spreading effects of the Afghan

1

war, changed the American posture toward Afghanistan from close alliance with the Mujahideen to benign neglect. The Islamic militants from the Middle East, Pakistan and Central Asia, and from other distant places quickly filled up the vacuum left by the great powers.[3] Afghanistan became the training ground, a sanctuary, and a safe base from where Islamic militants wanted to operate against their pro-West governments to realize their ideal of an Islamic state. Some of them, like Osama bin Laden, even had far-reaching goals of attacking the United States and Britain on their home turf; very few could consider such a threat serious enough to pay any attention to the collapsing state and society in Afghanistan until the tragedy struck in New York and Washington, D.C., on September 11, 2001. Perhaps this tragedy could have been averted if the western world had not left Afghanistan to fend for itself in a vacuum of power and statelessness.

The Afghans, having made great sacrifices in contributing to the fall of the Soviet empire, deserved a better deal than isolation and having been left in a state of anarchy due to feuding between the various warlords after the end of the Cold War era. The flight of the Western countries from the Afghan scene left a bitter taste of foreign involvement and a widespread feeling among more reflective, nationalist Afghans that they had unwittingly been a proxy in a confrontation scripted in foreign capitals. This sentiment is not out of place, as we can look at the Afghan tragedy with greater clarity and coolness than we could in the heat of the Cold War geopolitics. The bitter truth is that the people of Afghanistan, their territories, and the country as a whole became a battleground of superpower rivalry, in the making of which they had no role. An element of fate, wickedness of Afghan leaders, or perhaps their poor knowledge of world affairs, and the strategic confrontation of the two superpowers has made them the victims of a long cycle of unending war for the last thirty years.[4]

One of the most destructive dimensions of the Afghan war is the internal strife among factions organized around tribal, ethnic, religious, and ideological lines. With the caving in of the state, which had historically maintained some kind of balance and peace among different communities, the struggle for autonomy, power, and influence became so desperate that it resulted in the worst kind of communal and intergroup violence the country had ever seen. Afghanistan's history is replete with violent outbursts, but what the country experienced during the rise and reign of the Taliban was perhaps one of the most tragic periods both in its incivility and human degradation as well as in terms of its long-term effects on ethnic and social relations. In addition to the popular perceptions of the Taliban as the religious movement driven by the zeal of Islamic fundamentalism, the ethnic undertones of the movement cannot be dismissed as irrelevant to the analysis of its social support base. For the ethnic minorities, the Taliban was both a symbol of Islamic conservatism as well as a reflection of Pashtun ethnic chauvinism that aimed at recapturing political power and reasserting its dominance. We cannot understand the Afghan civil war exclusively in reference to religious dimension alone, which is one of the central forces in shaping the Taliban movement, but not the solitary one.

The Taliban's political slogans and apparent agenda of peace, stability, justice, ending warlordism, and creating national unity appeared to be attractive to many Afghans, even on the other side of the ethnic divide for a while.[5] The people of Afghanistan were exhausted with warfare, insecurity, and frequency of violence and found the Taliban a better alternative to the warlords that had divided the country into fiefdoms. But that honeymoon was very brief. The ethnic minorities closed their ranks and became unified to confront a common adversary in the Pashtun Taliban. While protecting their ethnic turfs, they portrayed the Taliban as "foreign" funded, trained, and equipped by neighboring Pakistan for its own strategic interests.[6] The national unity, peace, and stability that the Taliban promised were contested by the Tajiks, Uzbeks, and Hazaras as false and deceptive; these latter groups resolved to fight back to reclaim their territories and stake equal claim to power in Afghanistan. The ensuing turmoil further eroded the social capacities of the ethnic groups, conflict-ridden political factions, and discredited leaders of all political colors to rebuild their state and society.

A brief comment on the nature of the Taliban regime, leadership, and ideological makeup is necessary here to gain an idea about how Afghanistan lost its sense of direction and the traditional balance of power among various groups. The Taliban leaders, guided by the spirit of creating an Islamic state in the image of Deobandi interpretation of Islam mixed with Pashtun traditionalism, attempted to establish a highly centralized political order. All the commands flowed top down from Mullah Omar, the chief of the movement, to the lower rungs of clerical hierarchy and functionaries of the regime. The power structure was rigidly conservative in outlook, antimodern and anti-West in ethos and beliefs. A pan-Islamic feeling and a self-perception that the Taliban regime could play a vanguard role in supporting Islamic movements in other countries brought all kinds of militants from Central Asia, Pakistan, and the Middle Eastern countries into Afghanistan. Each foreign militant group in Afghanistan found the regime supportive of their respective religious and political struggles in their home countries. All states, perhaps with the exception of Pakistan, which supported the Taliban, became increasingly apprehensive about the fallout of a stable Islamic state in Afghanistan under the Taliban. Their fears about insurgency by the Islamist groups operating from Afghanistan were not unfounded.[7] Therefore, these states persistently raised questions about the wisdom of Pakistan to lend support to the religious militia, which Pakistan continued to deny in the face of considerable evidence.[8]

The United States and Western powers first saw in the Taliban some vague prospects for stability, but soon realized the dangers of helping a militant

Islamic movement that had the potential to spell disaster throughout the region.[9] It took them longer than it should have to recognize how dangerous Afghanistan had become under the Taliban. Not even the attacks on U.S. naval vessel S.S. Cole and two embassies in East Africa caused any major shift in U.S. policy except lobbing off cruise missiles in August 1998 at the hideout of Osama bin Laden and seeking Pakistan's collaboration to capture him. Never was the U.S. security establishment clear about the ability of Mr. Laden and his underground network of transnational militants to strike at the symbols of its power and prestige at home ground.[10] The tragedy of 9/11 established beyond a doubt two facts of international life in the emerging post–Cold War world order. First, ungoverned spaces in failed or collapsing states can become secure and comfortable zones for terrorists to wage their wars against the West and other states opposing their worldview if they are not filled with credible authority. Second, the United States, leading the Western world, can no longer define security in traditional narrow terms or confine its strategy to defending certain strategic zones against states, but it needs to extend defense to non-state actors in distant places, and employ its forces to change regimes and build new ones.

These considerations guided the American invasion of Afghanistan when it sought authorization from the United Nations and attempted to form a broad international coalition to remove the Taliban regime. Six years after U.S. forces landed in Afghanistan, it is nowhere close to completing the major task of state and nation building. Along with NATO, the United States continues to fight insurgency mainly in the Pashtun regions close to the border with Pakistan. There are troubling questions about a strategic failure in Afghanistan and how it will adversely affect stability and peace of the neighboring states.[11] Afghanistan, with all the international security and economic assistance that it has been receiving for the past many years, still remains within the zone of uncertainty. The peace and security with effective, functional state that the Afghans expected to achieve are not within their reach yet. Economic and political gains are only partial, and the reconstruction process too slow. There are genuine difficulties in building peace and reconstructing Afghan state and society, which cannot be described entirely as a post-conflict situation, as limited, unconventional war and counterinsurgency operations still continue.

Afghanistan has acquired a strategic position in countering terrorism and the Taliban movement throughout the region more for its weaknesses than strengths. Future stability and peace of the region hinges a great deal on the success of a stable and unified Afghanistan. Therefore, leaving the business of state and nation building unfinished is not a rational or prudent option. However, there can be a debate about setting the priorities of reconstruction, choice and adequacy of means, cultural or social relevance of policies, nature and extent of inclusion of social groups, questions of power sharing, and internal contestation in the process.

The purpose of this book is to engage in this debate with a focus on how thirty years of war has affected the Afghan state, ethnicity, ethnic balance among microsocial communities, and contestation over power. The basic argument of this book is that war has significantly altered the balance of social and political forces in Afghanistan, polarizing and strengthening ethnic, tribal, territorial, and religious identities. Fresh efforts to reconstruct the post-Taliban Afghan state will have to take into account ethnic rivalries, territorial fragmentation, and interests of regional and great powers that have influenced the pattern of internal conflict and territorial fragmentation in Afghanistan.

THEMES AND PROPOSITIONS

The fundamental question this book raises and tries to answer is; what effect has war had on Afghanistan as a nation, its ethnic communities, its state and institutions. The central premise of the book is that primordial ethnic identity and Islam emerged as powerful tools of social and political mobilization at the end of the long years of war. Islam and ethnicity, however produced two different types of resistance movements against the state that has had equally disastrous effects on the capacity of the Afghan state. The Islamic resistance of the Mujahideen targeted the Marxist state as a client of Soviet imperialism and played a critical role in delegitimizing it. Weakened by internal opposition, and finally left alone to defend itself after the collapse of communism, the communist Afghan state disintegrated. The state got destroyed in its early phase of modernization when its institutional base was infirm. The Marxist revolution, resistance, civil war among the Mujahideen factions, and the rise of the Taliban chipped away the structure of the Afghan state piece by piece. The warlords, ethnic fiefdoms, and transnational militants quickly filled the ungoverned spaces and found the vacuum of authority and power to their advantage.

This study covers three major themes—ethnicity, state, and war. Four sets of propositions predicate discussion on these subjects that run through various chapters. (1) The wars in Afghanistan have sharpened ethnic and regional identities that now present greater challenges than before to manage and govern a multiethnic society with each group having larger ethnic affiliations across the borders; (2) Political polarization and multilevel confrontations that evolved in the course of the wars have fragmented Afghan society, leaving a narrow space for social contact and political consensus; (3) The Islamic militants of Afghanistan from a wide variety of states that joined Afghanistan's wars under different motivation present a serious threat to its peace and stability, as they are down but not out; (4) Afghanistan has accumulated dangerous social, economic, and security legacies of wars that it cannot face on its own. The conflict consumed its indigenous social energies and traditional authority and institutions. In the absence of these prerequisites of revival, it requires long-term, effective, and positive engagement of its neighbors and international community to rebuild itself. Left on its own, the country may plunge back into civil war, intercommunal violence, and statelessness.

THE MAKING OF THE FRONTIER STATE

The idea of frontier is very interesting and much debated in American historiography, which argues that American "democracy and social progress and national mores have been chiefly, if unconsciously, the creation of frontiersmen, as these, in an epic sweep westward across the continent, successively wrested new free lands from wilderness and the Indians and there, 'as nowhere else in recorded history, set up institutions relatively free from coercion by either law or habit.'"[12] The frontier is a very distinctive idea that reinforced the "isolationist state of mind," and recognized the diversity of immigrant populations to promote a vigorous sense of nationalism. One may argue how much the United States was different in being a "new world" and how much it owed its civilization to European roots or the "old world," but there may be a great deal of agreement on how factors of geography and distance shaped its sense of uniqueness. It would be useful to make it clear that we do not wish to use the concept of the frontier state in the same sense or even draw the same meanings, as American historians do. However, we are tempted to use the frontier state as a geopolitical conception with the following characteristics: remoteness, existing on the margins of regional and global systems, weak authority structure, internal fragmentation and conflict among competing groups, transnational ethnicities, legitimacy of internal conquest, and preemptive and reactive intervention by neighbors. There is yet another dimension to the frontier character of Afghanistan, which is that the ethnic boundaries of its populations are shared by at least six states. Historically, Afghanistan emerged as a buffer state out of the territorial space vacated by old declining empires on the edges of two advancing European powers: Czarist Russia and Britain in the eighteenth century. Earlier, it served as the frontier of the Mughal Empire, and even before that of the Delhi Sultans.[13]

The areas which now comprise Afghanistan were always at the crossroads as well as the frontiers of ancient empire-building in the region; it was both a gateway to foreign armies as well as a source of invasions. These areas changed hands with the rise and fall of the Turkoc-Mongol and Persian empires. It was only in the eighteenth century that, after the decline in power of these empires, the Abdali Pashtun tribes founded the Afghan kingdom in 1747 under the leadership of Ahmad Khan. He first united other Pashtun tribes and then, with increasing power, conquered Hazara, and Uzbek and Tajik areas, declaring himself the Shah (king).[14]

Afghanistan essentially remained a weak state. The authority structure at the top, as well as the state institutions, were rooted in social traditions of the country and reflected vertical hierarchies. Unfortunately, while Afghanistan suffered the humiliation of colonial control, it did not receive any positive benefits, which countries like India under the direct British rule did. Western education, modern professions, industry, capital accumulation, and a long political struggle for independence against the *Raj* created new sectors in the Indian society which have aided the process of state formation. Afghanistan was hardly touched by these changes and hence was unable to reap the limited benefits its neighbors extolled from colonialism. But absence of these benefits generated among the Afghans other qualities: independence and the will to resist outside control.

External linkages of the Afghan state with the international system were not much help in taking root in the society, either. Dependence on foreign aid isolated the state from society. Individuals and social groups interacted with the state not as citizens in any modern sense but as members of a tribe, ethnic community, religious sect, or other kinship networks. These traditional institutions maintained their own political space and allowed the state limited access to its members. A political culture based on the autonomy of the tribes and other social groups constrained the growth of the state.[15] Therefore, the Afghan state never emerged as a focal point in Afghan citizens' identity.[16] It remained underdeveloped both in terms of modern institutions, with the exception of the armed forces, as well as in its political capacity to extend direct and effective control over all subjects and territories.

The introduction of the 1964 constitution opened up Afghan politics for the first time as it marked the beginning of a relatively free debate on national issues. New press laws allowed the political groups to publish magazines and newspapers for articulating their points of view. With the parliamentary elections, new informal political organizations along leftist and Islamist lines emerged. However, the traditional power structure of Afghanistan remained unaffected by both the free debates in the parliament and its criticism in the press. Elections only legitimized the power of the tribal chiefs. Out of the 216 elected members, 146 were tribal leaders and next to them religious leaders constituted the largest professional group.[17] Monarchy retained all powers of the state. All laws passed by the parliament had to had sanction and approval of the king, which reduced the parliament to a debating forum. This experiment only sharpened the ideological divisions within the country primarily between Soviet-supported Marxists and the Islamists.

The central system of the state functioned on an oligarchic pattern through networks of patron-client relationships. Powerful and socially influential groups participated in the system to maintain their status. Informal power-sharing among elite groups, largely based on tradition, gave the political order stability and legitimacy.[18] Due to its exclusivity, the system remained closed. Recruitment to higher administrative positions and political roles was restricted to the influential members of the patrimonial elite.

The old power elite, satisfied with the distribution of power and autonomy in their local affairs, remained loyal to the system. Family ties among the elite and their overlapping participation into religious and social networks further promoted their integration into the power arrangements at the top. The ruling establishment of Afghanistan, like any other in the Third World, had a stake in preserving the lopsided distribution of power and privileges in the society, which came through ascription rather than personal achievement. In part, it was the underdevelopment of the civil society, evident in the absence of any organized protest, that the traditional institutions, and the groups operating them, maintained a monopoly over exercising social and political control.[19]

Autonomous structures of local authority have long existed parallel to the state.[20] They have proved capable of blocking access of the state to the local population in the critical areas of political power and identity of the individual. In this broad polarization of state-based power and local authority, two factors, inherent in the social and economic structures of Afghanistan, have frustrated the attempts to integrate the state with the fragmented society. The first factor relates to the organization of social and political power in the vast and autonomous periphery of the state. The *mullahs* (clerics), landlords, and tribal chiefs have exercised far greater influence than the state. Blood ties, kinship, tribal ties, and the hold on local economies have immensely contributed to the power of the nonstate societal elites. The local patron-client relationships and the exercise of authority, though within the bounds of tradition, has been socially accepted and generally perceived benevolent compared to an alien and intrusive image of the state.[21]

Second, the political economy of agricultural production has constrained the growth of the state. Since arable land and water resources were limited and scattered, agriculture remained largely subsistence-oriented.[22] Production was localized and just enough to sustain the local population, economic transactions or trade across the local boundaries did not develop.[23] Consequently, a national market system that could integrate the subsistence-oriented rural economies did not take off. Underdeveloped infrastructure further added to the fragmentation of the economy. With the construction of a few highways and the introduction of mechanized cultivation on a limited scale, agriculture began to commercialize in the decades of the 1960s and 1970s. But changes in agricultural economy were restricted to few areas and its benefits confined to influential landowners who had easy access to the government-sponsored loans.[24] The modern sectors of the economy, such as industry, commerce, and finance, did not show any growth either. The important thing to show is that the political economy based on agricultural production could not generate enough resources for the state to strengthen its central authority.[25]

The traditional political order of the "rentier" state,[26] based on somewhat elite consensus could not go on unchallenged. The selective modernization of the state apparatus through foreign resources brought forth a new class of administrators and intellectuals. This segment of the Afghan society, though small, highly influenced the political outlook of volatile young groups, who were socialized in a relatively modern atmosphere of the school. Social mobility and the prestige that the administrative and professional positions achieved served as a catalyst for the expansion and influence of modern educational institutions.[27]

The ideological orientation and the ethos of the groups that emerged from the modern school system directly clashed with the interests of the old power elites. Their aspirations for representation and a share in power per force challenged the traditional relations of authority. The attendant desire for political restructuring introduced a new intellectual discourse on competing ideas and ideologies. The debates and controversies concerning replacing the authoritarian system of monarchy primarily focused on socialism, democracy, and Islamism.[28]

These conflicting ideologies of the aspiring political groups within and outside the state might explain the origin of multipolar confrontations that have ravaged Afghanistan for the past thirty years. Two broader categories were the Marxism of the Parcham (banner) and Khalq (people), the two factions of the former Peoples Democratic Party of Afghanistan (PDPA), and Islamism of the radical Mujahideen groups.[29] Their ideological frameworks were distinctive in terms of the basis of claims to political power and contradictory visions of Afghanistan's political and economic restructuring. But these opposite ideological camps were never homogeneous even in their own ranks. Their inner factionalism that has been responsible for decades of conflict needs to be explained.

First is the issue of interpretation of Islam as a state and ideology, which beyond rhetoric, lacks consensus among the Islamic communities throughout the world. The Islamist Mujahideen groups were no exception.[30] The Marxist groups were unable to form coalitions anywhere, let alone in the political milieu of Afghanistan.[31] Class background, the socialization process of leaders, and the absence of a democratic, pluralistic political culture are some of the variables that help us explain confrontations among various ideological groups. Social and cultural orientations of the members of these groups were incompatible with the political values that would allow accommodation with those opposed to their beliefs.[32] Not surprisingly, they became poised to confront each other even in the preliminary stages of their formation.

The conflict and hostility along Afghanistan's nascent ideological camps sharpened more with the introduction of the electoral process under, by Afghan standards, the liberal constitution of 1964. Clear lines were drawn between the so-called modernists and the Islamists, who had their genesis in the polarization of 1920s, which was generated by the modernization program of King Amanullah.[33] It is necessary to state from the outset that neither of these camps was politically broad-based. They functioned more in the urban environment, and mostly among the politically aware and literate sections of the society. In each group there existed traditionalists and moderates, both of Islamic and secular variety, who favored a more gradualist approach to development and reform of the traditional institutions.[34]

This was the familiar pattern of ideological discourse witnessed in most postcolonial Islamic societies. The modernist camp was comprised of elements from nationalist, secularist, and Marxist groups. Although the motivations and social origins of these groups were different, their political interests converged on confronting the rising power of the Islamist groups, who were equally opposed by the conservative religious establishment for what they called their modern interpretation of Islam.[35] It was a rather grand coalition of diverse interests that developed more expediently, and was not adequately structured.

While modernization, development, and social reforms appeared to be the common political agenda of both groups, inherent social class contradictions remained unresolved. Each group waited for the opportune moment to outflank the other. This became apparent when the coalition captured power in 1973, under the leadership of Sardar Daoud, a former premier and member of the royal family.[36] He was a convenient choice of the modernist coalition in that he had earned the image of a true nationalist, and was credited with the expansion and modernization of the Afghan Armed Forces through the enormous Soviet assistance.

The Marxist groups that had existed independently were definitely encouraged by the growing partnership of the Soviet Union with their country, which was initiated by Daoud during his premiership (1953–1963). In the wake of increasing Soviet interest, activities of the left-wing groups were no longer confined to the barren intellectual debates of the drawing rooms. They found an audience in educational institutions and among the Afghan Army personnel that were trained in the Soviet Union and were consequently quite receptive to their political propaganda. The revolutionary strategy of the Marxist groups from the very beginning stressed a sort of united front of all the progressive sections of the Afghan society.[37] Recruiting and indoctrinating a cadre within the Afghan Armed Forces figured central in their political campaign. Otherwise, the obstacles to a mass revolutionary line abounded. The society at large was religious, conservative, and traditional in its values. Foreign influence, let alone the Soviet brand of socialism, was generally perceived as atheistic and anti-Islamic, and was considered an affront to the cultural sensibilities of a largely peasant society.[38]

The modernist elements felt that the political order established by the 1964 constitution helped the traditional elite to perpetuate their social and political control.[39] They also feared that the increasing power of the religious establishment was pressing the king to introduce Islamic laws, ban communist groups and sever ties with Moscow. Daoud, who had been excluded from participating in elections,[40] exploited the frustration of the military and bureaucratic circles and staged a coup in 1973 that put an end to the so-called democratic experience. Daoud represented the ethos of a state created by the middle class and military establishment. The modernist coalition under Daoud, which also included socialists, in the beginning had three objectives: block the Islamists from gaining power, end the monopoly of oligarchic elite over state institutions, and modernize the country.[41] It will be out of place to go into detail the conflicts and contradictions within this coalition, but at the end Soviet-supported military officers and the Marxists murdered Daoud and staged a successful revolution on 27 April 1978, that opened a new tragic chapter in the political history of Afghanistan.[42]

While in power, the new socialist elite demonstrated a serious lack of pragmatism. Moreover, their approach to restructuring the state was based on a sort of textbook revolutionary thinking, and Marxist romanticism rather than practicality. Their political ethos expressed in rhetorical terms and their obsession with creating new social relations put the Marxists on a collision course with the mass society.[43] The collision occurred before the Marxists had achieved complete control over all the institutions. They had not managed to develop any political consensus, even among themselves. Conversely, the leaders of the PDPA thought that by dominating the coercive institutions at the top, they would effectively suppress the opposition, and resistance from, what they frequently referred to as the "vested interests," and "reactionary" elements. Attempts to subordinate the state and society to a Leninist party through coercive means were, indeed, an old practice, which backfired in the Islamic social and cultural environment of Afghanistan.

Two factors, largely missing in the political analysis of the Marxist regime, added to its difficulties. First was the fact that the revolution was primarily a political change at the top through a military coup d'etat. Even within the armed forces, there was hardly any consensus on the meaning and direction of the revolution. The so-called revolutionary legitimacy, quite often cited in the case of such authoritarian regimes in the Third World, did nothing to win the hearts and minds of the Afghan population.[44] If social structures are important, and they are, in the acceptance and stability of the power elite, then the Marxist rulers of Afghanistan were definitely outsiders. They had neither social claims to power nor any basis for making a convincing political case for being where they were. In the context of Afghan political culture, they were nonentities. Military leaders in many Third World countries crashed the doors of political power but many of them spoke in a political idiom that was compatible with the common values, or at least not openly too offensive to popular beliefs. In Afghanistan, popular perceptions of the revolution, Marxists, their ideology and links with Moscow were not conducive for even preliminary political communication with the masses.

Second, the heavy reliance on the application of state power against the rebellious masses, now self-evident, was counterproductive.[45] Many of the influential elements of the Afghan Marxist power structure were Stalinist in their approach to controlling dissent. Instead of initiating a meaningful dialogue in vernacular political vocabulary, they strengthened intelligence agencies, established torture cells, filled prisons beyond capacities, and resorted to general warfare against the common man. This was not an appropriate strategy of achieving transformation of the country. Nor was it capable of offering any basis of integrating the civil society into the new political order.

The administrative apparatus of the state, which was never strong, began to disintegrate in the wake of mass uprisings. Revolt grew stronger and stronger with each violent action of the *Khalq* functionaries. The popular resistance to the regime led by the socially influential sections of the society posed a serious challenge to the survival of the Marxist state. Fearing its collapse, the Soviet Union substantially increased its level of support. It poured more weapons and stationed more advisers to stabilize the shaky revolution and protect the insecure Afghan Marxists. The open collaboration and political identification with the Soviet Union further alienated the Afghan Marxists from mass society.

The gulf between the oppressive Marxist state and the civil society widened further with the Soviet intervention. The resistance parties, local groups, and the people rightly blamed the communists for occupation of their country and the cruelty that followed. Afghanistan got caught in a vicious conflict, which was shaped by internal confrontation and also by the strategic competition of the two great powers. Islam and nationalism inspired and mobilized the masses to take up arms against the state directly controlled by a foreign power. A "culture of *Jihad*"[46] (holy war) that had deep roots in the Afghan social tradition flourished with foreign arms, money, and political support, which after defeating the Soviet Union continues to fuel resistance against the international coalition led by the United States.

GEOPOLITICS OF THE FRONTIER STATE

Afghanistan occupies a central position at the junction of three strategic regions—central Asia, south Asia, and southwest Asia. Being landlocked, the country has remained relatively isolated from the regional and international systems. It was the colonial expansion of Czarist Russia and British India from opposite directions in the middle of the nineteenth century that brought Afghanistan to its strategic thinking. The British in India were too fearful of the Russian expansionism beyond Central Asia. They thought leaving Afghanistan alone would push it under the Russian influence. The British were very concerned about the Russian intention toward their colonial possessions in the Indian subcontinent.[47] To checkmate the Russian advance they adopted what is known as forward deployment policy in the northwest of India. The British established a formidable defense infrastructure in Balochistan and the North-West Frontier region, which now form part of Pakistan.

The central objective of the British policy was to keep Russia out of Afghanistan at any cost, even if it required military intervention. The British invaded Afghanistan in 1839–1842 and then again in the later part of the century in 1878–1880 to keep Afghanistan under its sphere of influence. The fierce resistance from the Afghans to the presence of Anglo-Indian forces inflicted massive casualties on the invaders and finally changed the British strategy. Britain had realized that internal domination of Afghanistan would be difficult, costly, and uncertain. The goal of keeping Russia out could easily be achieved by handling Afghanistan's foreign affairs and recognizing and strengthening internal autonomy of the Afghan rulers. In its reformed strategic vision, Afghanistan emerged as a middle space or a buffer between Russia and British India, separating the two from having direct territorial contact. Both the empires wanted to avoid direct contact between their colonies, and with the passage of time, reached a consensus on the buffer status of Afghanistan.

One of the most important aspects of buffering Afghanistan was to settle its boundaries, so that no power took advantage of undefined borders. The most notable of the boundary agreements was the Durand Line Border Agreement that British India drew with Afghanistan in 1893 settling the empire's eastern and southern frontiers.[48]

Afghanistan regained full sovereignty in 1919 after a brief war with British India. The timing of this declaration was propitious. The First World War had exhausted Britain, and the Russians were still preoccupied with consolidating their revolution. Russia, however, was the first to recognize Afghanistan's independence and offer her assistance and enter into a treaty of friendship.[49] The British also accepted Afghanistan's independence by concluding a new treaty at Rawalpindi the same year.[50] A number of European states began to assist Afghanistan, but the foreign aid was not enough to support the modernization program that the country's new modernist ruler Amanullah Khan had on his cards.

The departure of the British from the Indian subcontinent in 1947 drastically altered the geopolitical environment of Afghanistan and also later shaped its new alignments in foreign policy. It resented the inclusion of Pashtun areas into Pakistan although the Pashtuns of British India opted for Pakistan through their free will, which they expressed in a referendum that was conducted by the British. According to the partition plan all areas of British India had to join either India or Pakistan. The Pashtun nationalists on both sides of the border had demanded a third choice: independence for the Pashtuns. Failing to achieve this objective, the Afghan rulers raised the issue of the Durand line, the boundary settled by the British and Afghan king Amir Abdul Rehman in 1893. They also demanded creation of a Pashtunistan state by separating tribal areas of Pakistan. Isolated and poor, Afghanistan had neither the military power nor any external support to reshape its boundary with Pakistan.

Afghanistan's international environment changed for the better with the coming of the Cold War and the strategic rivalry between the Soviet Union and the United States in 1950s. Pakistan's decision to join the Western alliances against communism brought Afghanistan closer to the Soviet Union. Moscow extended large-scale economic and military assistance to Afghanistan, and as a rebuke to Pakistan, began to support Kabul's claims against Islamabad. Realizing Afghanistan's position as a historic buffer, now between the free developing world and communist expansionism, the United States also provided a significant amount of economic assistance to Afghanistan but declined requests for arms, which it feared could be used against her ally, Pakistan. Heavy dependence of Afghanistan on external sources can be explained from the fact that from 1955 to 1987 the former Soviet Union gave $1.27 billion in economic and $1.25 billion in military aid, while the United States poured economic assistance worth $533 million.[51] Afghanistan used foreign assistance in developing state institutions and economic infrastructure. It established new educational institutions, mostly in Kabul and other major towns, developed road and communication networks, and trained state administrators.

The United States, the postwar superpower, preferred a security alliance with Pakistan over Kabul for its containment strategy.[52] Though Washington provided considerable development assistance to Afghanistan, it did not match the growing influence of Moscow in the important areas of training and supply of military equipment.[53]

Dependency relations of the Afghan state with the Soviet Union in modernizing the armed forces and launching development projects increased its vulnerability to penetration in important areas of public policy and national security by big neighbors.[54] Moscow's involvement in the political affairs of Afghanistan further deepened with the Saur revolution of April 1978. Lacking domestic support, the Afghan Marxists leaned heavily on the Soviet Union to ensure their political survival. Without the Soviet commitment, and direct participation, the fragile political order, which they were attempting to build, could not stand in the face of a highly mobilized national resistance. Equally important was the convergence of the Soviet regional interests with a dependent Marxist regime in Afghanistan. These were: to counter the rising power of the Islamic movements in the region, which had the potential of influencing political developments in Soviet-controlled Central Asian Republics; to ensure stability in the bordering areas; and to demonstrate the ability to militarily intervene to defend allies in the region. More importantly, the Soviets did not fear any countermove by the United States as Washington's security arrangements in southwest Asia had collapsed with the success of the Islamic revolution in Iran.[55] The Soviet leaders, though a very limited group which participated in the decision to intervene in Afghanistan, assumed that military action could salvage the political situation in Afghanistan, which was fast slipping into anarchy.

The Soviet intervention invited counterintervention from Iran, Pakistan, Islamic states of the Middle East, and the Western powers. Soviet military presence across the Khyber Pass changed the buffer status of Afghanistan, complicating Pakistan's security dilemma, which faced a vastly powerful India along its eastern plank.[56] The inflow of refugees and Mujahideen further dragged Pakistan into accepting a "front-line" state role. But this policy decision, though influenced by geopolitical considerations, was not entirely independent of the domestic political process inside Pakistan. A military regime which was alienated found a splendid opportunity in the Soviet invasion of Afghanistan to attract Western support.[57]

The United States interpreted the Soviet move as a threat to the stability of the adjacent areas that are vital to the economies of the industrialized states. To safeguard the collective interests of the Western world, Washington declared that "any attempt by outside force to gain control of the Persian Gulf region will be repelled by any means, including military force."[58] Therefore, the conflict in Afghanistan, particularly following the Soviet invasion, was internationalized. Afghanistan was, from then on, a victim of not only its internal confrontations but also its geopolitical factors.

Linkages and interconnectedness between Afghanistan's internal political dynamics and its geopolitical environment need to be understood. This interplay might be explained through three factors—dependence of the state and counterelite on external factors, convergence of political and strategic interests of the Afghan partisans and their foreign supporters, and the involvement of transnational ideological groups.

Physical conditions of the country and the intensity of the resistance put up by the population frustrated the Soviet attempts to restore law and order and establish an effective government. The presence of the Soviet forces was offensive to the national sentiment of the Afghans, and thus counterproductive in resolving the crisis. Inviting the Soviets to secure their political survival further stigmatized the communist leaders, alienating them from the society.

The use of massive force against the civilian population, destruction of rural infrastructure, and ruthlessness of the "scorch earth" strategy strengthened the political support for the resistance, which took up arms against the Kabul regime. The more the Soviets escalated the level of their counterinsurgency operations, the more they moved the warring Afghan groups away from national reconciliation. The Soviet involvement in support of the Kabul regime was politically divisive, and a failure in terms of securing the objective of pacifying the country.

The defiance put up by the Afghan resistance forced the Soviet Union to fight a war of attrition, which worked to its disadvantage. The war took a heavy toll in men and material and seriously damaged the Soviet Union's international reputation. After failing to expand control beyond the cities, despite protracted counterinsurgency campaigns, it decided to seek a way out of the Afghan quagmire.[59] Political changes within the Soviet Union, especially new leadership committing itself to openness and restructuring, added to the previous urgency to end a war that was unpopular at home, and had generated tremendous opposition abroad, particularly from the West.

But the war also had devastating effects on the Afghan state and society. Almost everything that Afghanistan had built with its meager national resources and foreign assistance was destroyed. Most of the population became dislocated internally and in neighboring countries. The resistance parties that organized the insurgency failed to resolve their conflicts and this pushed the country to a civil war that lasted until 2001, when the Taliban was ousted from power. The failed state syndrome[60] created warlords, and brought in foreign elements that benefited from political and ethnic fragmentation. The rise of the Taliban was one of the disastrous outcomes of the conflict that continues to trouble Afghanistan. The effects of the Afghan war went beyond its borders and have spilled over into Pakistan, central Asia, and the Middle East. The tens of thousands of young men who volunteered to fight on the side of the Afghan Mujahideen went back home with war hardiness and training to launch military attacks against their own regimes. They also embraced a revolutionary Islamic ideology and armed struggle as their strategy to change traditional political order according to their vision of Islam that is antimodernity, anti-West, and obscurantist. Their imprints are too visible in acts of terrorism and violence throughout the region.

TRANSNATIONAL ISLAMIC MILITANTS

The role of transnational ideological groups and movements in subjecting Afghanistan to external intrusions is no less significant than the state actors. Not only did they mobilize political support in the Islamic countries and generate financial resources, but they also trained and sent their volunteers to fight along the Afghan Mujahideen groups.[61] The waging of *jihad* by the private transnational groups became linked to a broader Islamic revivalist movement. The foreign militants from the Middle East, Pakistan, and central Asian states found stateless Afghanistan a convenient place to train, hide, and plan attacks against the West and their own countries. They also became involved in local power struggles among the Afghan factions. The non-Afghan trans-Islamic groups like Al Qaeda offended popular religion, showed no regard for local culture, and contributed greatly to internal rifts. The terrorist networks created by the Al Qaeda have survived the ouster of the Taliban, and it seems the organization has reassembled in the border regions between Afghanistan and Pakistan from where suicide bombers have been attacking targets in both the countries. The Taliban and Al Qaeda are down but not out. Their presence in one of the most difficult terrains and their capacity to establish safe havens among the local populations are not positive signs for the state and nation building process in Afghanistan. Our argument is that the war on terrorism must be a collaborative enterprise, which requires the cooperation of regional states and major international actors. Afghanistan or even Pakistan may not be able to face the challenge of the Taliban and Al Qaeda–sponsored terrorism without international support and a long-term comprehensive strategy that must combine military offensives with economic and social development of the region.

ETHNIC FRAGMENTATION

The wars in Afghanistan have drastically altered the balance of power and influence among the traditional social and political forces in the country. Supplies of foreign arms, money, and patronage along with the illegal economy of drug trafficking and warlordism have sprung up new forces. The ethnic and social forces of Afghanistan are more conscious of their separate identities today than any time in the history of the country. The responses to the communist regime and the Soviet invasion were organized more or less on an ethnic and local basis. By ousting the communist state and its functionaries from their regions, they established a sort of self-government under their own ethnic leaders. Ethnic considerations subsequently caused political polarization among the Mujahideen groups, locking them into a bitter struggle for power after the fall of the Marxist regime in 1992.

The multipolar confrontation acquired dangerous sectarian and regional dimensions and gradually transformed itself into an ethnic conflict between the Pashtuns, fearing loss of power, and the coalition of Uzbek and Tajik groups from the north who had gained greater political influence in Kabul, which had been traditionally dominated by the Pashtun elite. In the absence of democratic institutions, the Afghan factions were unable to resolve their differences peacefully or maintain stable coalitions, which undermined national unity. The differences between the Pashtun majority groups and the minorities on the one hand, and political rift between the parties professing traditional and revolutionary Islam on the other, widened the conflict within the resistance after the departure of the common enemy, the Soviet Union, from the scene.

The rise of the Taliban movement, which sought reunification of the country through military conquest and established a highly centralized state apparatus run by a rigid theocratic line, also had Pashtun ethnic undertones. Their military offensive pushed the ethnic minorities to margins, causing the worst human rights violations.

The post-Taliban political arrangements were tilted in favor of the ethnic minority groups from the northern parts of the country. With the new constitution and elections for the parliament and provincial councils, Afghanistan's political system is gradually becoming more representative. The issue of ethnicity may get diffused with economic and political reconstruction. But the question of identity and regional interest will take a longer time to settle, depending on how the social groups of Afghanistan seek accommodation and live within a unified state like they had before the wars.

THE REVIVAL FRAMEWORK

The challenge for the Afghan leaders and the international community that are trying to rebuild the country is how to achieve, peace, stability, and normalize a society that has experienced one of the most devastating conflicts of our time. They are trying to reconstruct Afghanistan's political institutions, structure of governance, vital institutions of the state, infrastructure, and rural economy. The reconstruction model has ingredients of modernity with a focus on human development, representative institutions and an effective statehood. This is the vision that the silent majority of the Afghans, tired of vicious cycle of violence, would like to pursue.

There is realization among Afghan leaders and ordinary peoples that they need international assistance to overcome their difficulties, notably the stubborn legacies of the conflicts that continue to haunt them in the form of warlords, drug mafias, and remnants of the Taliban. There cannot be any two opinions about peace and stability being fundamental requirements for reconstruction. Conversely, progress on reconstruction of infrastructure and state institutions will have credible demonstrative effects on populations and wean them away from the warlords and the Taliban movement.

Rebuilding societies and states after longer periods of internal strife and external intervention is a difficult task and it requires long-term commitment and regular flow of resources until national leaders and their institutions can take care of themselves. One of the major obstacles in the way of reconstruction has been, and continues to be, the Taliban insurgency in the majority Pashtun regions. Their attacks on NATO and the Afghan security forces and the counterinsurgency operations against them have delayed the rehabilitation of populations and the revival of normal life patterns. One of the casualties of growing conflict is the diminishing trust between the International Security Assistance Force for Afghanistan (ISAF) and the local communities because of the collateral damage caused to the civilians.[62] The issue of winning the support of the civilian populations through reconstruction and security programs remains as important as ever before. The coalition forces face enormous odds in delivering these programs in a state of lawlessness in the Pashtun regions. The resurgence of the Taliban has slowed the pace of reconstruction somewhat, but the movement has not acquired the capacity to reverse the process and change the dynamics of politics in its favor.

Military action or counterinsurgency operations in situations like that of Afghanistan are essential but have to be linked to peace building, negotiations, and conflict resolution through a shared vision of good society and by integrating interests of all vital stakeholders. The international community may play a constructive role in bringing different factions of Afghanistan, including moderate Taliban and former Mujahideen leaders, to the negotiating table. A political solution to the conflict aiming at reconstituting broad and legitimate power arrangements would be credible only if it gathers the support of all the important Afghan groups. The involvement of foreign powers, no matter how well meaning it appears, may complicate the task of structuring national consensus among the Afghans, if the main actors impose solutions from above. In our view, foreign benefactors and friends are a poor substitute for indigenous political or social forces for mediating conflict among the old and new power elites or among the rival ethnic groups.

What is essential to recognize is that peace and stability in the fractured polity of Afghanistan might not be restored unless those engaged in a struggle for power, or outsiders, wishing to defuse it, seek new relationships among all the constituent groups—ethnic, regional, and religious. Any attempt to structure powerful centralized authority within the framework of the nation-state model would be self-defeating. Decentralization, regional autonomy, and revitalization of traditional patterns of authority would all strengthen accommodation. Political structuring under the catchy slogans of constitutionalism, electoral process, and even self-determination would lose significance, if it ignores the underlying social forces of the Afghan political culture that has not changed much after years of conflict.

NOTES

1. See some stories in Alex Klaits and Gulchin Gulmamadova-Klaits, *Love and War in Afghanistan* (New York: Seven Stories Press, 2005), pp. 63–64.

2. Bob Woodward, *Bush at War* (New York: Simon & Schuster, 2002).

3. Milton Bearden, "Afghanistan: Graveyard of Empires," *Foreign Affairs*, Vol. 80, No. 6 (November–December 2001), pp. 13–30.

4. William Maley, *Afghanistan Wars* (London: Palgrave Macmillan, 2002).

5. Kamal Matinuddin, *The Taliban Phenomenon: Afghanistan 1994–1997* (Karachi: Oxford University Press, 1999), pp. 22–34.

6. "Taliban 'havens' along border: U.S.," *Dawn*, December 17, 2006.

7. The Islamic Movement of Uzbekistan had links with the Taliban. Its military leader Juma Namangani took refuge in Afghanistan where he was killed after the ouster of the Taliban. See, testimony of Mr. R. Grant Smith in the Committee on the Judiciary, United States, Senate, March 13, 2002; "Terrorists or Mujahideen" (editorial), *Daily Times*, 22 March 2004.

8. Ahmed Rashid, "Pakistan and the Taliban," in William Maley, ed., *Fundamentalism Reborn?: Afghanistan and the Taliban* (London: Hurst & Company, 2001), pp. 72–89.

9. Initial view about the Taliban in the United States was that the religious students could serve positive objectives. See, Richard Mackenzie, "The United States and the Taliban," in William Maley, ed., *Fundamentalism Reborn?: Afghanistan and the Taliban*, op. cit., p. 96.

10. Anonymous, *Through Our Enemies' Eyes* (Washington, D.C.: Brassey's Inc., 2003), p. xviii.

11. "Afghan failure may lead to regime change in Pakistan: UK generals," *Daily Times*, 16 July 2007.

12. Carlton J. H. Hayes, "The American Frontier—Frontier of What?" *The American Historical Review*, Vol. 51, No. 2 (January 1946), p. 200; Ray Allen Billington, "The American Frontier Thesis," *The Huntington Library Quarterly*, Vol. 23, No. 3, May 1960, pp. 201–16.

13. Irfan Habib, *An Atlas of the Mughal Empire: Political and Economic Maps with Detailed Notes, Bibliography and Index* (New York and Delhi: Oxford University Press, 1982).

14. See Louis Dupree, *Afghanistan* (Princeton: Princeton University Press, 1980); Monstuart Elphinstone, *An Account of the Kingdom of Caubul and Its Dependencies in Persia, Tartary, and India* (Karachi: Oxford University Press, 1972, first edition 1815).

15. Jirga (grand assembly of elders and notables) and provincial councils of *sardars* (chiefs) were two traditional institutions that along with the religious establishment played an important role in confirming legitimacy on the Afghan kings, and approved constitutional and legal changes in the country. The institution of jirga also functioned at local levels to adjudicate disputes between individuals and tribes.

Looking at the evolution of the Afghan state, particularly its early phase and central system of governance, one can hardly miss the point that it rested on consent of the tribes and other socially influential groups. Allegiance to the state by them was conditioned by the unwritten but well-respected tradition of local autonomy. On this point see, A. Olesen, "Afghanistan: the Development of the Modern State," in K. Ferdinand and M. Mozaffari (eds), *Islam: State and Society* (London: Curzon, 1988), pp. 155–169; Jolanta Sierakowska-Dyndo, "The State in Afghanistan's Political and Economic System on the Eve of the April 1978 Coup," *Central Asian Survey*, vol. 9, no. 4, 1990. pp. 85–86. Leon B. Poullada has argued that originally the central government was in effect an emanation of a tribal confederation and the Amir was considered a paramount chief, a *primus inter pares*, by other tribal chiefs. Other factors that contributed to the autonomy of the tribes are: geographic location, tribal culture of defiance, dynastic quarrels, and the impact of "great game" between Britain and Russia, which, in particular, promoted the pugnacity of the Pashtun tribes. See, Poullada, "Political Modernization in Afghanistan: The Amanullah Reforms," in George Grassmuck et al., *Afghanistan: Some New Approaches* (Ann Arbor: The University of Michigan, 1969), pp. 116–17.

16. On the evolution and identity of the Afghan state and its relationship with the civil society, see Barnett R. Rubin, "Lineage of the State in Afghanistan," *Asian Survey*, November, 1988, pp. 1183–1209; M. Nazif Shahrani, "State Building and Social Fragmentation in Afghanistan: A Historical Perspective," in Ali Banuazizi and Myron Weiner, (eds), *The State, Religion, and Ethnic Politics: Afghanistan, Iran, and Pakistan* (Syracuse: Syracuse University Press, 1986), pp. 23–74.

17. Fred Halliday, "Revolution in Afghanistan," *New Left Review*, vol. 112, November–December, 1978, p. 19.

18. Three types of leadership may be identified that used links with the state to enhance their local power: elders of tribes and ethnic groups, *ulema* (scholars of Islam), and *rohanyun* (saintly figures), which included pirs (spiritual leaders), and *hazrats* (respectable on religious grounds). See, Nabi Misdaq, "Traditional Leadership in Afghan Society and the Issue of National Unity," *Central Asian Survey*, vol. 9, no. 4, 1990, pp. 109–12.

19. Although social class distinctions existed in Afghanistan, the basic identity of the common man in the villages was with a clan or tribe. The mystique of kinship relations prevented emergence of any challenge to the traditional authority.

20. On the nature of the political system of Afghanistan and its social and historical roots, see a pioneering study by Richard S. Newell, *The Politics of Afghanistan* (Ithaca: Cornell University Press, 1972.

21. For this analysis I have benefited from David Gibbs, "The Peasant as Counter-Revolutionary: The Rural Origins of the Afghan Insurgency," *Studies in Comparative International Development*, vol. 21, no. 1, Spring 1986, pp. 37–45.

22. Estimates of arable land vary. But it is generally believed that land area where something can be grown is about 12 percent, of which only 4 percent is cultivated mainly due to insufficient irrigation system. Louis Dupree, cited by Gibbs, in Ibid., p. 38.

23. Maxwell J. Fry, *The Afghan Economy: Money, Finance, and the Critical Constraints to Economic Development* (Leiden: E.J. Brill, 1974), p. 56.

24. Douglas G. Norvell, *Agricultural Credit in Afghanistan: A Review of Progress and Problems from 1954 Until 1972* (Kabul: Agricultural Division, United States Agency for International Development, 1972), pp. iii, 1.

25. Despite largest share of the agriculture in Afghanistan's economy, the government's farm-generated revenues were nominal. It is difficult to find statistics in this issue. Just to give an idea, the government's revenues in 1971–1972 were only 1.2 percent. K. Glaubitt, Saadeddin and B. Schafer, "Government Revenues and Economic Development of Afghanistan," *Afghanistan Journal*, vol. 4, no. 1, 1977, p. 1.

26. Barnett R. Rubin applies "rentier" state model to Afghanistan by suggesting that, since 1957, more than 40 percent of states' income came from foreign sources. See his "Political Elites in Afghanistan: Rentier State Building, Rentier State Wrecking," *International Journal of Middle East Studies*, no. 24, 1992, p. 78.

27. On the expansion and prestige of modern education, see, Wolfram Eberhard, "Afghanistan's Young Elites," *Asian Survey*, February 1962, pp. 3–22; Barnett R. Rubin, "The Old Regime in Afghanistan: Recruitment and Training of a State Elite," *Central Asian Survey*, vol. 10, no. 3, 1991, pp. 73–100; Olivier Roy, *Islam and Resistance in Afghanistan* (Cambridge: Cambridge University Press, 1986).

28. Tahir Amin, *Afghanistan Crisis: Implications and Options for Muslim World, Iran and Pakistan* (Islamabad: Institute of Policy Studies, 1982), pp. 95–106.

29. On the education, socialization, and development of ideological identities of the Marxist and islamist elites, see Rubin, "Political Elites in Afghanistan," *op. cit.*, pp. 78–99.

30. On political and ideological differences, see, Shah M. Tarzi, "Politics of the Afghan Resistance Movement: Cleavages, Disunity, and Fragmentation, " *Asian Survey*, vol. 31, no. 6, June 1991, pp. 479–511.

31. Raja Anwar has provided the most detailed and insightful analysis of this subject. See his *Tragedy of Afghanistan: A First Hand Account*, translated from Urdu by Khalid Hasan (London: Verso, 1988).

32. Both the Afghan Marxists and Islamist ideologues and political activists came largely from tribal and feudal social backgrounds. This is why they did not show any tolerance to each other. For Islamists, all Marxists were kafirs (atheists, nonbelievers) and agents of the Soviet Union, while Marxists regarded the Islamists as a fundamental obstacle to their rule and reform program.

33. Efforts of the Afghan state to modernize army and civilian bureaucracy began in the late nineteenth century (reign of Amir Abdul Rehman, 1880–1901), but it was King Amanullah who provided greater political will and commitment. See Leon B. Poullada, *Reform and Rebellion in Afghanistan, 1919–1929: King Amanullah's Failure to Modernize a Tribal Society* (Ithaca: Cornell University Press, 1973).

34. Amin Saikal provides excellent insights into the modern phase of Afghanistan's political history. See his *Modern Afghanistan: A History of Struggle and Survival* (London: I.B. Tauris, 2004).

35. Amin, *Afghanistan Crisis*, pp. 95–101.

36. For analysis of the overthrow of monarchy in 1973, see Louis Dupree, "A Note on Afghanistan 1974," *American University Field Staff Reports* (AUFS), South Asia Series, vol. 18, no. 6, 1974.

37. See the founding document of PDPA in Anthony Arnolds, *Afghanistan's Two-Party Communism* (Stanford: Hoover Institution Press, 1983), pp. 137–48.

38. M. Nazif Shahrani, "Introduction: Marxist 'Revolution' and Islamic Resistance in Afghanistan," in M. N. Shahrani and Robert L. Canfield (eds.), *Revolutions and Rebellions in Afghanistan* (Berkeley: Institute of International Studies, University of California, Berkeley, 1984), pp. 3–57.

39. Although social class distinctions existed in Afghanistan, the basic identity of the common man in the villages was with a clan or tribe. The mystique of kinship prevented emergence of a traditional authority.

40. Under the 1964 constitution no member of the royal family could contest elections. This provision was devised to keep Sardar Daoud out of politics.

41. For details see Hasan Kakar, "The Fall of the Afghan Monarchy in 1973," *International Journal of Middle Eastern Studies*, no. 9 (May 1978).

42. Hannah Negaan (Pseud.), "The Afghan Coup of April 1978: Revolution and International Security," *ORBIS*, vol. 23, no. 1 (spring 1979).

43. Imposition of alien revolutionary concepts on a largely feudal and tribal society without the proper understanding of its structures, values, and critical forces was, perhaps, the central cause of the revolt against the Marxist government.

44. William Maley has very convincingly demonstrated that the Leftist regime confronted a serious legitimacy crisis. See his "Political Legitimation in Contemporary Afghanistan," *Asian Survey*, vol. 27, no. 6, June 1987, pp. 705–25.

45. This can be gauged from the fact that in the first phase of the conflict (1978–1979), before the Soviet invasion 40,000 Afghans were killed in 1978 and 80,000 in 1979. The rate of casualties increased in the following years. It is estimated that between 1 million to 1.5 million might have been killed by the time Moscow pulled out its troops. Proportion of those incapacitated by the war is thirty-one per thousand of the entire population of the country. About one-third of the citizens became refugees in the neighboring countries, mostly (3.5 million) in Pakistan. See a well-documented study by Marek Sliwinski, "Afghanistan: The Decimation of a People," *ORBIS*, vol. 33, no. 1., Winter 1989, pp. 39–55.

46. Shahrani, "Introduction: Marxist 'Revolution' and Islamic Resistance in Afghanistan," pp. 25–40; see also Eden Naby, "The Concept of Jihad in Opposition to Communist Rule: Turkestan and Afghanistan," Studies in *Comparative Communism*, vol. 19, no. 3/4, Autumn/Winter 1986, pp. 287–300.

47. On Afghanistan's geopolitics and foreign relations, see, Ludwig W. Adamec, *Afghanistan, 1900–1923: A Diplomatic History* (Berkeley: University of California Press, 1967); L. W. Adamec, *Afghanistan's Foreign Affairs to the Mid-Twentieth Century: Relations with the USSR, Germany, and Britain* (Tucson: University of Arizona Press, 1974); V. Gregorian, *The Emergence of Modern Afghanistan: Politics of Reform and Modernization, 1880–1946* (Stanford: Stanford University Press, 1969); Olaf Caroe, *Soviet Empire*, (London: Macmillan, 1954); William P. Coates and K. Zelda, *A History of Anglo-Soviet Relations* (London: Lawrence and Wishart, 1943; Arnold Fletcher, *Afghanistan: Highway of Conquest* (Ithaca: Cornell University Press, 1965); David Fromkin, "The Great Game in Asia," *Foreign Affairs* vol. 58, no. 4, Spring 1980, pp. 936–951; Zalmay Khalilzad, *The Return of the Great Game* (Santa Monica, Ca.: California Seminar on International Security and Foreign Policy, September 1980).

48. Durand line is the present boundary between Afghanistan and Pakistan. An accord to draw this boundary was signed between Britain and Afghanistan in 1893. After the creation of Pakistan, Afghanistan insisted to redemarcate this boundary, which Pakistan has claimed final. Pashtunistan is the Afghan title for the tribal territories around the Durand line that form part of Pakistan. Afghan rulers have from time to time demanded inclusion of the tribal areas inhabited by the Pashtu-speaking ethnic groups to join Afghanistan or become an independent Pashtunistan state. These two issues caused considerable friction between the two neighboring states in the decades

of the 1950s and 1960s. Afghanistan's position considerably changed in 1976–1977 when Sardar Daoud decided to improve relations with Iran and Pakistan. These issues lost significance with the civil war, Soviet invasion, and Pakistan's support to the liberation of Afghanistan. Whether or not the future rulers of Afghanistan will take up old quarrels with Islamabad is yet to be seen. On the historical origins of these disputes, see, S. M. Burke and Lawrence Ziring, *Pakistan's Foreign Policy: A Historical Analysis* (Karachi: Oxford University, 1990), pp. 68–90; Ainslee T. Embree (ed), *Pakistan's Western Borderlands* (Durham, N.C.: Carolina Academic Press, 1977), Mehrunisa Ali, *Pak-Afghan Discord: A Historical Perspective, Documents 1853–1979* (Karachi: Pakistan Study Centre, Karachi University, 1990); Saedduddin Ahmad Dar (ed), *Selected Documents on Pakistan's Relations with Afghanistan 1947–1985* (Islamabad: National Institute of Pakistan Studies, Quaid-i-Azam University, 1986).

49. S. Fida Yunas, *The Durand Line Border Agreement* 1893, Special Issue (Peshawar: Area Study Centre, University of Peshawar, 2003), pp. 1–45.

50. Ibid., pp. 93–94.

51. Barnett R. Rubin, *The Fragmentation of Afghanistan: State Formation and Collapse in the International System*, pp. 63–68.

52. On this point see, Henery S. Bradsher, *Afghanistan and the Soviet Union* (Durham: Duke University Press, 1985).

53. In 1947 and then in 1955, the Afghan government had requested the United States for military aid. But Kabul's disputes with Pakistan complicated the affair. However, the United States supplied Afghanistan with $800 million in economic assistance between 1946 and 1978. The military assistance during this period amounted to only 5.6 million dollars. Milton Leitenberg, "United States Foreign Policy and the Soviet Invasion of Afghanistan," *Arms Control*, vol. 7, no. 3, December, 1986, pp. 272–73.

54. Amin Saikal notes that "by the turn of the 1970s—no major Afghan political decision could be taken or military operation initiated without the knowledge of Soviet advisers and embassy," Amin Saikal, "Russia and Afghanistan: A Turning Point?" *Asian Affairs*, vol. 20, (old series 76), part II, June, 1989, p. 173.

55. On December 8, 11, 15, 17, and 27, 1979, the United States conveyed its serious concern to the Soviet Union about the movement of her troops around Afghanistan. But capability of the United States to prevent the impending Soviet invasion or retaliate effectively was not taken seriously by Moscow. See, *East-West Relations*, op. cit., pp. 111–21.

56. Theodore L. Eliot, Jr., and Robert L. Pfaltzgraff, Jr., (eds), *Red Army on Pakistan's Borders* (Washington, D.C.: Pergamon-Brassey's, 1986); Francis Fukuyama, *The Security of Pakistan: A Trip Report*, Rand Report N-1584-RC (Santa Monica: Rand Corporation, September, 1980); Lawrence Ziring, "Soviet Policy on the Rim of Asia: Scenarios and Projections," *Asian Affairs*, vol. 9, no. 3, Jan.–Feb., 1982, pp. 135–46; Robert G. Wirsing, "Pakistan and the War in Afghanistan," *Asian Affairs, An American Review*, vol. 14, no. 2, Summer 1987, pp. 57–75.

57. See, Omar Noman, *Pakistan: Political and Economic History Since 1947* (London: Kegan Paul International, 1990), pp. 120–25; Shahid Javed Burki (ed), *Pakistan Under the Military: Eleven Years of Zia Ul-Haq* (Boulder: Westview Press, 1991).

58. On the U.S. response, see the following: Richard P. Cronin, *Afghanistan: Soviet Invasion and U.S. Response*, IB 80006 (Washington, D.C.: Congressional Research Service, Library of Congress, updated 24 November 1981); U.S. Congress, House, Committee on Foreign Affairs, Subcommittee on Europe and the Middle East, *Hearing: East-West Relations, United States-Soviet Relations*, 24 and 30 January 1980, 96th Congress, 2nd Session (Washington, D.C.: U.S. Government Printing Office, 1980); Zalmay Khalilzad, "Afghanistan and the Crisis in American Foreign Policy," *Survival*, vol. 22, no. 4, July–August, 1980, pp. 151–60; William E. Grifith, "Superpower Relations after Afghanistan," *Survival*, vol. 22, no. 4, July–August, 1980, pp. 146–50; U.S. Department of State, *Soviet Invasion of Afghanistan*, Special Report No. 70, April, 1980.

59. For the analysis of shifts in the Soviet approach to negotiations, see an excellent study by Riaz M. Khan, *Untying the Afghan Knot: Negotiating Soviet Withdrawal* (Durham: Duke University Press, 1991), pp. 242–84.

60. Gerald B. Helman and Steven R. Ratner, "Saving Failed States," *Foreign Policy*, 89 (Winter 1992–1993), p. 3.

61. There is hardly any documentation of the numbers of foreign Islamist volunteers involved in fighting along with the Mujahideen. According to the investigation of this author, the largest number was sent by the Islamicist parties of Pakistan, in particular by the *Jamat-i-Islami* (Islamic party). Youth affiliated with *Ikhawan Ul-Muslimoon* (Muslim Brotherhood) from the Middle Eastern countries and Far East came to wage holy war. The total number of all these groups was never more than a few thousands at any time. Interviews with Afghan party leaders in Peshawar, January 1990.

62. Luke Baker, "Taliban Growing Stronger in Afghanistan: UK Report," *Dawn*, 19 July 2007.

2

Ethnicity, Political Power, and Fragmentation

Wars, particularly long, destructive civil wars among local groups, create or sharpen existing ethnic identities by an exasperating sense of loss among some groups, while inducing a real or imagined sense of empowerment among others. A war with multiple domestic, regional, and international dimensions and lasting more than twenty-eight years has drastically changed the ethnic balance of power among Afghanistan's social groups. This development is troubling because it is bound to reflect in the reconstruction of the Afghan state, a process already under way with support from international influences. The question is how the social and political aspirations of ethnic groups are likely to be accommodated in the new framework of the Afghan state. It is an extremely difficult task to find a new balance in any politically fractured society that has experienced such a long spell of deadly conflict. Since the ouster of the Taliban regime, that largely consisted of the Pashtun majority ethnic group, the question of division of power among social groups, what role different communities would have in the central government and how they will be represented have been, and continue to remain, politically explosive issues. In this chapter, we will look at the question of identity construction in Afghanistan under different regimes, the structure of ethnic groups, the effects of war on ethnic communities, and why the ethnic fault lines may persist and under what conditions they may disappear.

Afghanistan has always been a multiethnic state, and like most postcolonial states, it has more than one ethnic group, speaks too many languages, and has multiple and multilayered identities.[1] Ethnicity however does present a challenge for the state formation process by itself. It requires a different kind of politics that is integrative, culturally sensitive, and politically participatory. In

27

many instances we have seen that failure to integrate ethnic groups into a national power structure or inability to grant them a fair degree of cultural and political autonomy has politicized many of them, leading to civil wars.[2] The collective nationhood experience of many postcolonial states provides mixed evidence about the success of creating national solidarity and a sense of common national identity. Not all states have really succeeded in nation-building based on equitable distribution of power or representation of all groups. Nor have they fallen apart as nation-states, despite many political strains in evolving institutions that would accommodate legitimate aspirations of ethnic groups. In the case of Afghanistan and other states in the neighborhood their identity markers are the same—common lineage, sect, history, location, and mores. Ethnic group identities have subjective orientations in terms of self-definition and conceptions of the other, which makes them different in some of the core values that the members of an ethnic group share among themselves.[3] Afghanistan's ethnic groups have also identified themselves with some of the above markers and, over the past two centuries or more, since the formation of Afghanistan as a state have retained their individuality and group consciousness.

ETHNIC DIVERSITY

The issue of ethnic identity is as complex as its many local, regional, and social forms. As a result of this complexity, ethnic, religious, and linguistic diversity of Afghanistan has presented enormous political difficulties in developing a coherent sense of nationhood. Afghan nationalism has been a contested issue and it is being contested increasingly by the minority ethnic groups because of its Pashtun social imprint and identity markers. Before we talk about each ethnic group and its demographic representation and social characteristics, two aspects of Afghan ethnicity need a mention. First is the ethnic affiliation of social groups within Afghanistan with ethnic groups in neighboring countries. The three sovereign ethnic states—Uzbekistan, Tajikistan, and Turkmenistan, all share a strong ethnic sentiment with similar social groups in Afghanistan. Additionally Afghanistan's fourth neighboring state, Pakistan, has two Pashtun-dominated provinces, Balochistan and Northwest Frontier Province, which have overlapping tribal affiliations across the border into Afghanistan. In crisis situations throughout Afghan history, the counterpart ethnic populations across the borders have served as a source of support and place of refuge and shelter. The transfer and migration of population as refugees and resistance fighters has been a two-way traffic. A good number of Uzbeks, some Tajiks, and Turkmen from central Asia came to Afghanistan to seek sanctuary in their war of resistance against the Russians in the late nineteenth century and the early part of the twentieth century. Afghanistan is a unique country in this respect, serving as a frontier state to so many diverse ethnic groups with their own states next door. Therein lies potential for regional fragmentation and the risk of redrawing of national boundaries if the present phase of nation-building under international patronage failed is to fail. The second aspect of Afghan ethnicity is the territorial and geographical divide between the north and south of the country. The areas north of the Hindu Kush are culturally, ethnically, and linguistically part of central Asia and share very little in common with the rest of the areas, except a common Afghan state. The southwestern parts of the country in demographic characteristics as well as topography are similar to Balochistan and the NWFP in Pakistan. This is yet another fault line in Afghanistan's fresh quest for state and nationhood. The historical memory of Afghanistan as a common homeland of all ethnic groups, an old political unit with international recognition and identity, and a notional middle ground among equally multiethnic states within the region may be a good starting point to reconstruct the frontier state. But the big question is how the issue of ethnic balance, sharing of power, and joint ownership of the new Afghanistan is settled among ethnically more politicized and fragmented communities.

In today's world when numbers are important for social group empowerment, political participation, communal mobilization, and representation, determining the demographic size of ethnic groups has become a highly politicized issue. This is truer of societies like Afghanistan that have witnessed long spells of conflicts and where no population census was ever fully conducted. Therefore, figures about the ethnic groups are rough estimates, and for political reasons each ethnic group in Afghanistan tends to exaggerate its numbers.

PASHTUNS

Pashtuns are the largest ethnic group in the country. Their numbers are estimated to be between 50 percent to 54 percent of the entire population. Some Pashtun nationalists put the figure much higher while minority ethnic groups tend to quote a smaller size of Pashtun population. The Pashtuns are concentrated in the southern and eastern parts of the country. The Pashtun tribes were settled with land grants in central, northern, and western parts of the country, by Amir Abdul Rehman, where they have formed local communities. Durrani and Ghilzai are two main tribal confederations among the Pashtuns, and have their territorial domains in the south and east of the country respectively. Historically and even in recent times they have been rivals and at times competition for power and resources have resulted in active hostility and prolonged periods of strife among subtribes of the two. Most of the Pashtun ruling class came from the Mohammadzai clan of the Durrani Pashtuns originally from the Kandhar region. Within each stream of Pashtun tribal confederacy, there are further tribal divisions and subdivisions with their own local leadership patterns. Ghilzai are more numerous but in social hierarchy and tribal order their position is lower than the Durranis. The Durrani ruling elites have always been marked by a consciousness of the numerical strength and jealousy of Ghilzai tribes. At times they forged closer alliances with them and sought their support in conflict situations. Without the passive or active alignment with the Ghilzai tribes, the Durrani elite perhaps couldn't succeed in establishing Pashtun domination in the nineteenth century. At other times, particularly in the twentieth century, they made their own political choices and refused to stay in alliance with the Durrani chieftains. The process of separation between the two lines of Pashtuns began with the modernization process in the later part of the twentieth century. Thereafter, the Durrani elites were no longer dependent on the tribal militia. They raised regular forces, recruiting educated urban Tajiks and other non-Pashtun groups. The links of the Durranis with their tribal Pashtun society were weakened further with their urban upbringing and the adoption of Dari or Persian as their mother tongue.

Pashtuns are distinguished from other ethnic communities on account of their tribal social structures and values of pride, independence, valor, and chivalry, which are known as Pashtunwali. The khans or clan chiefs play an important mediating role in the social hierarchy, maintaining social coherence and managing relations with other tribes and political authorities both in situation of peace and war. The war of resistance and then the civil war has greatly impacted on the Pashtun tribes and their relations with other social groups. The Ghilzai Pashtuns destroyed the Durrani dynasty by launching the Saur revolution from within the armed forces. The same eastern Pashtun tribes revolted against communism, crossed the border into Pakistan, and organized the toughest resistance against the Soviet forces. As a result of war, and its accompanying political fragmentation among the tribes and empowerment of other ethnic groups, the role played by the Pashtuns in the Afghan society and the emerging power structure has somewhat declined.[4]

TAJIKS

Tajiks form the second largest ethnic group after the Pashtuns and they are estimated to be roughly 26 to 30 percent of the population. They have emerged out of the two wars, the Soviet war and the civil war with the Pashtun Taliban, as the more powerful ethnic group, and in a way they seem to have dominated the post-Taliban power structure in the country. Compared to the Pashtuns, Tajiks are more skilled, better educated, and have a greater number of urban intellectuals, merchants, and entrepreneurs. During the reign of the Durrani dynasty, urbane and educated Tajiks joined the ranks of civil services, educational institutions, and modern professions like medical doctors, engineers, and lawyers. Their placement in the government departments and traditional role as merchants made their transition to middle class status faster than any other social group in the country. It was not because of any policy of ethnic preference but because of their better education and preparedness to work in the government, but mostly in politically subordinate positions. Being functionaries of the old regime that the Marxists dismantled, the Tajiks more than any other group suffered greatly as a social class.

It was partly the pattern of resistance, which formed along familiar lines of regional and local community-based leadership, and a strong sense of identity that Tajiks organized their own resistance groups under their own commanders. Ahmed Shah Masud was the most charismatic of them; he had national stature and had developed links with a number of foreign powers. The Tajik commanders were able to strike wider and deeper roots in their community and kept both the urban and rural sectors of their population more or less aligned with the aid of using the umbrella of the *Jamiat-i-Islami. Jamiat* was an important link with Pakistan and other countries as a vehicle of generating money and arms for the Tajik resistance forces, but it was the local dynamics of community interests and the logic of war that determined the resistance strategy of the Tajik commanders. One of the most important spin-off effects of the war of resistance was the claiming of local authority and control by evicting the government representatives from most of the countryside. War also catapulted the Tajiks on the regional scene in central Asia, Russia, and Iran in the West of the country. Their toughest period in the history of Afghan conflict was the resistance against the Taliban, which stretched their forces and capacity to the limits.

The fortunes of the Tajiks changed after 9/11 as the American war against the Taliban and their subsequent removal from power placed them in a dominant position. Since the Bonn Agreement, the Tajiks have emerged as a very powerful and influential group within the new evolving Afghan state and out of it in the economy and the fledgling civil society. They are better "positioned to provide a large share of the leadership and sophistication required for the unification and rebuilding of Afghanistan's polity."[5] But the way in which other communities, particularly the Pashtuns, though fragmented, accept the new balance among the social forces of Afghanistan would greatly determine the place and political role of the Tajiks in the new Afghan state.[6]

UZBEKS

Uzbeks are one of the smallest ethnic groups of the country, comprising only about 8 percent of the population. They have made transition to a nontribal society with large numbers in modern professions quite similar to the transition made by the Tajiks. Uzbeks are not natives to Afghanistan but settled in the country at the time of Turkish invasions, and later as refugees and fighters escaping the Russian armies and thereafter the Soviet forces in central Asia. Like Tajiks, they have an ethnic state next door and have family and clan affiliations across the borders. As an ethnic group, they occupy an important geopolitical landscape between the Hindu Kush and the central Asian region beyond the Amu Darya. Their language and culture is closer to people in Uzbekistan than mainstream Afghanistan but the majority of them speak Dari as a second language.[7] The Taliban forces twice occupied Uzbeks' major city, Mazar-i-Sharif, and there was fierce fighting and untellable revenge atrocities by the combatants of the two sides. A Shia party, *Hizb-i-Wahdat*, joined Uzbeks in their resistance against the Taliban. The post-Taliban political developments have placed the Uzbek national leadership in a better position to bargain for power and resources and claim authority over their region, which is occasionally contested by the Tajik militia leaders from the neighboring provinces. With peace and stability returning to Afghanistan, Mazar-i-Sharif and Uzbek provinces, because of their location as a gateway to central Asian states, would emerge as a focal point of regional commerce and trade.

HAZARAS

Hazaras represent about 7 percent of the population of Afghanistan. They are not natives to the land but, as tales from oral history go, came as a part of invading hordes of Genghis Khan in the thirteenth century. The Hazaras have very distinctive Mongolian physical features and their dialect, Hazaragi, has Turkish and Mongolian vocabulary. The original dialect and social structures have changed during the past few centuries. They have gradually adopted Persian or Dari as their language and Shia Islam as their religion, under the influence of Persian rule in the region. Socially, they are no longer nomadic people but have largely become settled farmers in the highland valleys of central Afghanistan, which after them is call Hazarajat or the land of the Hazaras.[8] Their tribal structures and hierarchies are still the same. Tribal Hazara Khans and Sayyids stand at the top in the hierarchy of influence and power and have greater wealth than ordinary folks. The Hazaras are the poorest and most marginalized of ethnic communities of Afghanistan. It is partly their barren landscape and partly long-standing discrimination against them that has placed them in an inferior economic and social position. Until the second decade of last century, it was common to enslave Hazaras. They experienced the most brutal internal colonization in the 1890s when Amir Abdul Rehman decided to bring their desolate region under stricter control of Kabul. This move was accompanied by the opening up of their region for settlement of Pashtun tribes. Since then Pashtun presence as traders and farmers has substantially increased.

Hazaras, like other minority communities, have emerged out of the war more empowered and greatly conscious of their place in the Afghan society. During the war of resistance against the Soviet forces, they turned to revolutionary Islamic Iran for political support, conserved their energies by not actively taking part in the war, and paid a great deal of attention to forging unity among diverse Hazara groups in the region. Under the influence of Iran, they created a common umbrella organization, Hizb-i-Wahdat, which has been demanding greater regional autonomy for the Hazaras and their adequate representation in the administrative and political institutions.

AIMAQ

The Aimaq are the Persian speaking semi-nomadic social group that straddles the area between Herat in the west and the highlands of Hazarajat in the East. Their numbers are somewhere between half a million to three-quarters of a million. They appear to be Mongolian in features but they are of mixed Mongolian and Turkish origin who migrated from Central Asia. They are divided into four distinctive clans—Jamshedis, Taimani, Taimuri, and Firozkohi. All of them have distinctive cultural traits and speak variants of the Dari language that is closer to Herati accent. Their areas, like the Hazarajat, have seen migration of the Pashtun, who share common grazing lands with them and some of which have now settled in this region. The relations between the two communities, unlike others, have been peaceful and cooperative.

OTHERS

The Turkmens, Nuristanis, and Balochis constitute smaller social groups that make up about 4 percent of the Afghan population.[9] Balochis of Afghanistan have much in common with the tribes of Balochistan in Pakistan and are socially closer to them than with any Afghan group. Nuristanis share history, ethnicity, and culture with the *Kafirs* (unbelievers) of Kafristan, a region in the northwest of Pakistan. The same community of Kafirs was converted to Islam by force in the late nineteenth century and the area was renamed Nuristan, meaning a region that embraced the light of Islam. This small group of Nuristanis is isolated from mainstream national life. The Afghan Turkmens share a border, ethnicity, and language with people across the border in Turkmenistan. They have a tribal social formation and have a semi-nomadic life style. A good number of them have settled in northern towns and engage in trade.

None of the main ethnic groups is homogenous in its internal composition or social structure. Pashtuns, for instance, have a large number of tribes and subtribes with whom they identify. Quite often, it is not the ethnic category but their place of residence that forms the basis for an individual's identity in Afghanistan. As elsewhere, identity is a multilayered conception in Afghanistan. A person can be an Afghan, a Pashtun, Gilzai, and Ghaznavi depending on the circumstances and the social context within which he is expressing identity. The questions of ethnic identity and group solidarity have gained political significance as the twenty-eight-year-long war has vastly changed the population landscape of the country. We will discuss some of the legacies of the conflict and how they impact upon reconstruction of social and political life in Afghanistan later in this chapter. There are still millions of Afghan refugees in Iran and Pakistan and a great number of them are physically dislocated inside the country. After a bitter armed conflict for many years, Afghanistan's social groups are in the process of readjusting to new social and political spaces. The purpose of our discussion about ethnicity is to make two points. First, historically, ethnic loyalties have been stronger than any other loyalty and have had varying degrees of intensity among different social groups. In the course of the long civil war, ethnicity has emerged as a powerful political force defining identity, group affiliation, and advancing claim for representation and access to power. Second, the issues of ethnicity, state, and political power in Afghanistan have a regional and geopolitical context because all major ethnic groups of Afghanistan spill over into the territories of neighboring states. This attracts the involvement of other regional states in support of one ethnic group or another.[10]

It is equally important to note that the two major ethnic groups of Afghanistan, the Pashtuns and Tajiks, are not socially coherent through a common language; this gives each of them a semblance of cultural unity. The Pashtuns are further subdivided along tribal lines, have social hierarchies, and there is a vertical division among them: Barakzais, Mohammadzais, the Durranis from Kandahar being higher than the Ghilzais of the eastern zones. The Dari-speaking Tajiks, the second largest ethnic community, don't have similar social divisions but do have horizontal subidentities, like Herati, Badakhshani, and Kabuli.[11] Some of the groups, mainly Pashtuns, are interspersed geographically due to deliberate state policy of their resettlement out of their historical homelands for land and water resources.[12] They have also intermingled in a few urban areas, like Herat, Kabul, and Mazar-i-Sharif. Trade, commerce, expansion of government activities before the Saur revolution, new opportunities for ed-

ucation, and government services have created social and political space for
ethnic groups to interact with one another. What we are suggesting is that ethnic group boundaries, despite the strong feelings of separate identities, were
porous because of overlapping layers of common religion, language, and sect.
Some of the groups became socially more integrated through marriage bonds,
which in the Afghan culture is more of a family affair that an individual act.
Social integration across ethnic groups in Afghanistan is quite common but it
has generally taken place more in the modern social and economic context of
the town than in the rural areas where the vast numbers live. In the rural setting they tend to gravitate around narrow family and subtribal identities.

Although 99 percent of the population is Muslim, relations among various sects have not been harmonious. The estimates of Sunni and Shia[13]
sects vary widely from one source to another. It is generally believed that
about 80 to 90 percent of the Afghans practice Sunni Islam, while 10 to 20
percent are followers of the Shia sect. The numbers and relative strength of
each have gained greater political significance than ever before, as they are
used to support demands and claims for a greater share in power. There is
a deep sense of persecution among the Shia religious minority, who are predominantly Hazaras. Last century, they were systematically attacked and
even enslaved by the Tajiks, Uzbeks, and Pashtuns.[14] However, it is necessary to dispel the notion that sectarian divide is along ethnic lines. Not all
Hazaras adhere to the Shia sect, nor are all Tajiks or Pashtuns Sunnis. Due
to inter-marriages and conversion from one Islamic sect to another, the religious divide has never been strictly along ethnic lines.

ETHNICITY AND NATION BUILDING

Historically, ethnic groups in Afghanistan have coexisted without major
conflict over resources or on the issue of representation. A sort of ethnic balance existed among the majority and minority groups. This notion of balance is based on terms of harmony, equilibrium, and stability of relationships among the ethnic groups and not in terms of any social, economic, or
political equality, which is hardly possible in real social situations. The
Pashtun groups that founded the Afghan state starting as a tribal confederacy dominated the superstructure of the state through its turbulent existence for more than two centuries.[15] The Afghan monarchs though Pashtun
in ethnic origin were ecstatic in embracing the social values, cultures, and
language other than Pashto, the national language of the Pashtun, on both
sides of the Afghanistan and Pakistan borders. They adopted Persian, which
in Afghanistan with local variance of idiom and accent is known as Dari for
its elegance and association with the high elite and the intellectual culture
of the Persian court. The Persian language and culture through Persian im-

perial domination of the region for centuries in Afghanistan, and beyond
into central Asia, has left enduring marks on local populations, including
Tajiks and the Afghan oligarchy.[16]

It is questionable whether the Afghan kings in the twentieth century
made any serious and deliberate attempt to construct an inclusive and composite national identity representative of the ethnic cultures, folklores, and
modern literary expressions. Many historians and observers of the contemporary society and politics of Afghanistan believe that Afghan nationalism
and identification of most of the ethnic groups with this idea, or some
might argue, ideal, subsumed other layers of divisive identities and gave
Afghanistan a coherent sense of national identity.[17] But non-Pashtun intellectuals and subnationalist elements have argued that the construction of a
single national identity had a Pashtun social base, as it rested on Pashtunwali, or the historical social code of the Pashtun tribes.[18] For this reason,
Pashtun groups have identified themselves with Afghan nationalism more
than other ethnic groups. Mainly Pashtun ethnic symbols and cultural expressions in dance and music were adopted as national culture. Since the
declaration of independence in 1919, after the Treaty of Rawalpindi between the British Indian government and King Amanullah Khan,[19]
Afghanistan used three different routes to channel the construction of a single national identity. These were: (a) strengthening and expanding the administrative capacity of the central government in order to penetrate into
different areas of the Afghan society; (b) perpetuating a uniform system of
education that was embedded in the Afghan/Pashtun national ethos; (c)
promoting a common identity disregarding ethnic and social diversity.[20]
Tajiks, Uzbeks, Hazaras and many other smaller ethnic communities didn't
see themselves through the Pashtun-based construction of a single national
identity. They resented nonrecognition of their individualities and their exclusion from the national identity–making process, but they had very few
channels to express grievances or seek access to power and resources beyond the narrow circles of ethnic elites tied to the Afghan oligarchy.

In any authoritarian system, the dominant ethnic groups write the script
of state and nationhood because this kind of politics is by nature exclusionary.[21] Afghanistan under the monarchy was no exception. In the absence of institutions for interest articulation or facilitating representation of
different social groups in the power structure, the monarch acting as the
chief patriarch determined who got what and why. In this kind of political
system, it is also easier to generate myths about national identity, nationalism, and nationhood, and sustain them in the absence of political participation.[22] We know that myths are important for generating support for national symbols and articulating a common sense of nationhood, but if
these myths and symbols are representatives of one single dominant group,
which in the case of Afghanistan was the Pashtun, other groups begin to

question the intentions and sincerity of such projects. The non-Pashtun groups were not comfortable with the Pashtun-oriented national solidarity and cultivation of national ethos.[23] But they were unable to present any serious challenge to the notion that all peoples living in Afghanistan were Afghans and that Afghan nationalism and national identity was inclusive of all groups within the society.

Did this project progress or succeed in its objectives under the monarchy? There is mixed evidence about its success. The outside world did recognize Afghan nationalism and its strong historical roots in resistance against foreign invaders, and the valor and sentiment of great sacrifice that the Afghans have demonstrated again and again to defend their country.[24] Within the country also a strong sense of Afghan national identity has prevailed, at least in the urban settings and among the educated classes. This sense did not travel deep into the rural society for the reason that the question of larger identity is irrelevant to their daily existence, and their identification is with narrower communities of family, clan, subtribe, tribe, locality, and region.[25] It is also a social fact in other developing countries where modernity has not crossed the frontiers of towns and cities. The policies aimed at increasing the writ of central government or fostering single nationhood did not end ethnic and social fragmentation of Afghanistan. National integration is a long and evolutionary historical process that can be accomplished by economic and social transformation of a society and by providing effective political tools of empowerment to different ethnic communities, recognizing their individuality and increasing their representation. Additionally, there is also a time factor, the duration of independence for maturing nationhood.[26] Regional and international environments determine the geopolitical fix that can impede or facilitate development of national integration. Afghanistan, being landlocked, having a poor resource base, and being on the margins of world politics was not lucky enough to obtain enough economic or political support. The change of its role from a historical buffer to an aligned state of the former Soviet Union further alienated her from alternative centers of world power.[27] The process of national consolidation gravely suffered with political instability, political polarization, and creeping influence of regional powers and internal confrontations that took both ideological as well as ethnic shapes.

ETHNICITY AND COMMUNIST REGIME

The leaders and ideologues of the Afghan communist factions were overly impressed by almost everything about Soviet communism, including nationalities policy. Even in the initial stages, when the new communist government had to find its feet on the shaky political ground on which it had landed it-

self, proclaimed that it would protect and advance the rights of the ethnic minorities and promote their languages and cultures.[28] This was in line with the
ideological orientation of the Marxists in other parts of the world, where they
have supported ethnic movements and their quest for autonomy and political rights, sometimes to cause dissent and fragmentation in states seen in the
opposite political camp.[29] The Afghan communists, driven by ideological
zeal, wanted to show that they were creating a different social and political order, and for that purpose, they wanted to redefine the relationship between
state and society, and among different ethnic communities. The nationality
tone became more emphasized when Babrak Karmal took over after getting
his arch political rival, Hafizullah Amin, killed. He talked about "ensuring a
new atmosphere of democratic legality, trust and cooperation between the
nationalities of Afghanistan," vowing that oppression and injustice were
things of the past.[30]

Ethnic policies under Karmal, at least at a rhetorical level, took four different expressions. First was the recognition of minority languages and expression of regional and local cultures associated with different social
groups. Before communist rule, Afghanistan's school education was bilin-
gual, with the choice of Persian or Pashto as the medium of instruction. It
was perhaps a natural choice, given the historical importance of the two
languages and tradition of imparting education in either of the two. The
Pashtun-dominated regions in the south and east of the country for historical reasons preferred Pashto, while the other parts of the country adopted
Persian, which has also been a language of interethnic communication. The
Afghan communists began to change the two-language educational system
by replacing it with multiple languages, giving a choice to the ethnic minorities like Uzbeks, Turkmens, Nuristanis and even a tiny minority, the
Balochis, to teach school children in their mother tongues. Disregarding the
question of practicality of the new languages project, the ideologues of the
new regime wanted to strike a departure from the past. Another factor in replacing Persian with regional languages was the growing cultural influence
of Iran, and the apprehension among the Afghan and Soviet communists
that Iran would revive the Persian language based culture in central Asia.[31]
It was partly the influence of the Pashtuns in the communist party of
Afghanistan that Pashto language teaching, learning, and literature began to
get more importance, hoping that it would take the place of Persian as an
inter-ethnic language.

The second part of communist ethnic policies emphasized decentralization of administrative powers to the provinces, districts, and to the lower
levels.[32] This policy was, however, limited to the official declarations, because the authority of the communist state under the stress of nationwide
resistance had crumbled, forcing the regime to rely on centralized measures
of security and political control. Two other areas of communist nationality

policy, political representation of minority and culture, are quite significant. The regime, in a perpetual political crisis and devoid of political legitimacy, thought it wiser to solicit the support of ethnic minorities to compensate for the loss of support from the majority groups that had taken up arms against it. The best way to make its overtures toward the minorities, known and felt in the hope of creating desirable political effect was to assign political responsibilities to the known and prominent members of ethnic minorities. It was not exactly political empowerment of the minorities but symbolism of inclusion in the political hierarchy. This sent out a powerful message to politically and culturally alienated groups. Finally, recognition of the multiethnic cultural character of Afghanistan opened up new avenues for cultural expression in the form of daily newspapers in ethnic languages, the formation of folk song and dance troupes, and wider publicity of ethnic poets and their works.[33] All the publications had a lot of Central Asian content and liberally borrowed the style and material of renowned intellectuals and poets who had earned name and fame in that region.

The question is how successful was the nationality policy of the communist regime? It is quite problematic to come up with any measurement of any policy in dynamic conditions of conflict. The impact of the nationality policy went beyond political symbolism in giving the ethnic minorities a feeling of recognition, political importance, and a sense of political participation. For that reason, the regime succeeded in generating a political effect in the north of the country where the resistance forces from other regions were not able to extend their political influence. That minority region remained the focus of the communist regime both in allocation of whatever resources it could spare from war and also as a source of raising local counterinsurgency militias.

Although the Afghan communist regime in the fashion of the Soviet Union set itself above ethnic considerations, the hard political fact was that individual identity and alliances and grouping within the party were seldom separated from ethnicity. The formation of communist factions and their attempts to establish control over power in Kabul showed tremendous political friction and polarization along ethnic lines. Personal ambitions of the top leaders further accentuated divisions and splits within the party. The most notable difference between the two major factions, the Khalq and the Parcham, was the different nature of the social support base along urban-rural, Pashtun and non-Pashtun dividing lines.[34] The Khalq and Parcham were so divided from the founding of the PDPA to its disintegration that in the view of Anthony Arnold, one of the early commentators on the subject, "loyalty to Moscow was a factor" in keeping factions together, but "incapable of reconciling their fundamental antagonism and intolerance of one another."[35] The self-destructive feuds subsequently consumed all of them, wrecking the political ideal of revolution and reform.

The Pashtuns more than any other ethnic group were against the communists; this enmity was not along the lines of the ethnic origins of the communists but against the foreignness of their ideology and the imperial influence of Moscow. Pashtuns' anger and their low level of resistance flared up into a national uprising when the Soviets installed Babrak Karmal, who besides being a Tajik was a replacement for the assassinated Pashtun leader Hafizullah Amin. Coupled with this was the way in which Babrak Karmal was brought into power and the outright invasion of the country by the Soviet Union. All this set the Pashtuns and all other social groups on the course of confrontation with the Afghan state. At this point, the Pashtun had seen power slipping away from them. The Pashtuns had more than one objective for fighting against the former Soviet Union and their local protégés. Liberation of the country being at the top in the hierarchies of objectives, one of their primary interests was in restoring Pashtun dominance in the central power structure because they thought it was their right justified by historical and demographic factors.

The Soviet Union in its multipronged strategy of pacifying Afghanistan also used ethnicity as one of its cards in countering insurgency. Divide and rule has been a time-tested strategic dogma of all imperial powers, and ethnic divisions provide ample opportunity to play this game. Although all the ethnic groups took up arms against the former Soviet Union, not all of them waged the war of resistance with the same nationalist or ideological zeal, intensity, and consistency. The Pashtuns, being numerous, having support among the coethnics in the bordering regions across Pakistan, and with strong official patronage from the host country were more determined to fight until the last Soviet soldier vacated their country. Some of the Afghan groups made compromises through their foreign supporters. Iran, isolated and being in the containment ring of the United States, did not encourage the Hazara groups to go all out after the Soviet forces but secured some kind of regional autonomy for them.[36] They became more interested in administering and defending the Hazarajat, their traditional geographical homeland, than engaging the Soviet or communist forces. In a way the Soviets succeeded in isolating the Shias from mainstream resistance. The only exception was that of Ayatullah Mohsini from the Kandhar region, who came to Pakistan, but he hardly had any forces to organize resistance. The Soviet Union concentrated its efforts to secure an ethnic support base among the Uzbeks around the Mazar-i-Sharif by giving weapons and training them to fight against the Mujahideen factions. Abdul Rashid Dostam first emerged as a warlord under the patronage of the Soviet forces. There is also considerable evidence to suggest that after the second Soviet incursion into the Panjsher valley in 1983 the Soviet Union entered into a deal with the Tajik commander Ahmad Shah Masud.[37] The deal was not, however, about winding up resistance forces but a sort of peaceful coexistence between the two and a mutual recognition of each other's interests.

RESISTANCE AND POLITICAL FRAGMENTATION

Unlike many of the national liberation movements that had a national command structure and presented themselves as united fronts of all the sectors of the society against the common enemy, the occupier or an imperial power, the Afghan resistance took an opposite direction. From the outset it was fragmented along tribal, ethnic, and local lines.[38] In our view, there are two reasons for its fragmentation. First, it was the spontaneity of national uprising against the Soviet invasion. Without any unified national call, all the ethnic groups and local communities, mostly outside Kabul, began to resist the communist government which was already under pressure from relatively more organized groups. The local community leader, village, or tribal chief, and later, as the resistance movement progressed, the local commander, emerged as the man on the scene, organizing, supervising, and controlling the armed men. All ethnic groups had a territorial base and they were not willing to hand over control of their historical homeland to other ethnic group leaders. In the tribal regions of the country, a tribe would not give up local control to any other. The resistance parties based in Pakistan had to go through the local commander, and in most cases, were not able to penetrate deeply into the local social structures. It was therefore easier to stay within the comfortable confines of the familiar territory where the resistance groups had a social support base, which they jealously guarded against the encroachment of other groups. The ethnic base of resistance parties, with a few exceptions in the Islamist groups, we believe, was the most crucial factor in causing ethnic fragmentation in the country, which continues to cast a heavy shadow on post-Taliban state reconstruction activities. The ethnic groups in the process of war against the former Soviet Union gained international recognition and support by developing horizontal relations with regional states for securing economic and military assistance.[39] By liberating their respective ethnic zones through denying control to the illegitimate central state which was under the control and influence of a foreign power, the non-Pashtun groups gained administrative autonomy, established self-governance, and with the militias or resistance forces of their own vastly empowered themselves, as never before in the modern history of Afghanistan. The story of the Pashtun-based resistance groups is very different. They were never unified under any single party or leader and their fragmentation was on regional, religious, and ideological lines. Six of the seven Mujahideen parties recognized by Pakistan were mainly Pashtun in ethnic origin.

The second important reason for ethnic character of the Afghan resistance, though overshadowed by a call for *Jihad* and liberation mythology at that time, was the absence of political institutions like political parties, free media, and press and political forums. Whatever political development Afghanistan achieved during the constitutional decade (1964–1973) was wiped out first by the republican coup of Sardar Daoud and then by the brutal and repressive communist takeover in April 1978.[40] Absence of political institutions perhaps could be compensated for by some kind of ethnic homogeneity, but even in such situations, political rivalries among leaders and groups have created fractured resistance movements. Had the king been wise in allowing the political parties to register and engage in open politics, perhaps many of the tragedies of Afghanistan might have been averted. The parties could have provided a common base, leadership, and organizational networks to gel the ethnic-based resistance groups together. There is also the role of the neighboring states in keeping the Afghan resistance movement divided. The Afghan intellectuals and leaders are not unjustified in their criticism of Pakistan and Iran in pumping support and extending patronage to selective resistance parties and their leaders.[41] Pakistan has been widely accused of giving undue preference to *Hizb-i-Islami* and its leader Gulbadin Hikmatyar, and also for recognizing seven parties as legitimate resistance groups, providing them sanctuary and support, while excluding others with moderate or nationalist credentials.[42] There is considerable evidence to support the view that Islamabad's policy toward the Afghan resistance had a strong bias in favor of the Islamist groups that were ideologically closer to the religious right of the country and the pan-Islamic vision of late General Zia ul-Haq, the military ruler at the time.

When in 1987 Moscow began to signal to the world community that it would withdraw from Afghanistan, a sign that some of the Mujahideen parties had read in the weakness of the Soviet counterinsurgency strategy, the resistance groups began to preposition themselves for future power struggles and to defend their own turfs against other Mujahideen rivals. The two major resistance parties, *Hizb-i-Islami* and *Jamiat-i-Islami*, which were both sort of Islamist in orientation but with very different ethnic social bases, wanted to conserve energies and resources to prepare for capturing power. We think the script for the battle of Kabul after the fall of Najibullah had been written well before the event, and the capture of the national seat of power by Jamiat's Ahmed Shah Masud and counterattacks by the Hizb to stake its claim on power were no accidents. The ethnic minorities or non-Pashtun social groups in Afghanistan, having tasted a great degree of autonomy and self-assertion through their individual security forces, were never willing to accept the traditional Pashtun domination; a fact that continues to trouble relations among the Pashtun majority and the rest of the communities.

The formation of the Mujahideen government under the Peshawar Accord in the early part of May 1992 was a political move to present the parties that had been involved in the resistance as larger than ethnic identities. The assumption behind this move was that the Mujahideen factions would work together and collectively undertake the enormous task of restoring peace, social order, and stability in the country. The vast devastation caused by the Soviet war was truly a national challenge and it was hoped that the leaders of the seven parties would rise to the occasion and guide the country out of the mess. It was a false hope because it rested on misconceived notions of social structures of the parties and their capacity to form a durable coalition. The rhetoric of Afghan and Islamic brotherhood and that the factions had common history and identical stakes in the future stability of the country didn't last the duration of the meetings called by friendly countries like Pakistan and Saudi Arabia that had supported them during the years of resistance. What was really at stake? It was the old, classic question of power. In the absence of political institutions to mediate conflict of interest, persuasion by external powers couldn't bring about a change in the attitudes of the Afghan parties, which had been marked by long years of mistrust among their leaders. Therefore, the Peshawar Accord for sharing power and constituting a coalition government began to show strains within months as multiple rivalries along ethnic, sectarian, and party lines spilled over into active and very deadly conflict in and around Kabul.[43] In the first few months after the arrival of the victorious Mujahideen parties in Kabul, the Wahabis of *Ittehad-i-Islami* of Professor Abdul Rab Rasul Siaf fought pitched battles against the Shia militia, the Tajik forces of Ahmed Shah Masud attacked the Uzbek forces of Dostam to get them out of the city, and *Hizb-i-Islami* forces of Hikmatyar camping at the outskirts rained the inhabitants with rockets in order to send the message that Hikmatyar was a serious contender for power. It was not the dawn of liberation that the citizens of Kabul or generally the people of Afghanistan had hoped and fought for. We have already alluded to some of the structural reasons for this kind of political outcome of the war. The single largest failure of Pakistan, the United States, and other powers that supported the Mujahideen parties against the former Soviet Union were in the area of managing the politics of the resistance. Either they were too optimistic about the ability of the Afghan factions that hardly had any experience in political coalitions to share power or they had no long-term political vision about Afghanistan beyond the retreat of the Soviet forces. This neglect was partly responsible for the conflict among most of them after the departure of the common adversary from the national scene.

The multiple confrontations among the Mujahideen parties turned the entire country into a war zone; each community, ethnic or subtribal, fending for itself. The absence of state and its institutions from the lives of these

communities encouraged the local structure of authority along ethnic and
still narrower clan and local levels. Regional or local autonomy that the social groups had enjoyed for more than a decade, since all of them had
turned against the central state, which was seen as an enemy controlled by
a foreign power during the Soviet war, changed the traditional power relations both among the ethnic communities as well as between these communities and the central state. During the Mujahideen rule that had placed
the Tajik ethnic group at the apex of power in Kabul, the Pashtun majority
began to feel that it had lost sovereign control over Afghanistan. Although
the majority of them were as marginalized as other social communities, the
ordinary Pashtun had a greater sense of security and ownership of the system in the Pashtun king and the Pashtun-dominated oligarchy ruling
Kabul. At social and psychological levels, the Pashtun identification with
the old system was stronger than other communities.

Although the Mujahideen government headed by Tajik president Burhanuddin Rabbani had many Pashtun elements, the ordinary Pashtuns and
their tribal and party leaders thought that they had been betrayed and the
Tajiks had unlawfully captured the power. They also found proof in the denial of power to Hikmatyar; a Pashtun party leader of a nonethnic ideological party, by the so-called Tajik-dominated government in violation of the
provisions of the Peshawar Accord. Along with this feeling of power loss,
political fragmentation, demographic dislocation, and the economic situation were perhaps worse than in other areas of the country. With the end of
foreign aid that was channeled through the Mujahideen parties mainly for
war efforts, the local commanders using the same arms resorted to criminal
activities. This included protection to heroin production and trafficking, extortion of money from traders by establishing checkpoints, and kidnapping
for ransom.[44] The countryside and smaller towns were plunged into total
chaos with the disintegration of the state. Many of these commanders who
emerged as local gendarmes frequently fought turf battles, and have seen it
as a profitable operation, many others joined the ranks of warlords con-
verting the entire country into fiefdoms. With no formal political authority,
or functional state institutions, the warlords ruled the country fragmenting
political power, society, and social cohesion everywhere.[45] But the effects of
political fragmentation were more pronounced in the Pashtun regions. The
failure of the Mujahideen parties to present a coherent, functional political
authority based on power-sharing arrangements produced the conditions
for localization and capture of power by ethnic and factional warlords.

TALIBAN AND THE PASHTUN ETHNICITY

The Taliban movement in the Pashtun areas was influenced by many factors
that we have examined in detail in a separate chapter, but anarchy, lawless-

ness, and excesses of the local commanders and warlords were the most immediate ones that triggered their uprising. However, their rapid rise and
popularity among the Pashtun tribes cannot be explained with reference to
their ability to provide security or restore social order alone.[46] Nor was coercion and intimidation a reason for the support that the Pashtuns extended to the Taliban leaders and their fighters. Why were the Taliban able
to get so much backing from the Pashtuns? As we have indicated elsewhere
in this volume, there was no single reason for Pashtun political interest in
the Taliban movement. Among other factors, Islam and ethnicity were the
most compelling reasons for the Pashtun community to support the Taliban. They did regard the Taliban as selfless young men devoted to the study
of religion, with the will to fight against the evil of warlordism and implement Islamic laws that the Mujahideen government had failed to do. But
underneath of all this there was a strong element of Pashtun ethnicity. The
Taliban and their leaders were ethnically Pashtun and their religious ethos,
much influenced by their traditional culture, were more or less the same.
However, some of their regional antagonists contend that the vast majority
of the Pashtuns practiced non-Wahabi traditional Islam of the Sufi saints.[47]
The fact is that during the war of resistance, even before the influence of
Whabi Islamic teaching and practices among the Pashtuns, had significantly
eroded the social base of traditional Islamic practices. That is evident on
both sides of the Afghan-Pakistan border in the proliferation of *madrasa*
networks. Disregarding this controversy, the Pashtuns saw in the Taliban a
genuine hope for restoring peace and reuniting the country.

However, their conception of reuniting the country was very different
from the rest of the ethnic groups. While other ethnic groups, now significantly empowered, wanted unity by redefining the terms of social contract
among various groups, the Pashtuns wanted continuity of the old relationships. The subject of the Taliban's efforts to construct a new identity, its relationship with Islam, and the role that the Pashtun ethnicity played in
their political project is very complex, and therefore it does not lend itself
to an easy explanation. Ostensibly, there is a contradiction between the uni-
versalistic identity of Islam that would subordinate other forms of identity
articulation and the Pashtun identity of the Taliban itself. Never did the Taliban leaders express themselves in ethnic terms, because in their worldview,
ethnic particularism stood opposite to the common Islamic faith that most
of the Afghans shared. Their view of common Islamic identity applied to
similar Islamic communities across the borders of Afghanistan. Such a pan-
Islamic view is very common among the Islamists in almost every country.
And that also partly explains why the Islamist activists from different countries descended on Afghanistan during and after the war of resistance. There
was a warm welcome for all of them and the Taliban needed their support
for their quest for power and also to turn their country into a hospitable
place for those seeking refuge from repressive governments and willing to

fight for Islamic rule.[48] However, the larger and overarching Islamic identity and pan-Islamic sentiments tend to hide the ethnic factor behind the Taliban movement. It is not only how a social group like the Taliban identifies itself, what the sociologists might call subjective identity, but also how a particular group is understood and recognized by others.[49] The non-Pashtuns, some of them equally Islamists on their own terms, did not accept the Taliban's self-projection as an entirely Islamic and nonethnic movement.[50] Nor was their claim of the movement and its leaders being above the ethnic considerations and the promise of accepting local autonomy of the ethnic groups in return for the acceptance of Taliban ideology and right to rule in Kabul regarded as real.[51]

The minority ethnic groups were hardly impressed by the unity calls of the Taliban under one Allah, one Quran, and one Islamic law.[52] They viewed them as essentially Pashtuns but even worse than the old Pashtun oligarchy because of their rigid and orthodox interpretation of Islamic law and its harsh implementation. All ethnic groups, the Tajiks, Uzbeks, and the Hazaras opposed the Taliban tooth and nail to defend their traditional territorial strongholds and claim to self-rule. These ethnic groups being relatively weak and fragmented themselves with a history of infighting among themselves now saw a more powerful enemy in the Taliban, and therefore decided to close their ranks. The Taliban's march beyond the Pashtun territories and onto Kabul provoked a new phase of civil war that was primarily defined by the questions of power and ethnicity. In the case of ethnically fragmented societies, the two cannot be separated. With the growth of ethnic identity and its politicization, the demands on sharing power at the center, seeking recognition of identity, and assertion of autonomy have all been common among minorities.[53] Afghanistan's minority groups had similar concerns, interests, and strategies of empowerment. At the same time, Afghanistan was and is a different country in two important respects. First, the long years of war have greatly affected the construction of identity by each ethnic group, and second, each one of the identities has gotten entangled into a web of relationships with neighboring foreign powers and similar ethnic groups across the national borders. These two factors contributed to the complexity of the civil war and the patterns of internal and external linkages that in many ways provided fuel to the civil war.

The conflict between the Northern Front that represented a wide mix of ethnic minorities supported by a good number of foreign powers, and the Taliban, supported by Pakistan, Saudi Arabia, and the United Arab Emirates in varying degrees, shows the ugly face of multiple confrontation that raged in and around Afghanistan over which of the Afghan groups would govern and what would be the degree of influence that external powers would exercise. The Taliban, while in power, reinforced the view that it wanted supremacy of Islamic law as it interpreted it, and second a veiled domination of the Pashtun majority. It is no surprise that Pashto, the language of the Pashtun ethnic group, got better recognition as almost all the Taliban leaders delivered their sermons in this language. Their press conferences and dialogue with representatives of foreign countries were also delivered in Pashto.[54] Not that Pashto replaced Dari in the urban areas, but being the language of the ruling militia, it became associated with power. All other ethnic groups reacted by focusing on their own particular identities and fought back to deny their territories to the Taliban. By any criterion or definition, this phase of the Afghan conflict was ethnic in orientation. The divide was primarily between the Pashtun Taliban and the non-Pashtun ethnic minority groups. There was only a very limited number of individuals on both sides who for political reasons stayed with the nonethnic side. The Taliban–Northern Front war was the most bitter in terms of revenge, brutality, and intragroup violence.[55] The atrocities committed by the Taliban against their enemies both times they took over Mazar-i-Sharif are horrific and well-documented. The atrocities that the Taliban committed while taking over Mazar-i-Sharif the second time, and what their enemies did to them when they evicted them the first time, are horrific and well-documented.[56] The Taliban, because of their zeal, commitment, numbers, resources, and foreign support were able to capture most of the country and were able to bottle up their opponents to a very narrow zone. The assassination of Ahmed Shah Masud on 9 September 2001, just two days before the 9/11 terrorist attacks in New York and Washington, D.C., made them virtually the new rulers of Afghanistan.[57] Their victory however began to change into their defeat and removal from power as the United States and the rest of world community came down very heavily on them because of their support of Osama bin Laden and his terror network, both of which they hosted within the country. Their refusal to hand over Osama and other leaders of his Al Qaeda organization to the U.S. authorities led to their defeat and expulsion from power.

POLITICAL RECONSTRUCTION AND ETHNICITY

The United States, in its war against the Taliban after the 9/11 tragedy, tried the time-tested strategy of courting the enemies of the enemy. In Afghanistan, the Northern Front emerged the natural ally of the United States, and the leaders of the Front, for a price, obliged the United States for its need for their territory, manpower, and intelligence gathering.[58] Both had a common interest in defeating the Taliban; the Northern Front, battered, humiliated, and pushed into a corner of the country by the Taliban, was rather too eager to jump on the American side and take the place of the Taliban in Kabul.

Therefore, it is necessary that one must assess the impact of ethnic factor in the reconstruction of the Afghan state and society by raising this question: is the emerging power structure well represented by all ethnic groups? Is there any feeling of exclusion or marginalization? The majority of the Pashtuns feel that they have been excluded because of the Pashtun background of the Taliban, and that their representation in the post-Taliban power arrangements has been far below their numbers in the population. There is a deep sense of loss of power within the Pashtun sectors of the Afghan society, but they neither have the political parties, institutions, or leaders in the opposition to present their grievances or articulate their interests. Individual leaders from the Pashtun area who have struck independent deals or have joined the post-Taliban political arrangements give a false impression about the Pashtuns having accepted the reality on the ground. Of course, there are many such important individuals with tribal or clan support, but there are doubts if they represent the mass sentiment of the largest community. The selection of Hamid Karzai during the Berlin conference in December 2001 as head of the transitional administration was a good political move as he is a Pashtun from Kandahar, the hometown of the Taliban.[59] But has it really assured the Pashtuns that they have an adequate share in political power at the center? Selection of Karzai, who has done relatively well in consolidating his own position and expanding the base of his government after the October 2004 elections, has not erased the impression that power has been captured by the Tajik warlords supported by the United States and that Karzai is just a frontman without any real power.[60] This perception was perhaps accurate in the initial stage when the United States was trying to put together the pieces of the Afghan political puzzle. And it owed a lot to the Northern Front leaders who for their own reasons welcomed the U.S. intervention to "liberate" their country from the Taliban. But over the last four years, things have begun to change.

Contrary to popular perceptions among the Pashtun social groups, Karzai has emerged as a central political figure due to international recognition and support. Karzai has also managed to strike pragmatic alliances, and has garnered the support of a large section of the Pashtun community, who voted for him in the presidential race in October 2004. Disregarding popular perceptions among the Pashtun social groups, Karzai has emerged as a central political figure by striking pragmatic alliances and has international recognition and support, but most importantly, a large section of the Pashtun community voted for him in the presidential race in October 2004.[61] The question is, was it due to genuine feelings for Karzai or a sign of protest and ethnic revulsion against his rival candidate, Mr. Yunis Qanooni, a Tajik warlord? Many observers believe that the presidential election demonstrated a sharp ethnic divide in the country. The Pashtuns voted for Karzai because he was a Pashtun, and the Tajiks voted mainly for the Tajik candidate and others for the members of their own communities. The results of presidential elections reflect a sort of national census on ethnicity. There was no major shift in voting across the ethnic lines, except where some important leader of an ethnic group entered into an alliance with a leader from another group. Such kind of voting behavior, however, is very common in the developing countries, particularly in south Asia, where people vote along the lines of caste, tribe, subtribe, clan, and extended networks of family or bridari.[62] Although Afghanistan is not an exception in this regard, the memory of intraethnic violence and social effects of a long civil war may have long-term effects on the balance of power among the ethnic groups. The most troubling aspect of the ethnic divide is that the majority group, the Pashtun, which had never defined itself in a narrow ethnic category and had symbolized the ethos of Afghan nationalism, has begun to nurture ethnic feelings. Scholars of ethnic studies have found different reasons for the rise of ethnic feelings, and it is not always the minority becoming politically alienated and marginalized.[63] Any community or ethnic group that enjoyed power for part of a country's history but saw decline in its share of power as other social groups got better representation had its ethnic identity become politicized.[64] The question of why Pashtuns supported the Taliban or why they remain relatively alienated from the power arrangements in Afghanistan cannot be addressed without examining ethnic fragmentation and disruption of traditional ethnic balance among the social groups.

A large section of the political and intellectual elite of the Pashtun community has held the view that the Pashtuns, who traditionally exercised relatively greater influence in Afghanistan, have lost power. It began to happen with the ouster of the communist regime of Najibullah.[65] Anwar-ul-Haq Ahady, a former professor of political science at Providence College, Rhode Island, and the governor of the State Bank of Afghanistan since the ouster of Taliban, attributes the decline of the Pashtuns to five major factors. These are: capture of Kabul by the coalition of ethnic minorities, fragmentation and conflict of interest among the Pashtun groups, the disconnect between the Pashtun resistance parties and the society at a grassroots level, negative Western feelings toward the Pashtun community because of its support and association with groups like the one led by Hikmatyar, and the competition for influence in Afghanistan among its neighbors.[66] For the last four years, the American war efforts to stabilize Afghanistan very much like the Soviet counterinsurgency strategy have focused on the Pashtun areas. The reasons for concentration of military operations against the Pashtun territory are identical, although the historical settings and driving force for military intervention by the superpowers are very different. Chief among them is the historical tradition of resistance among the Pashtuns against the presence of foreign powers in Afghanistan and a popular perception at present that their country has been invaded and occupied by the United States. The popular discourse and discussion on Afghanistan by the media ignores this fact, and rather it centers on the Taliban, Al Qaeda, and terrorism.[67] It is true that the

Taliban is still active and its attacks against the United States and fledgling Afghan national army troops seemed to have increased since 2005. Also, the leaders of the Taliban and Al Qaeda organizations have continued to evade arrest and prosecution. Nor has terrorism emanating from Pashtun-dominated regions across the Afghanistan-Pakistan border been completely eliminated. The activism of the Taliban and presence of fugitive leaders in the border regions between the two countries raises the question of why some sections of the Pashtuns, if not the majority, support them against the American forces even at a heavy cost of military reprisals and regular aerial attacks and ground operations.[68] Even if one concedes the point that there has been progress in winning over tribal loyalties in the Pashtun areas, and there has been progress of reconstruction projects, enlarging presence of security forces, and some rehabilitation of agricultural economy, the problem of insecurity, fear, and the presence of the Taliban persist. One may also raise the question of whether the Taliban is the right kind of identification of the forces that are resisting the presence of American forces and American support to the government in Kabul.

It would also not be irrelevant to study the political history of Afghanistan in similar situations, the two wars the British fought in the nineteenth century, and the one imposed by the Soviet Union in the last quarter of the twentieth century. On these three occasions, the Pashtuns took a larger part of the responsibility of defending the country and for that reason bore the brunt of the foreign wars. Two of the major characteristics of their earlier historical encounters with the foreign powers are relevant to the new war launched by the United States, though in a totally different context. First is the growth of wider support for the militias at the societal level and the involvement of more than one group. In the present situation which appears to be more complex, we see support from the Pashtun tribes on the Pakistani side of the border, joining of the insurgency activities by *Hizb-i-Islami* of Hikmatyar and also by the underworld of smugglers and drug traffickers.[69] The second characteristic is a sense of historical burden that the Pashtun seem to carry on their shoulders to defend Afghanistan. Such a sense has negative effects on interethnic relations in the country because it casts the minorities out of patriotic mythology and labels them as collaborators with foreign powers. This sense also existed at the time of the communist governments, particularly when the Soviets installed Babrak Karmal (1980–1986). By design and policy Karmal under Soviet guidance brought the ethnic minorities closer to the regime, to serve as a political counterweight to the Pashtuns who accounted for the bulk of anticommunist resistance forces.[70] The U.S. policy in a similar vein started with the cooptation of the ethnic minorities, and at least for three years, paid greater attention to leaders of ethnic minorities than to the Pashtuns. The reasons for this tilt or choice were obvious. The ethnic minorities driven out of power by the Taliban militia were more open to welcoming and supporting the U.S. forces than the Pashtun community that provided a strong political and ethnic base to the Taliban. In every situation, like the post-Taliban conditions of Afghanistan, some of the tribal leaders and strong individuals with local and regional influence from Pashtun areas have sided with the central government and cooperated with the foreign powers.

Ethnicity is an issue in all multiethnic societies.[71] But it is an issue of deeper concern and graver consequences in societies going through post-conflict reconstruction, which Afghanistan is today. The reason for this concern is the impact of stubborn legacies of the conflict on interethnic and intersocietal relationships. In Afghanistan ethnic communities have been guilty of genocidal acts, ethnic cleansing, and brutality against one another. As that phase of conflict is over and Afghanistan is rebuilding itself as a new state, the question of ethnic balance, equity, fair share in power, and adequate representation have become important. The non-Pashtun ethnic groups are greatly empowered, more self-confident, and have maintained control over their regions for decades now. Pashtuns who claim majority in the population think power has shifted to minority groups, notably the Tajiks, a view which is contested. Some of the Afghan scholars however argue that "there are no majority or minority ethnic groups" in Afghanistan because such a characterization is offensive and pejorative.[72] In our view nonrecognition of ethnicity as a factor in Afghanistan's present and future politics will not make this issue disappear, rather it would haunt the policy makers with its powerful influence on perceptions about power, identity, and marginality in Afghanistan. Our argument is that Afghanistan has changed vastly in terms of ethnic balance due to civil war, foreign intervention, and state failure. Defining Afghan nationalism in singular terms, therefore, is no longer a political possibility. As reconstruction is the overarching political theme in Afghanistan, perhaps its identity politics need reconstruction by recognizing the reality of ethnic empowerment of minorities and providing institutionalized balance and representation of all groups in the political, economic, and cultural life of the country. Afghanistan and its majority community, the Pashtuns, need to understand the political logic of a reconstruction of identity as a composite nationhood that would be accommodative and not exclusionary. Recognition of ethnicity and legitimacy of the claim of each group for space in all spheres of national life will have positive political implications about rights, representation, autonomy, and a sense of worth and right to participate in the power arrangements of the country. With the growth in the capacity of the state, as reconstruction projects in different areas of national life spin off positive political effects, the ethnic groups may find a new balance among themselves.

NOTES

1. Nazif M. Shahrani, "War, Factionalism, and the State in Afghanistan," *American Anthropologist* Vol. 104, No. 3 (September 2002), pp. 715–22.

2. Selig Harrison, "Nightmare in Baluchistan," *Foreign Policy*, No. 32 (Autumn 1978), pp. 136–60.

3. See debate on definitions of ethnicity, Stanley J. Tambiah, "Ethnic Conflict in the World Today," *American Ethnologist*, Vol. 16, No. 2 (May 1989) p. 335.

4. Richard Newell, one of the first-generation American scholars on Afghanistan's political history well before the emergence of the Taliban, commented that "Persisting divisions among them (Pashtuns) have weakened their claim to dominance. . . ." See his "Post-Soviet Afghanistan: The Position of the Minorities," *Asian Survey*, Vol. 29, No. 11 (November, 1989), p. 1094.

5. Ibid., p. 1096.

6. I am using the new Afghan state in terms of the evolving political structure of the country in the light of new constitution and post-Taliban political developments.

7. Harvey H. Smith, et al., *Area Handbook for Afghanistan* (Washington, D.C.: U.S. Government Printing Office, 1969), p. 75.

8. Ibid., pp. 72–74.

9. As mentioned in the text, these figures are not authentic. One may use the following sources: Louis Dupree, *Afghanistan* (Princeton, N.J.: Princeton University Press, 1973); Richard F. Nyrop and Donald M. Seekins, eds., *Afghanistan: A Country Study*, 5th edition (Washington, D.C.: U.S. Government Printing Office, 1986); Harvey H. Smith et al., *Area Handbook for Afghanistan* (Washington, D.C.: U.S. Government Printing Office, 1969).

10. Rupinder Kaur Bajwa, "Kin-State Intervention in Ethnic Conflicts: A Study of Afghanistan," in Gurnam Singh, *Ethno-Nationalism and Emerging World (Dis) Order*, pp. 168–82; Rajat Ganguly, *Kin-State Intervention: Lessons from South Asia* (New Delhi: Sage, 1998).

11. As Tajiks don't have tribal affiliation, they tend to identify themselves with a place of residence. See Harvey H. Smith et al., *Area Handbook for Afghanistan* (Washington, D.C.: U.S. Government Printing Office, 1969), p. 61.

12. Anwar-ul-Haq Ahady, "The Decline of the Pashtuns in Afghanistan," *Asian Survey*, Vol. 35, No. 7 (July 1995), p. 622.

13. The Sunnis are orthodox Muslims. In Afghanistan, they follow the Hanafi school of Islamic jurisprudence that was found by Abu Hanifa. The Hanafi school is one of the four schools of sunni jurisprudence, which are concerned with the interpretation of Sharia, the Islamic law. The shia sect is predominantly practiced in Iran. Followers of this sect believe that Ali, son-in-law of the Prophet of Islam, was the spiritual leader of religion after Prophet, and should have been the first Caliph. The history of Islam, particularly its early phase, has largely defined the positions of sunni and shia sects.

14. Hyman, op.cit., p. 8.

15. Louis Dupree, *Afghanistan* (Princeton: Princeton University Press, 1980); Gregorian, V., *The Emergence of Modern Afghanistan: Politics of Reform and Modernization, 1880–1946* (Stanford: Stanford University Press, 1969); G.P. Tate, *The Kingdom of*

Afghanistan: A Historical Sketch (Karachi: Indus Publications, 1973); S. Fida Yunas, *Afghanistan: A Political History*, two volumes (Peshawar: self-published, 2002); Senzil Nawid, "The State, the Clergy, and British Imperial Policy in Afghanistan during the 19th and Early 20th Centuries," *International Journal of Middle East Studies*, Vol. 29, No. 4 (November 1997), p. 582.

16. On the influence of Persian language in Afghanistan and Central Asia, see Edmund Herzig, "Regionalism, Iran and Central Asia," *International Affairs*, Vol. 80, No. 3 (May 2004) p. 511.

17. Ahady, op. cit., p. 622.

18. Elements of Pashtunwali code are: hospitality, giving refuge and protection to fugitives, and revenge.

19. On the Treaty of Rawalpindi, see *Pak-Afghan Discord A Historical Perspective (Documents 1855–1979)*, Ed. Mehrunnisa Ali, Pakistan Study Center, University of Karachi, 1990.

20. Barnett R. Rubin, "Lineages of the State in Afghanistan," *Asian Survey*, Vol. 28, No. 11 (November 1988) pp. 1196–99.

21. Perry Anderson, *Lineages of the Absolutist State* (London: Verso, 1974), pp. 462–550.

22. E. J. Hobsbawm, *Nations and Nationalism Since 1780: Programme, Myth, Reality* (Cambridge: Cambridge University Press, 1990).

23. In reaction to the perceived Pashtun domination, groups like Sitam-i-Milli emerged and they propagated an ideology of ethnic rights. Ralph Magnus and Eden Naby, "Afghanistan and Central Asia: Mirrors and Models," *Asian Survey*, Vol. 35, No. 7 (July 1995).

24. There are many accounts of Afghans fighting for the liberation of their country. For the Soviet-Afghan war, see for instance, Barnett R. Rubin, *The Search for Peace in Afghanistan: From Buffer State to Failed State* (New Haven and London: Yale University Press, 1995).

25. Syed Askar Mousavi, *The Hazaras of Afghanistan: An Historical, Cultural, Economic and Political Study* (Surrey: Curzon, 1998), pp. 168–74.

26. B. C. Upreti, "Ethnic Identity Consciousness and Nation-Building in Plural Societies: Some Observations," Gurnam Singh, ed., *Ethno-Nationalism and Emerging Word (Dis) Order* (New Delhi: Kanishka Publishers, Distributors, 2002), pp. 1–12.

27. Anthony Arnold, *Afghanistan: The Soviet Invasion in Perspective*, revised and enlarged edition (Stanford: Hoover Institution Press, 1985).

28. Beverely Male, *Revolution in Afghanistan: A Reappraisal* (London: Croom Helm, 1982), pp. 177–87.

29. Pakistan is a good example where the former Soviet Union and local Pakistani Marxists with Moscow's ideological orientation supported Baloch and Pashtun nationalities. See for example, Harrison, *In the Shadow of Afghanistan: Baluch Nationalism*.

30. Cited in Sauri P. Bhattacharya, "Soviet Nationality Policy in Afghanistan," *Asian Affairs*, June 1984, p. 130.

31. Eden Naby, "Ethnic Factor in Soviet-Afghan Relations," *Asian Survey*, Vol. 20, No. 3, March 1980, pp. 241–42.

32. Eliza van Hollen, "Afghanistan: 18 Months of Occupation," U.S. Department of the State, Public Affairs Bureau, Special Report No. 86, August 1981, pp. 1–3.

33. Following were the weekly newspapers that the Khalq government began to print and circulate about six to eight months after the revolution: Uzbek, *Yulduz* (Star), Turkmen, *Gurash* (Struggle), and the Baloch, *Soub*. This information is taken from Eden Naby, "Ethnic Factor in Soviet-Afghan Relations," pp. 242–43.

34. Anthony Arnold, *Afghanistan's Two-Party Communism: Parcham and Khalq* (Stanford: Hoover Institution Press, Stanford University, 1983), p. 36.

35. Ibid.

36. S. A. Mousavi, *The Hazaras of Afghanistan*, (Surrey: Curzon Press, 1998), pp. 175–202.

37. Author's interview with several officers of the ISI who worked with the Afghan resistance, Islamabad, June 2005.

38. Shah M. Tarzi, "Politics of the Afghan Resistance Movement: Cleavages, Disunity, and Fragmentation," *Asian Survey*, Vol. 31, No. 6 (June 1991), pp. 479–95.

39. Iran supported mainly Shia groups from Hazarajat; Pakistan's support was extended to all largely Tajik and Pashtun parties, though it also allowed refugees and leaders from other ethnic groups to base themselves on its territory. During the civil war years, the linkages of the Afghan groups with regional states took ethnic lines. S. A. Mousavi, "The Hazaras of Afghanistan: An Historical, Cultural, Economic and Political Study," (Surrey: Curzon Press, 1998), pp. 180–86.

40. General Umarzai, *Nights in Kabul: Actions behind the Curtain During the Last Two Decades in Afghanistan*, translated by Dr. Sher Zaman Taizi (Peshawar: Area Study Centre, Peshawar University, 2004).

41. Marvin G. Weinbaum, "Pakistan and Afghanistan: The Strategic Relationship," *Asian Survey*, Vol. 31, No. 6 (June 1991), pp. 496–511.

42. Author's interview with Afrasiab Khattak, Peshawar, 21 June 2005.

43. Amin Saikal, Modern *Afghanistan: A History of Struggle and Survival* (London, New York: I.B. Tauris, 2004), pp. 209–25.

44. Astri Suhrke, "Afghanistan: Re-tribalization of the War," *Journal of Peace Research*, Vol. 27, No. 3 (August 1990), pp. 241–46.

45. Ibid.

46. Nasreen Ghufran, "The Taliban and the Civil War Entanglement in Afghanistan," *Asian Survey*, Vol. 41, No. 3 (May–June 2001) p. 462.

47. That was the view of Pir Gilani and others.

48. Ahmed Rashid, "The Taliban: Exporting Extremism," *Foreign Affairs*, Vol. 78, No. 6 (November–December, 1999), 22–35.

49. On the question of identity formation, see John Rex, "Ethnic Identity and the Nation State: The Political Sociology of Multi-cultural Societies," *Social Identities*, Vol. 1 (1974) pp. 15–42.

50. The non-Pashtuns didn't accept the Taliban as above ethnic considerations. S. A. Mousavi, "*The Hazaras of Afghanistan*," p. 201.

51. The Taliban showed willingness to grant some sort of local autonomy to governors that they appointed in the areas that they captured. But such functionaries were their trustees although they belonged to the local communities. They also maintained their militia to defend them.

52. Ghufran, op. cit., p. 467.

53. On conditions under which ethnic identity grows, see Richard Jenkins, "Ethnicity etcetera: Social Anthropological Points of View," in Martin Bulmer and John

Solomos, eds., *Ethnic and Racial Studies Today* (London, New York: Routledge 1999), pp. 85–97; Paul Brass, *Ethnicity and Nationalism: Theory and Comparison* (Newbury Park, CA: Sage Publications, 1991), p. 8.

54. Olivier Roy, "Rivalries and Power Plays in Afghanistan: The Taliban, the Shari'a and the Pipeline," *Middle East Report*, No. 202 (Winter, 1996), pp. 37–38.

55. Amnesty International and Asia Watch reports on brutalities by Taliban and Northern Front. *Amnesty International, Annual Report 2000*.

56. On details of the atrocities committed in Mazar-i-Sharif, see complete Human Rights Watch report at: http://hrw.org/reports98/afghan/.

57. *Dawn*, 10 September 2001.

58. Bob Woodward, *Bush at War*, op.cit.

59. *Dawn*, 6 December 2001.

60. This impression is widespread among the Pashtuns on both sides of the borders. Author's interviews with Pashtun intellectuals and political activists in Peshawar, Jalalabad, and Kabul, August, 2004.

61. *Washington Times*, 12 October 2004. http://www.washtimes.com/upi-breaking/20041012-031213-5906r.htm.

62. Mohammad Waseem, *Democratization in Pakistan: A Study of the 2002 Elections* (Karachi: Oxford University Press, 2006), p. 157.

63. Joane Nagel & Susan Olzak, "Ethnic Mobilization in New and Old States: An Extension of the Competition Model," *Social Problems*, Vol. 30, No. 2 (December, 1982), pp. 127–43.

64. The case of Muhajirs, the Muslim immigrants from India who dominated the Pakistani state in the first two and a half decades developed a deep sense of loss as the native social groups began to compete with them for jobs, business, urban space, and bureaucratic and political power. Farhat Haq, "Rise of the MQM in Pakistan: Politics of Ethnic Mobilization," *Asian Survey*, Vol. 35, No. 11 (Nov, 1995), pp. 990–1004.

65. Anwar-ul-Haq Ahady, "The Decline of the Pashtuns in Afghanistan," *Asian Survey*, Vol. 35, No. 7, July 1995, pp. 621–34.

66. Ibid., pp. 625–28.

67. U.S. President George W. Bush, October 7, 2001. See http://www.whitehouse.gov/news/releases/2001/10/print/20011007-8.html.

68. "Karzai questions nature of military operations in Afghanistan," (based on an interview with Robert Chesal, 23 September, 2005) (http://www2.rnw.nl/rnw/en/currentaffairs/region/centralasia/afg050923?view=Standard#gerelateerdeArtikelen).

69. Drug mafia and smugglers who control the illegal border trade between Afghanistan and Pakistan have been and continue to be part of the militant outfits for pragmatic reasons.

70. Sauri P. Bhattacharya, "Soviet Nationality Policy in Afghanistan," *Asian Affairs* June 1984, pp. 125–37.

71. See John Coakley, ed., *Territorial Management of Ethnic Conflict*, 2nd revised and expanded edition (London: Frank Crass 2003); Gurrnam Singh, ed., *Ethno-Nationalism and Emerging World (Dis) Order* (New Delhi: Kanishka Publishers, Distributors, 2002).

72. Presentation of Nasreen Goss at a seminar in Karachi, 2–3 March 2005.

3

Rise of the Taliban and Civil War

The sudden rise of the Taliban movement raises many questions. How and why did the Taliban succeed in capturing more than two-thirds of the territory without any major resistance until they pushed across the areas populated by ethnic minorities? Why did the Taliban emerge from and remain confined to the Pashtun-dominated regions? Was religion the only driving force behind the Taliban movement or did Pashtun ethnicity play any role? What was the national and world outlook of the Taliban? Was the Islamic fundamentalism of the Taliban different from that of similar groups in other Islamic countries? Is there any relationship between the cultural and religious definition of good and how does that influence the politics of Islam in Afghanistan and other Muslim societies? These are complex questions, but any student of Afghanistan and Islamic politics would need to address them to explain Islamic social and political movements and determine why they have a tendency to turn violent. Instead of taking each question independently, we will try to address them together with some added focus on a few of them. Before doing this however, it would be useful to examine how the existing literature on Afghanistan, which has proliferated because of global demand in understanding the society and politics, depicts the Taliban movement and its rise to power. The discourses about the Taliban may be grouped essentially into two categories with some variations. Even these four categories that we have suggested are more heuristic devices than definite explanations, and they have many overlapping characteristics.

The first is the incomplete politics of Mujahideen resistance; the countries that supported the war of resistance against the former Soviet Union, notably the United States and Pakistan, did not pay any or enough attention to the postconflict political and economic reconstruction. For them that was too distant in the future, and the task at hand was how to defeat the Soviet Union. Washington, in the first few years of the war, was not even convinced whether the Soviet Union would ever quit the country or could be forced to do so.[1] Its assistance to the Afghan resistance was motivated largely by Cold War concerns against the rival superpower and by the need to rehabilitate its credibility as guarantor of security in the anxiety-stricken neighboring Gulf region.

The scale of national uprising against the communists was so wide and intense that there emerged all kinds of leaders, groups, and forces, at all levels of society; all wanting to liberate the country but with very little in common in terms of political vision or leadership. Some have also argued that it served the interests of Pakistan to keep the resistance divided in recognizing seven groups by confirming legitimacy to them and entitling them to economic and military assistance.[2] None of the major outside players wanted to address the issue of internal cohesion among the Mujahideen groups or help create some kind of common political and military forums from the outset of the war of resistance. Either they thought these were lofty goals or believed that placing fighting men and material in the field was too pressing to pay attention to the mechanics of political organization. One could understand this logic for the first couple of years, but not for the next eight years when there was ample time and opportunity, and when later there were clear signs of the Mujahideen victory.

One also needs to keep in mind the dynamics of war inside the country and the international climate created by the Soviet occupation. In the intensity of war and efforts to sustain it for a long haul, the supporters of resistance failed to examine the long-term consequences and likely impact of the new forces produced by the conflict on the Afghan society and the adjacent regions. One of the abiding criticisms of Pakistan's policy toward Afghanistan is that Pakistan deliberately sidelined the moderate factions within the Afghan resistance, putting its weight behind the Islamist radical Mujahideen groups.[3] In the final years of the resistance, there were opportunities to explore the issue of power transition with the Moscow-backed government in Kabul.[4] Overtures by Moscow, which was keen to negotiate a coalition government, and similar moves by Najibullah were conveniently spurned, as Pakistan smelled victory for the Mujahideen in the air.

With the benefit of hindsight one may term Pakistani and American strategy in Afghanistan as myopic. But one may also consider a human as well as institutional dilemma of state bureaucracies to visualize political events in distant futures. Islamists and radicals who are now branded as terrorists were genuinely aligned with the West during the Cold War against communism, and Afghanistan was their common battleground. The United States and Pakistan formulated and pursued goals in the objective environment of the 1980s. The American goals in the resistance were confined to defeating the Soviet aggression, while Pakistan wanted to establish a government that would be friendly or would at least deny influence to Pakistan's regional rivals in Afghanistan. Thus, neither of the two key players backing the resistance showed consistent interest in shaping political institutions among the resistance groups for future peace and stability.

Learning from the experience of other insurgencies and nationalist movements in the colonial world, some forms of partnership and coalition building might have been introduced. The political future of Afghanistan was left to the good intentions of the domestic political players that were constantly being manipulated by Pakistan and others; these players, even during the intense periods of war against Moscow, were interlocked into turf battles. There was no evidence at that time that the bitter factionalism among the Afghan Mujahideen parties would get resolved on its own or produce any political coherence when the Soviet troops departed from their country. They had neither any common political institutions to interact with nor were able to develop a political process that could generate social capacity and linkages between their strategy of war and politics of peace once they defeated the common enemy. This neglect resulted in a political vacuum among the Mujahideen groups. Pakistan, their main handler, preferred to deal with each of the seven groups separately, assigning different value and importance to each according to its estimation of role in the war efforts and commitment to the overall strategy that its planners behind the lines drew in closed offices.[5] One may also argue that keeping the Mujahideen divided was a convenient strategy to exercise greater control over them; but in terms of creating stable and peaceful Afghanistan, it was disastrous. We have dealt with some of these points in a chapter on Islamic resistance. What we have tried to argue is that the roots of the Taliban movement may be traced to the factional politics of the Mujahideen parties. Political capacity of the Mujahideen parties to govern Afghanistan together and revive its old traditions and build new institutions to sustain peace and economic reconstruction would have prevented the outbreak of the costly civil war that followed the collapse of the Najibullah regime. But this is only one of the many explanations about the rise of the Taliban movement. Our contention is that in order to understand how the Taliban emerged as rulers of the country one may need to look at other factors that are peculiar to Afghanistan, notably its ambitious neighbors, geopolitical environment, and more importantly, the internal dynamics of its social, political, and ethnic divisions.

The second set of explanations relate to the destruction of the Afghan state and its institutions.[6] While the general chaos, disorder, political fragmentation, and ethnic rivalries and unsettled issue of political power among the Mujahideen groups created circumstances that facilitated the rise of the Taliban, the most important thing to note is that there was no state apparatus

with any capacity to check or confront them. The insurgency against the Soviet Union had crippled the Afghan state, and whatever was left of it was further destroyed by the ensuing civil war among the Mujahideen parties. The
political void created by the defeat and departure of the former Soviet Union
increased the vulnerability of the beleaguered and demoralized Marxist state
that Moscow had left behind to largely fend off itself against the Mujahideen
and ambitious neighbors. It is remarkable that without the presence of the
Soviet forces and with limited flow of arms, the Najibullah regime survived
for more than three years. The Mujahideen parties failed to capture a single
town even in the peripheral regions like Jalalabad.[7] A limited success against
the rural town of Khost, on the border of Pakistan, was more a result of bargaining and cash flow than a real military victory. What was the reason for
the failure of the Mujahideen parties to capture any territory and establish
control inside the country? They were neither trained nor willing to fight a
conventional battle against the Afghan army that had maintained a good degree of internal cohesion until the end of 1991. The Mujahideen factions
preferred to conserve their energy, resources, material, and manpower for a
final showdown among themselves hoping that after the disintegration of
the Soviet Union, the Marxist regime in Kabul would also collapse. The fact
is once the common enemy was about to fade off, the factionalized Mujahideen parties set their sights on how to control power in Kabul. A prior
agreement to share power that Pakistan, Iran, and Saudi Arabia hastily brokered in Peshawar in the last week of April 1992 failed to prevent the outbreak of civil war that many had feared would erupt.[8] While the Mujahideen
leaders were quarrelling over the fine lines of the Peshawar Accord, Najibullah's hold over power had begun to loosen up with the defection of many
army generals from non-Pashtun minorities to Commander Ahmed Shah
Masud toward the last week of April 1992. The defecting generals paved the
way for Massoud and orchestrated a secret entry of his troops into Kabul out-
flanking his rivals, particularly the *Hizb-i-Islami* of Hikmatyar. All others followed the movement of the militia controlled by Massoud. Most of them
fought ferociously over the control of Kabul, staking claims over parts of it,
virtually dividing the city into separate territorial domains. There is consensus among the Afghans as well as outside observers that Kabul, which remained hitherto unharmed, was destroyed by the turf battles of the Mujahideen parties, particularly the *Hizb-i-Islami* of Gulbadin Hikmatyar.

    The weakened position of the Afghan state in terms of its vital institutions
and political capacity was further compounded by the question of legitimacy
of those who controlled it—the coalition dominated by Ahmed Shah Masud
and Burhanuddin Rabbani. Encouraged by their foreign sponsors, notably
Iran and Russia, they decided to stay on even after the short tenure of office
stipulated in the Peshawar Accord expired.[9] Disregard to the veracity of
claims of legitimacy by the rival factions and the genuineness of their griev-

ances, armed confrontation among them crippled their individual and collective capacity to revive the dead Afghan state. The conflict among the warring factions that had begun to shape along ethnic and regional lines dashed the hope about peace and normal life of millions of Afghans dislocated inside the country and living in exile in refugee camps in neighboring Iran and Pakistan. The Mujahideen lost their credibility, among the population that supported them during the war of resistance, to govern the country. All groups, with disregard to ethnicity, became greatly disillusioned with their selfish and individualist quest for power, lawlessness of former commanders who became local warlords, and inability of the Mujahideen factions to work together to maintain social peace and order.

Another point which is necessary to note about the statelessness of Afghanistan is that the foreign sponsors of the Mujahideen resistance failed to fully comprehend the political and security implications of removal of the Marxist government by force or its sudden collapse from within, which was actually the case. The United Nations representatives had partially succeeded in brokering an agreement that could result in the peaceful transfer of power in the last week of April.[10] But it was too late and not all the factions were willing to share power according to the vision of the peace plan. Peaceful power transition should have been one of the central themes of negotiations and should have come as a part of the larger package of the Geneva Accords that were signed in April 1988.[11] This question was left to be negotiated later through the agency of the UN. The Afghan groups and their regional backers were, in our opinion, more interested in capturing power by force than negotiating a political deal with the Marxist government. A negotiated settlement and peaceful transition would have saved hundreds of thousands of lives and some capacity of the Afghan state including its National Army to maintain peace and order. As a result of this failure, Afghanistan sunk into a civil war that created large stretches of no man's land where private militias and stateless terrorists began to operate with impunity. A state with no capacity, political or material, to defend itself was no match for the zealous religious forces of the Taliban that had snowballed into the second largest mobilization after the national uprising that followed the Soviet invasion of the country.

In most of the works that have so far been produced on the rise and rule of the Taliban, there is exclusive emphasis on their religious background, ideology, and anti-Western world outlook.[12] In our opinion, we need to carefully assess the social base of the Taliban. Their links with antimodern and anti-West transnational Islamic radical networks like Al Qaeda and sectarian outfits of Pakistan have obscured the Pashtun ethnic origin of the movement. In order to explore the Pashtun ethnicity and how it became a social base of the Taliban movement, we will have to digress a little bit and go into the larger issue of war and the rise of ethnicity among the minority groups. In the first place, Afghanistan was never an ethnically integrated nation; throughout its history, it has been a split nation, divided and further subdivided into tribes and narrow territorially defined entities. Social interaction, mixing up, and exchanges among the various groups took place only in a few urban settings. The growth of institutions of higher learning concentrated in Kabul, expansion of bureaucracy, open and some clandestine political activity brought the diverse ethnic groups together, but without modern economic and political processes each group tended to gravitate around the narrow zones of subtribal and subethnic identities. There was not enough trust or cultural sensitivity toward one another to produce any greater degree of social or political solidarity beyond a fuzzy and notional symbolism of Afghan nationalism whose definition remains contested. Afghanistan remained deficient in the process of nation building under both the monarchy and during the chaos of Marxist rule. Pashtuns as a majority ethnic community and as a ruling group had a perception of political dominance, but the historical balance that the Afghan rulers had created accommodated some interests and aspirations of other social groups. Non-Pashtun ethnic groups made significant gains through educational opportunity and the opening up of new professions along with traditional trade and commerce. But the Pashtun-dominated oligarchy exclusively took the responsibility of defining Afghan nationalism and articulating the vision of nation and statehood. The Pashtun-dominated political order had a stable balance but it was neither symmetrical nor representative of all regional and ethnic interests. It would be pertinent to mention that some scholars of Afghanistan studies question the entire notion of Pashtun dominance by raising questions about which groups actually dominated culture, modern sectors of the economy, urban life, and jobs in the state machinery. In their view, even the Afghan monarchy was alien to its Pashtun roots, as it embraced Persian language and cultivated a Persian urban mannerism and court culture.[13]

Once the old order broke down with the end of monarchy in 1973, new forms of politics began to emerge, which had destabilizing effects on state institutions, society, and intergroup relationships. In brief, three dimensions of new era politics can be mentioned to get an idea about how multidimensional polarization was taking place in a traditional society. The alliance of Parcham and Khalq, the two communist factions with Daoud, took the debate on to new ideologies; Marxism and Islam came out of the drawing rooms and into the open forums of educational institutions. The debate involved large groups of educated urban sections of the population and factionalized them along narrow loyalties to individuals and small groups. Second, political rivalry between the Marxists and Islamists turned violent as the former used agency of the state and partnership with Daoud to eliminate political threat from the Islamist groups. Third, Soviet penetration of the

Afghan state institutions, and counterintervention by Pakistan to force Daoud to change his policy added a strong external factor to internally po-larized politics of Afghanistan. Although Daoud's modernist, nationalist vi-sion of Afghanistan was consistent with his reputation and known political ideals, the Marxist forces that backed his capture of power had a different agenda and had pressure points outside the country. Therefore, the republi-can regime that Daoud attempted to structure had big political holes and dangerous ideological fault lines. When he realized the danger of becoming ensnared by the Moscow-controlled Marxist groups, it was already too late for him. Daoud and immediate members of his family were killed when the Soviet-trained and ideologically indoctrinated air force and army officers staged the coup, which was directed by Hafizullah Amin, leader of the Khalq faction on 27 April 1978. This tragic episode of Afghan history buried the dream of a modern Afghanistan with common bonds of culture, history, and Afghan nationalism. We have discussed these aspects of Afghan politics and society in detail earlier. The Marxist groups that took over control of the gov-ernment were factionalized along personal, regional, and ethnic lines. Nei-ther the communist ideology nor the common benefactor and patron, the Communist Party of the Soviet Union, was able to resolve their unending feuds. The disintegration of the already fragile social, economic, and politi-cal institutions created unprecedented chaos, insecurity, and social disorder.

The unstructured national resistance that quickly began to rise against the Soviet military march into Afghanistan, in December 1980, also took local, regional, and ethnic forms. A fierce struggle for power among the various Afghan Mujahideen parties that had a weak and loosely defined relation-ship with the local commanders inside the country gradually acquired an ethnic and regional dimension. A cursory look at the pattern of civil wars in the Third World, which have abounded,[14] will show that they have been fu-eled by ethnic considerations and the cycles of violence they created have further strengthened ethnic identities. In the case of Afghanistan, non-Pash-tun groups through foreign support and alliances gained control of their own areas, established local structures of authority, and considerably em-powered themselves through the different phases of war. This begs the ques-tion of what impact has this left on the Pashtun ethnicity and how this con-tributed to the rise of the Taliban.

Pashtuns bore the brunt of the Soviet war, faced the greatest challenge of physical and social dislocation, and fought back heroically. They rallied around their resistance leaders and local commanders in the name of Afghan nationalism and Islam, the two recurrent themes in the history of their struggles against foreign powers that attempted to dominate their country. The resistance parties in the Pashtun areas had many shades and colors but the most defining one was the Pashtun ethos and values that gel well with traditional Islam in the cultural sense of the word. These twin

sides of the inner consciousness of the Pashtuns were instrumental in denying the Soviet forces control over their territories and populations. At the
end of Soviet occupation and the later collapse of the Marxist regime of Najibullah, the Pashtuns saw the power shift to the Tajik minority with Rabbani as president and their strongman Ahmad Shah Massoud as the guarantor of security of the new political arrangements in Kabul. The Pashtuns
in the National Army and in other positions of power in the waning years
of the Marxist rule tried to facilitate the Pashtun parties notably of Gulbadin Hikmatyar, but lost the game to their ethnic rivals in similar positions.[15] Once officially in control, Rabbani and Massoud gained in international stature, and obtained the resources and recognition necessary to
consolidate their hold on power. Efforts by Hikmatyar, a Pashtun who commanded the most formidable force at that time, failed to get a share in
power through negotiations or the use of force. Other Pashtun groups were
too small, weak, and divided, but were never averse to the repeated attempts
that Hikmatyar had made to capture Kabul. Pashtuns at large felt humiliated, powerless, and without a leader who could reunify them. Some of
them looked toward former King Zahir Shah, but he neither had an army
nor the political will or vigor to return and lead his divided nation. He
knew well how Afghanistan, through the war of resistance and foreign intervention, had changed with the emergence of new forces. The traditional
Pashtun oligarchy and tribal notables that wanted to see him back were
mostly in exile and marginalized by the Pakistani authorities. Pakistan preferred Islamists like Gulbadin Hikmatyar as it felt threatened from political
mobilization and unity of the Pashtun groups around the traditional notion of Afghan nationalism that evoked fears of raising questions about the
border issue.[16]

The security situation in the Pashtun areas was another important reason
why the cross-section of the population from ordinary villagers to trades-
men, commanders of the Afghan army and former members of the communist party welcomed the Taliban. Why was there such mass-based appeal
of the Taliban vis-à-vis the security situation? The people were sick and tired
of the checkpoints on roads and highways by different local warlords who
forced passengers and traders to pay them for a safe passage. Indiscriminate
murders and kidnapping created social chaos. Defying the will of the warlords would lead to beating, detainment, and, worse, loss of life and property. The major resistance parties lost control over the local commanders
when their sources of funding dried up. The former commanders in many
areas assumed the role of local thugs. Most, if not all of them, began to prey
on their own populations to extort resources to maintain their power. This
was not the dawn of liberation and security that they had expected after the
defeat of the Soviet Union and its Afghan clients. The chaos and disorder
resulted primarily from the destruction of the Afghan state and its institu-

tions; though historically fragile they had had presence and some capacity to deal with rogue elements even in the peripheral regions. The traditional power structure of elderly tribesmen and locally influential persons got pushed to the margins with the rise of strongmen with guns, foreign monies, and militiamen on the payrolls of the warlords.

As discussed earlier, observers of Afghanistan's political history fail to understand the social origin of the Taliban because it is convenient to cast them as a group motivated by the desire of creating an Islamic state. There is no doubt about their ideological inclinations or commitment to an ideal of Islamic state, which we will delve into a little later. But there are questions about whether it was a planned force with a well-defined idea about how to capture power and rule Afghanistan, the way the Taliban did when it actually gained control over most of the country. The view that the Taliban was an accidental force and a local affair cannot be dismissed out of hand. When the distressed local population approached the Taliban madrasa headed by former Mujahideen warrior Mullah Omer to recover a boy who was kidnapped and molested by a rogue commander, the Taliban and its leaders had no plans to capture political power.[17] How, then, did their motive change is a question that we need to address with reference to the human need for security and trust. Afghanistan was truly in a state of nature; a state so vividly described by the eighteenth century English philosopher Thomas Hobbes, to drive the point home that without the strong arm of state, the society would lose its peace because the selfish nature of mankind would lead them to violate rights of other human beings, particularly the weak ones who might lack the power to defend themselves.[18] The social conditions in Afghanistan mirrored the chaos of the state of nature in turmoil, "every one against every one," and "life was short, brutish and nasty."[19] Under such conditions it was natural for the ordinary Afghans to accept the protection that the newly emerging Taliban force offered. The Taliban's slogans of peace, justice, and security of life and property were attractive. And they were not empty slogans, they enforced their vision of just order by gentle persuasion first, and when that failed, by brutal use of force. The Taliban movement filled a vacuum left by the collapse of the state.

Secondly, the Taliban accumulated trust and confidence of the Pashtun community to which they belonged. Their personal character, strong commitment to what they believed in, and sentiment of sacrifice for religion and the country invoked a tremendous amount of sympathy and support among the Pashtuns. As the force began to gather credibility, self confidence, and gained control of territories, the Pashtun peasants, former army men and Mujahideen fighters who had fought on opposite sides, looking for a new assignment, began to join them in hordes. It was a Pashtun whirlwind that gathered more momentum with each falling commander and successive withering away of the Mujahideen parties, which had lost local respect and support. Trust in all cultures is an important asset to build relationships and networks, what in modern social science inquiry is referred to as social capital.[20] We are using trust as a basic cultural expression that exists among tribal networks. In these societies, it is the honor and sanctity of word that matters more than a written contract. The Taliban delivered on what it promised on the issue of security both by word and deed, and it earned more trust and support. Afghans in the Pashtun zones wanted security of life and property and some degree of certainty. The Taliban gave them just that but on the condition of total obedience to the order it wanted to create. Haunted by the ghost of local warlords, it was not a bad bargain. Moreover, the Taliban's conception of justice, order, and Islamic piety was close to the customary Islam that the Pashtun tribes have practiced for centuries.

Having brought Pashtun ethnicity to the debate about the emergence of the Taliban, it is necessary to qualify our position. The ethnic consciousness was largely latent, unarticulated, and was never brought to the level of political discourse or rhetoric. As the movement was shaped by many complex internal and external forces, its emergence cannot and shouldn't be explained with reference to any single set of factors. This is what we have tried to argue in the previous sections by looking at the failure of Mujahideen parties, terror of the warlords, social disorder, political vacuum, and ethnicity. Let us now turn to what role religion had in the making of the Taliban rule. The Taliban movement was Islamic in character and in agreement with the way Islam is understood and practiced in the Pashtun territories both on the Pakistan as well as the Afghanistan side. Its ambitions rose from accidental security force to a regional movement with the ideal of establishing an Islamic state. Its victories were quicker than anybody could imagine because the society needed some credible security force to counter political anarchy. The society at large was exhausted and had lost the strength of its institutions. Battered for eighteen years, the local populations had no eagerness or vigor to resist any new force hovering over them or to risk their lives to support the discredited local commanders, rogue warlords, or warring Mujahideen factions that were in total disarray. The Taliban rode on the wave of general frustration, despair, and unending anxiety among the populations, particularly among the Pashtuns.

Among all these factors in our judgment, the undercurrents of Pashtun nationalism, though, subdued by the Islamic rhetoric of the Taliban, served as a bedrock for the growth of the movement. Largely for this reason the movement captured more than two-thirds of the country without any major resistance and its social support base remained largely confined to the Pashtun-dominated regions where it emerged. The leaders of the movement had remarkable success in reunifying the Pashtun belt, using Islamic symbolism and security as tool of political mobilization. What motivated the Pashtuns and set them behind the Taliban was a general concern that they had lost power over the state to the Tajiks and Uzbeks, and the Taliban was the right kind of force to secure their country and establish order. The Pashtuns had difficulty in accepting the fact that ethnic and religious minorities had grown vastly powerful, and had created autonomous regional fiefdoms.[21] Pashtuns, on the other hand, wanted to reestablish a reunified, centralized Afghan state under their domination. This still remains a fundamental point of consensus among them.

PAKISTANI CONNECTION

The Afghan groups internally opposed to the Taliban movement and most foreign observers have tended to place too much emphasis, if not entire credit or blame, on Pakistan and on independent religious groups based there for the Taliban's rise to the conquest of the larger parts of Afghanistan.[22] Pakistan has played a key role in the internal politics of the country from organizing, training, and funding the Mujahideen resistance to switching its support to the Taliban movement. How much of the rise of the Taliban can be attributed to the Pakistani connection and how much of it was on account of domestic and regional factors is a question that will perhaps never be settled because of the political controversies that have surrounded this question. Enough has already been written on it.[23] And more needs to be done to search the social, political, and economic roots of the Taliban movement. In most of the literature on Afghanistan, the societal factors seem to have been relegated to secondary importance, or ignored, stressing the Pakistani connection more than anything else. We think that any discussion about the rise of the Taliban will be incomplete without explaining the kind of support that Pakistan extended, for what reasons and to what effects. The motives, interests, and strategy of Pakistan also needs to be explained to answer why it supported the Taliban movement, and whether or not it was the right kind of strategy. How much weight and influence Pakistan carried with the Taliban leaders is another important question that we need to answer.

We must recognize the fact that the rise of the Taliban movement took place at a time of internal contestation in Afghanistan and bitter rivalry among its neighbors. All the regional states, notably Iran, Central Asian states,[24] and Pakistan, stepped up their efforts to bolster their favorite Afghan factions to increase and maintain their respective influence in the future politics of Afghanistan. Pakistan was better poised to exercise influence than others because of its wartime linkages and dependency relationships that it had created during the anti-Soviet war. But soon after a Mujahideen government was installed through the Peshawar Accord, which Pakistan was instrumental in brokering, Pakistan's influence had begun to wane with other regional powers also stepping in and supporting various groups that would be compatible with their vision of politics and regional security. The Mujahideen government in Kabul was freer to interact with external powers and no longer was it under the obligation of its former patrons in Islamabad to shape its foreign or domestic policies. Had the Mujahideen groups been united or succeeded in building a workable coalition among them, perhaps the external influence over some groups inside the country might have gradually disappeared. That was not to be the case; rather Afghan politics took an opposite direction.

The designated prime minister Gulbadin Hikmatyar, and Ahmed Shah Masud, the gendarme of the Rabbani regime, locked themselves in a bitter feud over the control of Kabul, which would determine who ruled Afghanistan. Their rivalry and unending conflict forced them to turn to foreign benefactors. Masud turned to Iran, Russia, Tajikistan, and India, while Hikmatyar continued to receive support from Pakistan.[25] Iran and Russia openly encouraged Rabbani to stay in power, reneging on the obligation to convene a consultative assembly to draft a new constitution and finally hold elections in the country. Violating the Peshawar Accord had four adverse consequences for the Rabbani regime and for the stability of the country. First was the question of political legitimacy; irrespective of what the nature of a political system is, it is an important issue for those who exercise political authority and they cannot escape from it. Let us take its simplest connotation, popular acceptance, which was not there beyond the narrow margins of some Tajik ethnic groups. Or let us consider any loose criteria of control or exercise of political authority as a mark of institutional capacity to govern, which never went beyond certain pockets of the capital city. Neither the Afghan tradition of consultation nor persuasion by friendly countries succeeded in resolving the question of legitimacy and power: who will exercise power, on what basis, and for how long, once the Peshawar Accord was thrown into the proverbial "dustbin of history."

The second negative consequence of going back on the commitments spelled out in the Peshawar Accord was that war reemerged as the essential instrument of settling political differences on access to power. All Mujahideen factions, who were distrustful of one another, had begun to prepare for capturing Kabul well before the departure of the Soviet forces from their country. Particularly, the two most powerful of them, *Hizb* and *Jamiat*, had their strategy, manpower and stock of weapons in place, and it seems neither of them wanted to live by any agreement reached between them by the intervention of friendly countries. Therefore, refusal by Rabbani to step down accelerated factional strife. Rabbani and Masud wanted to stay in power by force, and others who wanted to remove them had to resort to the same. Afghanistan was once again in deep turmoil, now with Afghans fighting Afghans.

Third, the new phase of war among the Mujahideen parties necessitated that they look for partners among the regional powers, who, as indicated earlier, wanted to support them to increase their influence inside the country. It can be argued that had the Mujahideen parties settled their political differences peacefully, the regional rivalry could perhaps have been reduced and even directed toward positive competition for reconstruction of Afghanistan. Since security, power, and political dominance were the goods that the Afghan factions wanted to have, it required them to seek foreign patronage, which they did without any moral restraint or good of the country. They were blinded by their particularistic interests into grabbing more, rather than rising above these considerations to collectively face the gigantic task of rebuilding Afghanistan.

The fourth impact of the collapse of the Peshawar Accord was on the economic and social situation of the country. Afghans, dislocated both internally and externally, living in the refugee camps in Iran and Pakistan, had hoped to return to their country after the end of communist rule. The new phase of conflict dashed their hopes as the fighting, social anarchy, and lack of any economic opportunity prevented them from coming back to the country. Those in Kabul and the other few cities that had been spared by the Mujahideen-Soviet war got trapped into the new war. In fact, a new wave of refugees from Kabul began to trickle down to Pakistan and other countries. Many Afghans who were on the sidelines or had passively accepted the Soviet intervention were quite skeptical about the ability of the Mujahideen parties to stay together in one political fold and their ability to govern the country. Their doubts were not unfounded and proved to be true. The fighting among the Mujahideen parties shows how a decentralized resistance movement was able to deny the Soviet Union effective control over the country, but at the same time, it established that without some common structure of ideology, leadership, and institutions it degenerated into local fiefdoms. In the eyes of the Afghan public it lost the image of nationalist warriors fighting for the glory of Islam and liberation of Afghanistan. This partly explains why the Taliban, as a new social movement, emerged in an environment of unending conflict.

Two other factors that we have already alluded to, undercurrents of Pashtun nationalism and the role played by external forces, proved disastrous in dividing Afghans into factions. The Taliban leaders very effectively exploited conditions of anarchy, foreign intervention, warlordism, and lawlessness to shape their struggle and seek social energy from Kandhar and its environs to their rule over Kabul and beyond.

The Taliban movement rising from the Pashtun areas adjacent to Pakistan had multilayered linkages with the Pakistani state, society, and religious parties that made it a natural partner of Pakistan. All other states interested in fielding a local force in Afghanistan found the politics and religious orthodoxy of the

Taliban too offensive to look toward them as partners. The Taliban became popular with the rural Pashtun population partly as a reaction to the influence that powers like Iran had in the internal affairs of Afghanistan under the Rabbani government. On theological matters, both Iran and the Taliban were poles apart and the sectarian gulf between the two competing interpretations of Islam was just too wide.[26] Therefore, it was natural for the Taliban to look toward Pakistan for whatever assistance it needed. Pakistan, under the compulsive security environment of the region, needed the Taliban on its side to deny influence to its rivals in Afghanistan and also to effectuate its theory of "strategic depth" that one of its prominent generals, Mirza Aslam Beg, had articulated in 1990.[27] In my opinion, it was more of a marriage of convenience between Taliban and Pakistan than any ideological affinity between the two. How much the Taliban owes its rise, strength, and successive victories to Pakistan and how much can be attributed to its own domestic power base is open to question. But Pakistan did play an important role in allowing the Taliban four key elements in its struggle. These were: access to food and medical supplies, provision of fuels[28] that the Taliban badly needed to run and move their war machine, recruit fighters, and raise funds through private sources, and finally a diplomatic link to the outside world that Pakistan gladly offered by recognizing its regime as the legitimate one. Pakistan offered them intelligence support and strategic advice in their key battles, and helped them negotiate political deals with local commanders and warlords.[29]

Why did Pakistan shift its policy from the former Mujahideen parties to the Taliban? There is no single answer to this question, nor is there any single factor that influenced Pakistan's new Afghan policy. Pakistan's policy toward the new emerging Taliban militia at first was a result of political expediency. There was hardly any serious thinking beyond the assessment that they had manpower, ideological zeal, and a political vacuum in the Pashtun regions of Afghanistan that they could very quickly fill. Those who were responsible for Afghan policy in Islamabad thought that aligning with the Taliban would serve Pakistan's interests better than the old policy of supporting the feuding Mujahideen parties or serving as a mediator among them. But it is also interesting to analyze who really shaped Pakistan's Afghan policy during the Taliban period. Much of the literature focuses on the Inter Services Intelligence (ISI), the agency that managed the Afghan resistance against the former Soviet Union.[30] The idea that the ISI wanted to change horses in Afghanistan to pursue the same policy sounds convincing but ignores the complex domestic environment and the various actors that shaped Pakistan's Afghan policy. The objectives of that policy-friendly, stable, and peaceful Afghanistan were the same, but the instruments of the policy and the strategy of achieving them were constantly reviewed and their effectiveness reassessed at every turning point in the troubled political history of Afghanistan and Pakistan. Pakistan had a new elected government under

Benazir Bhutto, a lady with liberal credentials and benefits of Western education. This begs the question of why her government embraced the Taliban movement as new allies. The simplest answer would be that like any pragmatic politician, she was interested more in advancing Pakistan's interests than in religion, ideology, and political behavior of a movement across the border. There is also another convenient explanation: she had no control over Pakistan's policy toward Afghanistan. In order to explain why Pakistan supported the Taliban, we need to look at the complexity of Pakistan's decision-making environment and the actors that tried to influence Pakistan's policy of lending support to the Taliban. They were three major actors; governmental, primarily the ISI; the ethnic, Pakistani Pashtuns; and religious, essentially the Deobandis of *Jamiat Ulema-i-Islam*.[31] Their interests converged on supporting the Taliban. The government of Pakistan for its declared, and not so declared, objectives in Afghanistan embraced the Taliban. Although the prominent Pashtun leaders in Pakistan remained mostly silent on the subject of the Taliban, the tribal and other leaders at the grass-root level did support the Taliban.[32] The JUI for both Deobandi as well as the madrasa networks considered the Taliban its own boys. But deep down there was a common ethnic factor binding all these elements. The Pashtun officers in the army as well as in the ISI who generally thought that it was their prerogative to handle the Afghan question had fraternal feelings for the Taliban and had shared its grief after the loss of power in Afghanistan at the hands of the Tajiks and Uzbeks.[33] The top leaders Fazal ur-Rehman and Sami ul-Haq, heading two different factions of the JUI, though always placing their religious identity before any other, including ethnic, happen to be Pashtuns. Both of them and the religious organizations and parties aligned with the Deobandi movement threw all their weight behind the Taliban. If there is any single individual who can be credited or discredited for the shift in Pakistan's policy toward the Taliban is a retired general of the Pakistan Army, Nasirullah Babar, who is an ethnic Pashtun. He was interior minister during the second tenure of Benazir Bhutto, from 1994–1997. Prime Minister Bhutto assigned him the responsibility of reshaping Pakistan's Afghan policy, and in doing so, he had full authority and control.[34] It did not take him much time to assemble the Pashtuns in the right place to build a consensus on supporting the Taliban. The JUI provided yet another layer of support outside the governmental bureaucracy. It is important to mention that the JUI was a coalition partner in the Bhutto government. Some analysts in Pakistan have argued that the Taliban was the brainchild of Nasirullah Babar.[35] In his vision of Afghanistan, the Pakistani interests converged with the Pashtun majority both for historical and ethnic, as well as geopolitical reasons. He thought they were natural partners and that they had to work together to reunite and stabilize Afghanistan.[36] This vision goes deep in Pakistan's policy-making circles. And why does it? Because the assumption is that the ethnic fragmentation of Afghanistan is a political fact and what affects Pakistan's security, stability, and political arrangements in the two bordering provinces, Balochistan and North-West Frontier Province, is how satisfied or alienated the Pashtuns on the other side of the border are.[37] Instability, chaos, disorder, and conflict on the other side of the border would engulf the Pakistani Pashtun regions in turmoil. The troubles Pakistan has been facing in the tribal regions of north and south Waziristan for the past three years are a case in point.[38]

The motives of the JUI were quite different from those of the official bureaucracy of Pakistan; they were both religious as well as political. Politically, the JUI had had very close connections with the Taliban leaders and their fighters. Most of them had gone through the madrasa network of Deobandis in the North-West Frontier Province (NWFP) and Balochistan.[39] They had a sectarian bonding with the Taliban as well, as they distinguished themselves from the rest of the Sunni and Shia categories by preaching and practicing more conservative and puritanical Islam. Historically, the ulema of the Deobandi sect, and especially the JUI, had aligned itself with the Pashtun nationalists in the above two provinces, and unlike *Jamat-i-Islami* they never viewed ethnic nationalism as contradictory to their identification with Islam.[40] The JUI and most of the Deobandis in Pakistan saw the Taliban government in Afghanistan as a first step toward the Islamization of their own country. The Taliban had captured larger parts of Afghanistan, had a great transnational support network, good Muslim leadership in their historical images of pious Islamic leaders, and a large number of fighters from so many different countries to establish an Islamic state next to the Islamic Republic of Iran that is based on a Shia model of Islamic state. Establishment of an Islamic state and its consolidation in Afghanistan would have served as a base for bringing about a similar Islamic transformation in the adjacent Islamic countries, notably Pakistan and the Central Asian states in the north. Afghanistan was a great territorial prize for the Pakistani Deobandis, who wanted to use their expanded networks to further their religious and political agenda across the region. Some of their fronts and offshoots like the *Sipah-i-Sahaba* Pakistan (army of the companions of the Prophet) found sanctuary in Afghanistan for training and launching terrorist attacks against their sectarian rivals, the Shia in Pakistan. Most of the wanted terrorists of the SSP were captured back in the country only after the overthrow of the Taliban by the American forces.[41] The Taliban leaders had always claimed ignorance about the presence of these sectarian terrorists.[42] Many of the Taliban fighters had interpersonal and institutional links with some, if not all, Pakistani sectarian terrorists who took refuge in their country. They had a mutual support system and strategic ties that were forged during the anti-Soviet resistance movement and during their common training in some of the madrasas in Pakistan. A common religious ethos, socialization in the madrasas, an identical worldview, and similar approach to social and political issues in their respective societies helped forge the ties that have survived even after the ouster of the Taliban from power.

All religions serve a common ground for political action among the communities that use it for political purposes. With Islamic resurgence on the rise and militant groups mushrooming in the democratic void of the region, both the Taliban and their supporters in Pakistan found Islam a great mobilizing force as well as a common political cause in it to establish a preferred political order, the rule of *Shariah* or Islamic law. Doctrinally, the Deobandis and other variants of Islamic groups objectify the rule of *Shariah* as an article of faith, and a will of Allah for founding good political order.

The support of the religious groups was not totally confined to the Deobandis or major factions of the JUI and went beyond these narrow dividing lines. Most of the religious groups and parties, usually those that had roots in the madrasa networks, extended full support to the Taliban, from their very rise to their control of Kabul and territories beyond the Hindukush mountains, when they confronted their ethnic rivals in the north of the country. What kind of support did the Pakistani groups provide? It ranged from everything from food stuffs to money and young fighters who were motivated to fight against the fellow Muslims belonging to ethnic minorities of Afghanistan believing they were fulfilling a religious responsibility of *jihad* or holy war against the "infidels." They went in tens of thousands to fight along with the Taliban against the forces of the Northern Alliance. But Pakistanis were not the only outsiders helping them; thousands of Arabs, along with Chechens and Uzbeks, were part of the Taliban support base. They were there not only to assist their hosts but also to plan against their own governments who they thought were 'enemies of the people' in being close to the United States and other Western powers. The United States, and the leaders and regimes in Islamic countries that were aligned with Washington, figured prominently in their propaganda and were marked on the top of their target list.

Besides the government of Pakistan and the Deobandis of JUI, there were Afghan-Pakistan businessmen interested in stability and order, in Afghanistan, that supported the Taliban. In the formative phase, the Afghan traders and transporters came forward with whatever means were necessary to bolster the Taliban. They saw the new militia as an emerging force that would eradicate the menace of checkpoints at the turn of every major road, confront the local warlords that took money from them, and establish the order necessary for the flourishing of businesses.[43] The degeneration of the Mujahideen resistance into proliferation of warlordism all over the country had deeply disappointed the Afghan traders and their powerful allies in the trading communities of Pakistan who were involved in the smuggling of goods. Chaos, disorder, and lawlessness had gravely affected the trading communities as well as tribes in the border regions who had an interest in smuggling commodities and third-party goods across the established caravan routes in and out of Afghanistan, with the connivance of Pakistani custom officials, through Chaman, a Pashtun border town in the Balochistan province of Pakistan, and through other entry and exit points. The Afghan traders had a vested interest in stability in the country and the restoration of the writ of law and governmental authority without any ideological preference for any group. Their choice for the Taliban was pragmatic because it was the only force capable of restoring peace. The harsh measures that the Taliban took to deal with robbers, thieves, and those involved in crimes against life and property did not matter to the traders and transporters. Rather, they demanded harsh measures to arrest the deteriorating climate of security. It suited their business interests to restore order no matter who did it and what measures they resorted to. To conclude this section, one can say that there were multiple interests, forces, and actors interested in promoting the Taliban and the social and political conditions in Afghanistan were just right for the emergence of such a movement.

IDEOLOGY OF THE TALIBAN

What the Taliban stood for has become obscured in the Western media by too much emphasis on Islamic fundamentalism and Islamic militancy. The Taliban has been grouped with other Islamist movements that have emerged in almost every Muslim country over the past fifty years. Although there is a common yearning for self-revival and an effort to retrieve the mythical glorious past from the cultural mix of colonialism, the Islamist movements are not the same. The orientalist writings on the subject of Islamic fundamentalism are flawed in not differentiating the social and cultural variants within what is broadly called the Islamic civilization.[44] As their social, political, and historical contexts vary, their vision of what is Islamic and what is not and what is the best strategy to achieve the ultimate objective of establishing an Islamic state varies greatly from one Islamic movement, and country, to another. A tendency to see the Taliban in the image of other, well-established or mature, Islamic movements and parties with great degree of political experience and standing will be an analytical fallacy. Until now, we have looked at the Taliban's ethnic roots and its popularity among the Pashtun tribes and the reasons why it was successful. Since the Taliban leaders themselves and their foreign observers have focused on their Islamic characteristics, it would be necessary to explain their view of Islam and the ideology that they stood and fought for.

The Taliban leaders put their ideology and politics in the simplest form; the Quran, and the Sunnah (the tradition of the Prophet) were their constitution, law, and political system.[45] But this belief, very common among most of the Islamic sects, has never resolved the complex interpretive issues, or even the methodologies of interpretation. All theological and sectarian divides including political factionalism among the Islamic movements rest on the question of interpretation of Quran and Sunnah. Each sect defines the Islamic religious mosaic both in harmony and disorder depending on the established theological lineages of the interpreter and decides what is authentically Islamic and what is not.[46] The political circumstances of different communities, in most cases the postcolonial troubles of state and nation formation, and the contestation of power to exercise control over state along with its social dynamics have generally shaped the ideologies of the postnationalist phase of politics in many Islamic countries. Afghanistan went through the same type of ideological conflict. Additionally, different Islamic groups differ on the fundamental question of what the Islamic state is, what purpose it will have, and how it would be established. In the case of the Taliban, it had to be through a military conquest and subjugation of all opposition and the population to the Taliban's will through the force of arms. The circumstances of their birth—the failure of the Mujahideen parties to create an Islamic state or provide some sort of law and order, their religious and political socialization in the atmosphere of the madrasa, and the experience of jihad, all contributed to the ideological mind-set of the Taliban. Besides these influences, their Deobandi theological lineage, the vision of Islamic law and society that was rooted in that theology shaped their enterprise of structuring an Islamic state.

It is interesting that the relatively more established Islamist groups like *Jamat-i-Islami* distanced themselves from the Taliban.[47] The Jamat and other similar groups perceived the Taliban as more traditional in orientation than reformist or modernist in the understanding of the Islam state, or how it could be constructed. The Jamat leaders were openly critical on some policies of the Taliban, but their opposition generally remained muted due to political considerations, notably their desire to play the role of mediator among the Afghan groups. In our view, the Taliban ideology was influenced as much by the question of political power as it was by its Pashtun ethnicity, tribal traditions, and premodern world outlook. There are three characteristics of their ideology that stand very salient—Islamic formalism, nonmodern traditionalism, and Pashtun tribalism. All these characteristics have a long history of development. Its political roots go back to the constitutional period (1964–1973) when the ulema, particularly after the second election in 1969, demanded the implementation of *Shariah* or Islamic law from the monarch. The Taliban thought of an Islamic order more in terms of implementing Islamic law in the light of Sunni-Hanafi school of jurisprudence and awarding Islamic punishments for petty offences and major crimes than of a political system in any sort of modern sense. One of the sections of the Deobandi Taliban and their followers and sympathizers in Afghanistan and Pakistan believe that the observation of the *Shariah* in letter and spirit on individual as well as on a collective level through the agency of the state is their central religious goal in life. Formal practices of Islam, like five daily prayers; fasting in the month of Ramadan; making pilgrimages to Mecca; paying Zakat (the religious tax); Islamic punishments like cutting the hands of thieves, stoning to death for adultery (in the case of married couples), and engaging in jihad against the infidels form the core of their political beliefs. Although Islamic formalism is not confined to the Taliban alone, it received tremendous support from the Pashtun society for what it preached and practiced because of the synergy between its ideology and the Pashtun traditions, namely the *Pashtunwali*.[48] In the traditional Pashtun society, Islam is practiced more or less as a way of life and there has always been greater emphasis on Islamic law and punishments than anywhere, with the exception of Saudi Arabia, in contemporary Islamic societies. The Pashtun population in general supported the Taliban for its religious fervor as well as for being close to the fundamental values of their society.

In the Deobandi religious order in general, and the Taliban in particular, there has been a strong sectarian sentiment against the Shiites.[49] Quite often they have declared this sect both privately as well as publicly as being out of the pale of Islam.[50] The massacre of Shia in Mazar-i-Sharif in the north when the Taliban captured the city was largely for sectarian hatred, but revenge and ethnicity also contributed to the violence. Intolerance of other sects and beliefs came as a part of religious training at early stages of their socialization with sectarian-minded teachers and colleagues.[51] They extended religion intolerance to the religious minorities, Hindus and Sikhs that had lived in Afghanistan for centuries in peaceful coexistence. The Taliban made them wear distinctive colors for identification, which amounted to humiliation. Likewise they were equally intolerant toward those Muslims who didn't observe the religious rituals, and the Taliban publicly humiliated them by whipping them. The religious police of the Taliban was the most feared and repressive; they ordered people to grow long beards, say prayers five times a day, and adopt the social behavior of puritanical Islam.[52]

In pursing a puritanical Islam rooted more in the Pashtun traditions than a modern interpretation of Islam and its application, the Taliban adopted *Khilafat* or caliphate as its ideal form of Islamic state.[53] The essence of this system is that the loyalty to the *Amir* (leader) is a sort of religious obligation, and the Amir knows better than others what is good for the community. In making decisions, he may consult those capable of giving advice but not necessarily be bound by any such consultation. This is a nonmodern political outlook, as it excludes popular sovereignty and representative government. But the Taliban was more concerned with the issue of religious legitimacy and how in its view that could best be created than with modern norms of politics.

The Taliban viewed the Muslim societies including that of Afghanistan as being corrupted by Western influences that included dress, food habits, political institutions, social customs, music, culture, education, and even viewing of television. The West as imagined by the Taliban was the enemy of Islam and the Muslims. The Taliban presented a very selective historical narrative of Muslims being the victim and of others, particularly the United States and Western powers, being immoral, materialistic, corrupt, and licentious. They interpreted the West more or less in Huntingtonian terms of the clash of civilizations.[54] The oppressive West had to be confronted and it had to start with overthrowing the pro-Western regimes in the Muslim world, which in the Taliban's view served foreign interests more than the interests of the Muslims. For this, the Taliban was open to collaboration with likeminded groups from the Muslim countries. It was their worldview and the facility of sanctuary that attracted tens of thousands of Islamic militants, who poured into Afghanistan to fight along with them.

THE AL QAEDA CONNECTION

Starting from the years of Mujahideen resistance, the Arab Islamic radicals had joined the jihad against the communists in large numbers. Their backers, Pakistan, Saudi Arabia, and the United States, rather encouraged political mobilization of the Islamists because they were training their guns at the communists. They did not give a serious thought to where the non-Afghan Mujahideen would go and what would be their new targets. The three consequences of introducing Islamic militants from so many Islamic countries to Afghanistan are quite obvious now. First, the militants succeeded in establishing transnational linkages, a common support system, and a worldwide network of organizations with many hidden layers. These networks continue to trouble all the countries involved in fighting terrorism in Afghanistan and Pakistan. It is difficult to uncover which organization is giving support to whom for what purpose. Second, Islamist groups from other Islamic countries trained their workers in Afghanistan in guerrilla warfighting capabilities, general military skills and in building transnational connections among similar groups. Third, all of them found a sanctuary in Afghanistan to hide, organize, and plan activities against their pro-West national governments, and later against the United States and other Western powers. Although Al Qaeda was founded much later, its top leaders and many fighters had the benefit of experience in Afghanistan.[55] And in the time of need they maintained contact with different leaders in Afghanistan during the unstable and chaotic Mujahideen government. When Osama bin Laden was ousted from Sudan under American pressure in 1994, he found a refuge in Afghanistan.[56] He didn't come alone, however; he brought with him the entire top echelon of his organization, his security outfit, gradually getting thousands of his Arab fighters into Afghanistan. Since his years of war against the Soviet forces, bin Laden was familiar with the tribal networks, leaders of the Mujahideen, and the terrain. He had grown quite deft at striking alliances with locally influential figures.

An interesting question is why bin Laden chose to settle in the Pashtun territories of southern and eastern parts of Afghanistan. One plausible explanation is that his earlier Afghan experience was in these areas, and not in the non-Pashtun regions of the country. Second, the brand of Islamic ideology, anti-American sentiments, and the general world outlook he held found acceptance with the leaders of the Taliban movement, some of with whom bin Laden had very close personal relationships. Among all the factors linking Osama and Al Qaeda with the Taliban, the most important is the fact that they needed each other badly for their own respective purposes. Bin Laden and his outfit needed a secure sanctuary from where they could plan and execute their political and military agenda against their targets in the Middle East and the world over, including the United States of America. To this end, a stateless Afghanistan which was remote, desolate, thinly populated, and difficult to approach was an ideal place for the Al Qaeda network to hide, and plan and act against its targets. The Taliban leaders welcomed Al Qaeda operatives and justified Taliban protection to them on the alleged grounds that the Al Qaeda members were "Islamic fighters," "refugees" seeking shelter against "tyrannical regimes."[57] There were material, strategic, and political reasons that also need to be looked into. The Taliban needed the material resources and the most trained and hardy fighters of the Al Qaeda army to fight its war against the Northern Front. The Al Qaeda members also proved to be a strategic asset in mobilizing fighters and financial assistance from some of the key Islamic countries. And also, there was a political consensus among the religious organizations in Pakistan, Afghanistan, and the Middle East to support the alliance between the Taliban and Al Qaeda. Behind the scenes, important *ulema* or scholars of Islamic theology played an important role in linking the two groups together.[58]

The United States began to focus on Al Qaeda and its presence in Afghanistan more seriously after the bombing of two of its embassies in East Africa, in Nairobi and Dar es Salaam, on 6 August 1998.[59] As a retaliation, the U.S. naval forces present in the Arabian Sea fired scores of cruise missiles on the camp of Osama bin Laden in Eastern Afghanistan on August 28, 1998, killing close to a hundred militant trainees.[60] Bin Laden had left the camp before the missiles were fired. The United States pursued a two-pronged strategy to apprehend bin Laden and destroy his organization. The first was the hiring and training of Afghans familiar with the region to follow bin Laden and provide real-time intelligence about his whereabouts, or arrest and kill him if they found an opportunity to do so. Despite repeated failures, the United States has not given up this option. The search for bin Laden and his close associates goes on as of the writing of these lines. The second prong was the application of direct and indirect pressure on the Taliban leadership to evict or hand over bin Laden to the Americans. Washington used the good offices of Pakistan to communicate regularly to Mullah Omar on the question of Al Qaeda. There was equal pressure on Pakistan to get bin Laden out of Afghanistan by using its connections with the Taliban leadership. Nothing worked. The Taliban leaders claimed innocence of bin Laden and demanded hard evidence against him, and claimed that if and when they would be satisfied, they would try bin Laden in their own courts. There is sketchy evidence of the Taliban attempting to use Bin Laden as a bargaining chip for recognition of their regime and a seat in the United Nations. Repeated attempts by Pakistan to negotiate a deal with Taliban failed miserably, as the inflexible, obstinate, and somewhat irrational leadership of the Taliban would refuse any compromise. As an alternative, Pakistan offered its own agencies to capture bin Laden on Afghanistan's territory and hand him over to the Americans. It trained a slick group of sixty commandoes under American guidance to arrest bin Laden.[61] The plan failed because of military takeover and change of government in October 1999.

The tragic events of 9/11 changed the way America looked at the world. Caught unprepared, its focus turned to the real source of trouble, Afghanistan's Taliban rulers and its militant guests from the Arabian Peninsula. While preparing for the worst—that is an attack against Afghanistan to remove the Taliban and capture Osama bin Laden the United States made repeated attempts through Pakistani and Saudi emissaries to convince the Taliban leaders to hand over bin Laden and his organization. In their meetings with Mullah Omar there was the always the question of evidence of bin Laden's involvement in the New York and Washington, D.C. terrorist attacks, and there was insistence on the right of Afghanistan to try them, if they were convinced about their complicity. The only flexibility they showed was to the extent that bin Laden and his associates would be tried by a council of Islamic jurists from Islamic countries. Even a very clear warning by the director general of the ISI about what was in store for the Taliban if it failed to deliver bin Laden didn't make the reclusive leader of the Taliban budge.[62] What happened to Taliban rule and the Taliban has been discussed in chapter 4. The question is, had the Taliban agreed to surrender bin Laden, could Afghanistan have been spared the wrath of an American war? In our view, it could have. Occupation of Afghanistan or ruling such a remote country was

never the primary objective of the United States. In the political and psychological environment created by the ramming of airliners into the
World Trade Center towers and the Pentagon, the United States could not
take no for an answer from the Taliban. Had the Taliban leaders been realistic or had some capacity to think as rationally as normal leaders who
run the modern states think about the questions of war and peace, they
could have avoided the imposition of war on them and their subsequent
destruction and removal. They could have saved their regime, and even
gotten the international recognition that they had been demanding since
a few years prior to the American attack on Afghanistan. The Taliban leaders chose rather the opposite track of refusal and confrontation. Perhaps
it is too early to judge the outcome of American war and the Taliban resistance to the regime that they have constructed. But with whatever benefit of history we have, there was room for negotiations and a concession
by the Taliban leaders. Their dogmatism and inflexibility ruined them and
brought untold misery to their followers and supporters.

IS THE TALIBAN GONE FOREVER?

Any discussion of the Taliban movement will be incomplete without addressing the question of the continuing Taliban resistance against the American
forces in Afghanistan and the new regime. Do they really pose a challenge to
the survival of the regime? What capacity do they have to destabilize
Afghanistan or prevent the Karzai regime from reconstruction and political
consolidation? Will they fade off in the mist of history or remain as a key
player in the future politics and security of Afghanistan? Our first reaction to
these questions is that the Taliban is down but not out. The top leaders are still
at large, and without the protection and cover of local populations they cannot remain out of the reach of American forces for long. However, consistent
and massive destruction of their camps, now routinely reported in the international press, suggest that regular bombardments have neither deterred the
Taliban fighters nor have they finished off their sources of recruitment, training, and deployment. In the summer of 2005, the Taliban staged daring attacks
against the Karzai regime's outposts and against the American forces that have
concentrated their counterinsurgency operations in Pashtun-dominated eastern and southern provinces of Afghanistan.[63] Although the Taliban is somewhat scattered, less organized, and fatigued, it has survived as a fighting force.
It is still, however, not in a position to pose a real challenge to the stability of
the Karzai regime. Its capacity is, at the moment, limited to peripheral regions
in the Pashtun countryside and areas close to the Pakistani tribal belt, like
Waziristan.[64] Its strategy is to menace the Afghan security forces at the weakest
points and deny the government an opportunity to rehabilitate communication infrastructure and rebuild security institutions.

The Taliban leaders and fighters are operating with two assumptions in mind. First, that the United States will not stay in Afghanistan forever, and one day will have to vacate the country. Second, the United States cannot afford the economic and political cost of occupation. Therefore, keeping the United States engaged in the periphery sends an important political message of insecurity to Kabul as well as to the local population: that foreign forces are vulnerable to the Taliban fighters.

What really makes the Taliban go on fighting has a lot to do with the post-Taliban politics of Afghanistan. Three aspects of political reconstruction and war strategy have directly and indirectly fueled anger and frustration among the majority of the Pashtuns who are continually supporting the rebel groups. First is the real and perceived exclusion of the Pashtuns in the post-Taliban government that the warlords from the Northern Front dominated for quite a while. Although the situation has changed since the October 2004 presidential elections and the placement of many Pashtuns in top governmental ministries, the image of the entire political enterprise is that of an American puppet. Second is the targeting of Pashtun areas to destroy the Taliban and its foreign allies present in regions close to Pakistan. From an American point of view, it would make sense to concentrate war efforts in these areas because a persistent resistance emanates from there. But this helps the Taliban propaganda machine in portraying the United States as an enemy of the Pashtun, and an occupation force in Afghanistan. Going by the norms and call of jihad against the former Soviet Union, the evidence of daily killings, bombardments, and capturing of Pashtun Taliban provokes a good degree of negative images about the United States and the government in Kabul that it supports. The third factor is related to the previous one but it has a significance of its own. It is the perception of a foreign force in occupation and being present on the Afghan territory and engaged in hostile activities. Historically, on three different occasions—twice in the nineteenth century against the British and a third time against the former Soviet Union last century—the Afghans fought against the invading forces. The United States like any power in such a situation has presented itself as "liberator" and "nation builder" but the claim is not universally accepted inside Afghanistan or out of the country.

During the past two years, the Taliban fighters have been joined by other anti-American forces. And these include the same multinational mix that troubled the Soviet forces for a decade. There are reports that Arabs, Pakistanis, and some from Central Asian states are joining the Taliban.[65] In our assessment, the forces engaged against the United States may become increasingly diverse with a united front strategy and a single focus on the removal of the United States from Afghanistan. The accounts of the activities of these forces in 2005 suggest that they have a constant flow of money, are better equipped, even using shoulder-held antiaircraft missiles.[66] The emerging nature of the resistance against the U.S. forces should be seen in

light of the general atmosphere of anti-Americanism in the Muslim countries. The situation in Iraq, the strength of insurgency there, and the popular perception that the United States is part of the problems of the Muslim
world feeds into the insurgency in Afghanistan. There is enough empirical
evidence to support the view that territorial problems in Islamic lands have
not remained confined just to people there but have attracted Muslims
from other part of the world to support them.[67] Based on this evidence, we
might say that the United States may confront this combination of Islamic
forces of which Taliban will be a significant part. Ultimately, in such conflicts, it is the question of the hearts and minds of the people; who really
wins them will determine the final outcome. Today, the situation is unclear,
ambiguous, and fuzzy. We have to bear in mind the question of economic
and political reconstruction of Afghanistan, how quickly this gigantic task
of state and nation building is accomplished. And also, the issue of Pashtun integration into the economic and political system is equally important
to isolate the Taliban and anti-American forces. Progress in state and nation
building that is under way may gradually reduce the Pashtun ethnic support
to the Taliban. Moderates among them, as it is evident from the September
2005 parliamentary elections, may choose to give up armed resistance and
isolate the extremist fringe.

NOTES

1. Alan J. Kuperman, "The Stinger Missile and U.S. Intervention in Afghanistan,"
Political Science Quarterly, Vol. 114, No. 2. (Summer, 1999), pp. 219–63.

2. Some of the individuals involved with the Mujahideen parties in official capacity in Pakistan argue that it was deliberate on the part of the government of Pakistan
to keep the Mujahideen factions divided for easier control and manipulation. Author's
interview with Mr. Abdullah, the first commissioner of Afghan Refugees, Peshawar, 21
June 2005. See also, Jessica Stern, "Pakistan's Jihad Culture." *Foreign Affairs*, Vol. 79
Issue 6, November–December 2000, p. 115, 12p, 1bw (check with Zain).

3. Author's interview with Mr. Afrasiab Khattack, Peshawar, 20 June 2005. See
also, Kristel Halter, "The Unholy Alliance: Pakistan, the Taliban, and Osama bin
Laden," *Washington Report on Middle East Affairs*, Vol. 20, No. 9, 2001, pp. 2, 89; M.
Ehsan Ahrari, "China, Pakistan, and the Taliban Syndrome," *Asian Survey*, Vol. 40,
No. 4., Jul.–Aug., 2000, pp. 658–71.

4. The intelligence chief of the Afghan government under Dr. Najibullah had a
meeting with the director general of Pakistan's Inter-Services Intelligence in Germany. Author's interview with former D.G. ISI, General (retired) Asad Durrani.
Rawalpindi, June, 2004.

5. On Pakistan's strategy, see Brigadier Mohammad Yousuf and Major Mark Adkin, *The Bear Trap: Afghanistan's Untold Story* (Lahore: Jang Publishers Press, 1993).

6. See Barnett R. Rubin, *The Fragmentation of Afghanistan: State Formation and Collapse in the International System* (New Haven & London: Yale University Press, 1995).

7. Offensive against Jalalabad was motivated by the consideration of placing an interim Afghan government inside the country to establish its credibility and political capacity to get international recognition. The United States and Pakistan made the decision together. Pakistan's ISI puts the blame squarely on the United States for pushing it to prematurely capture the city. See details in Marvin Weinbaum, *Pakistan and Afghanistan: Resistance and Reconstruction* (Boulder: Westview Press, 1994), pp. 39–41.

8. The Peshawar Accord was brokered by Pakistan in the last week of April 1992 quite in haste when the fall of the Najibullah regime appeared imminent. Iran, Saudi Arabia, the Pakistani government under Nawaz Sharif, and some religious political parities that had some influence with the Mujahideen leaders brokered the accord. The parties agreed to establish a fifty-member council that had thirty field commanders on it. *Dawn*, 28 April 1998.

9. Rasul Bakhsh Rais, "Afghanistan and the Regional Powers," *Asian Survey*, Vol. 33, No. 9. (Sep. 1993), pp. 905–22.

10. See details of the negotiations in Riaz M. Khan, *Untying the Afghan Knot: Negotiating Soviet Withdrawal* (Durham: Duke University Press, 1991).

11. UN Press Release SG/1860, April 14 1988.

12. William Maley, *Fundamentalism Reborn?: Afghanistan and the Taliban* (London: Hurst & Company, 2001).

13. Author's discussion with Dr. Shah Mahmoud Hanifi, assistant professor of Middle Eastern and South Asian History, James Madison University. Istanbul, Turkey, 7–9 May 2005.

14. *SIPRI Yearbook* (Oxford: Oxford University Press, 1995), p. 21.

15. Defense Minister Shah Nawaz Tanai in collaboration with Gulbadin Hikmatyar attempted a coup but failed to capture power, and fled to Pakistan.

16. Author's interview with Afrasiab Khattak, Peshawar, 20 June 2005.

17. This story has been repeated in the author's interviews in Pakistan and is documented in early journalistic works. See for instance, John K. Cooley, *Unholy Wars: Afghanistan, America and International Terrorism* (London: Pluto Press, 2001), pp. 143–61.

18. Thomas Hobbes, *Leviathan*, 1588–1679. (Oxford: Basil Blackwell, 1955).

19. Ibid.

20. Francis Fukuyama, *Trust: the Social Virtues and the Creation of Prosperity* (New York: Free Press Paperbacks, 1995); Francis Fukuyama, "Social Capital," Lawrence Harrison and Samuel P. Huntington, eds., *Culture Matters* (New York: Basic Books, 2000), pp. 98–111.

21. See a report in *Nation* (Islamabad) 14 July 1997.

22. Frederic Grare, *Pakistan and the Afghan Conflict, 1979–1985: With an Afterword Covering Events from 1985–2001* (Karachi: Oxford University Press, 2003), p. 194.

23. Ahmed Rashid, *Taliban: Islam, Oil and the New Great Game in Central Asia* (London: I. B. Tauris, 2001); Kamal Matinuddin, *The Taliban Phenomenon: Afghanistan 1994–1997* (Karachi: Oxford University Press, 1999); Neamatollah Nojumi, *The Rise of the Taliban in Afghanistan: Mass Mobilization, Civil War, and the Future of the Region* (New York: Palgrave, 2002).

24. Central Asian states, particularly Uzbekistan and Tajikistan, were concerned about the security threat from the Taliban ideology and their security links with the

Islamist opposition forces on their territory. Rajan Menon. "The New Great Game in Central Asia," *Survival*, no. 45 (2003), pp. 187–204.

25. Zalmay Khalilzad, "Afghanistan in 1995: Civil War and a Mini Great Game," *Asian Survey*, Vol. 36, No. 2, Part II. Feb., 1996, pp. 190–95.

26. Scott Peterson, "Rifts in Islamic World Deepen" (cover story), *Christian Science Monitor,*Vol. 90, No. 208 21 September 1998, p. 1.

27. The theory of "strategic depth" was postulated by General Aslam Beg, who was chief of army staff at that time in 1990. He thought in the event of a long war with India, Afghanistan could provide secure bases for military operations, since it has a relatively narrow band of width. Rais A. Khan, "Pakistan in 1991: Light and Shadows," *Asian Survey*, Vol. 32, No. 2, Part II. February 1992, pp. 197–206.

28. Fuel supplies from Pakistan were a critical resource because Iran had closed down official channels, and smuggling by camels from Iran was costly, inefficient, and not enough to meet the need of fighting a war. Author's interview with one of the top officials of the ISI, Lahore, 7 January 2005.

29. Pakistan brokered an agreement with General Abdul Rashid Dostam in Mazar-i-Sharif for the entry of the Taliban and joint rule on the basis of regional autonomy. Ibid.

30. See a report by Afghanistan's intelligence authority, "ISI Protecting Omar," *Dawn*, 18 January 2007.

31. Deobandis are a Sunni sect of Islam. They are conservative in Islamic outlook and emerged as Islamic reformers in the nineteenth century in India to purify Islam of Hindu and other practices that they thought had crept into religious practices of the Muslims in Subcontinent. They have taken their name from the place, Deoband in Uttar Paradesh in India. In postindependent Pakistan, the Deobandis have increased their following, madras networks, and religiopolitical fronts.

32. Conspicuous for not taking a political position was the Awami National Party, which has an historically long and abiding interest in the politics of Afghanistan because of its traditional ideology of Pashtun nationalism.

33. Some Pashtun nationalist leaders on the Pakistan side contest this view. They argue that the Punjabi officers on the top handled the Afghan issues and had Pashtun officers in junior positions who were not involved in strategic decision making, but only confined to carrying out the orders. Author's interview with Afrasiab Khattack. Peshawar, 21 June 2005.

34. Ralph H. Magnus , "Afghanistan in 1996: Year of the Taliban," *Asian Survey*, Vol. 37, No. 2, Part II. February, 1997, pp. 111–17.

35. Matinuddin, pp. 21–34.

36. See an interview of Naseerullah Babar, "Straight Talk," by Raza Khan, *The News on Sunday*, 18 February 2007.

37. See a critique of Pakistan's policy in support of the Taliban. Najam Sethi. "Pakistan's Folly," *The Wall Street Journal*, 12 October 2001.

38. North and South Waziristan are part of the several tribal agencies bordering Afghanistan that the federal government of Pakistan controls. During the anti-Soviet insurgency in the 1980s, these areas were major transit points for weapons and the Mujahideen into Afghanistan. Many of the transnational Islamic militants settled here after the end of the war. Pakistani forces have been operating against them in these regions, equally targeting the tribesmen who have given shelter to these

elements. See for instance, reference Shabana Fayyaz, "Towards a Durable Peace in a Waziristan," (Bradford: Pakistan Security Research Unit, Bradford University), 23 April 2007.

39. See two reports prepared by the International Crisis Group on the issue of Madrasas in Pakistan. "Pakistan: Madrasas, Extremism And the Military," *Asia Report,* No. 36, 29 July 2002; "Pakistan: Karachi's madrasas and Violent Extremism," *Asia Report,* No. 130.

40. After the 1970 elections in united Pakistan, the JUI formed a coalition government with the National Awami Party in Balochistan and the North-West Frontier Province. The National Awami Party was formed by the nationalists who espoused ethnic and regional rights for Balochis and Pashtuns. M. Rashiduzzaman, "The National Awami Party of Pakistan: Leftist Politics in Crisis," *Pacific Affairs,* Vol. 43, No. 3. Autumn, 1970, pp. 394–409.

41. See a report by Howard W. French, "For Militant, No Glorified End, but Death in the Dust," *The New York Times,* 19 May 2002, p. 8.

42. Taliban leaders claimed ignorance about the presence of sectarian terrorists. Author's interview with a former director general of the ISI. Lahore, October 25, 2005.

43. Author's interview with Agha Amin, Lahore, 15 September 2007.

44. Samuel P. Huntington, "The Clash of Civilizations?" *Foreign Affairs,* Vol. 72, No. 3, Summer 1993, pp. 22–28; Bernard Lewis, "The Roots of Muslim Rage," *Atlantic Monthly,* Vol. 266, no. 3, September 1990, p. 47.

45. Mula Ma'soun Afghani, "Our Goal Is to Restore Peace and Establish a Pure and Clean Islamic State in Afghanistan" Interview with Mula Ma'soum Afghani, official spokesperson of the Taliban Movement18th issue of *Nida'ul Islam* magazine, eighteenth issue. islam.org.au, April–May 1997.

46. Among the Sunni Muslims there are four: Hanafi, Humbli, Shaafi, and Shiite. The Shia follow Imam Jafar Sadiq and his compilation of jurisprudence. See Emmanuel Sivan, "Sunni Radicalism in the Middle East and the Iranian Revolution," *International Journal of Middle East Studies,* Vol. 21, No. 1., February 1989, pp. 1–30.

47. Matinuddin, note 64, pp. 39–40. Qazi Hussain Ahmed, chief of the Jamat-i-Islami, questioned the credentials of the Taliban as true representatives of Islam. He was critical of their treatment of women, particularly the closing of girls' schools.

48. It is a code of honor that the Pashtuns have lived with for centuries. It has somewhat colored their view of Islam as well. The *Pashtunwali* code includes: honor, revenge, hospitality, and shelter. It was in this tradition that the Taliban sheltered Al Qaeda fighters and their leaders.

49. It would be wrong to assume that all the Deobandis are sectarian. One section of the Deobandis has branched off and become sectarian.

50. This has been one of the prominent slogans of the sectarian Deobandis in Pakistan, which amounts to communal hatred against Shia. They have demonstrated this in their wall chalking and speeches during big rallies.

51. Olivier Roy, "Rivalries and Power Plays in Afghanistan: The Taliban, the Shari'a and the Pipeline,"*Middle East Report,* No. 202, Winter, 1996, pp. 37–40.

52. Matinuddin, pp. 34–40.

53. Khilafat was the system of Islamic governance that followed the death of the Holy Prophet. Four pious Caliphs, Abubakar, Umar, Usman, and Ali succeeded the Prophet in this order. Many Deobandis wanted to create the same system without

explaining how they would like to achieve this objective. In the case of Afghanistan it was easier, as the Taliban captured the state and enforced its own preferred system over the population.

54. Huntington, "The Clash of Civilizations?" op. cit.

55. Yonah Alexander and Michael S. Swetnam, *Usama bin Laden's al-Qaida: Profile of Terrorist Network* (Ardsley, NY.: Transnational Publishers, Inc., 2001).

56. There is lot of controversy over why the United States failed to seize Osama in Afghanistan. The 9/11 Commission report affirms the evidence that the CIA had ample evidence about Osama's involvement in terror networks in the Middle East. See *The 9/11 Commission Report: Final Report of the National Commission on Terrorist Attacks upon the United States* (New York: W.W. Norton & Company, 2004), pp. 108–21.

57. Anonymous, *Through Our Enemies' Eyes: Osama bin Laden, Radical Islam, and the Future of America* (Washington, D.C.: Brassey's Inc. 2002), pp. 154–67.

58. Author's interviews in Peshawar with observers of the Afghan scene suggest that Maulana Shamazai of Jamia Banuri, Karachi, who was assassinated in 2005, played a key role in the alliance between the Taliban leader Mullah Omar and Osama bin Laden.

59. *Dawn*, 7 August 1998.

60. *The News*, 29 August 1998.

61. Author's interview with former general Zia Uddin Butt, who was director general of ISI at that time. Lahore, 25 October 2005.

62. By many accounts, Mullah Omar was discourteous and even impolite to the Pakistani delegation, ridiculing them for pursuing the American line. *The 9/11 Commission Report* mentions a shouting match between Prince Turkey Bin Faisal, who went with the Pakistanis to Kandhar to negotiate expulsion of Osama from Afghanistan. *The 9/11 Commission Report*, p. 122.

63. The Taliban attacked an American MH-47 helicopter carrying Navy Seal commandos and other special operations personnel aboard. See, Carlotta Gall, "U.S. Troops Still Missing After Crash in Afghanistan," *The New York Times*, www.nytimes.com, 2 July 2005.

64. Pakistan has reportedly deployed 70,000 troops along the border with Afghanistan to control infiltration of Taliban militants seeking refuge in the tribal regions of Pakistan. It was for the first time in history that Pakistan sent troops in these areas which confronted heavy opposition. "Kabul's Failure Cannot Be Laid at Pakistan's Door," (editorial) *Daily Times* (Lahore), 22 June 2005.

65. Carlotta Gall and Thom Shanker, "Commando Saved in Afghanistan," *New York Times*, nytimes.com, 4 July 2005.

66. Ibid.

67. The Soviet war experience in Afghanistan, insurgency in Indian-administered Kashmir, Chechnya, Iraq, and to some degree Kosovo, suggest that fighters from Muslim countries joined them on the grounds of Islamic fraternity and solidarity. According to Pakistani retired general Aslam Beg, the war of resistance against the former Soviet Union created a "Global Resistance Force" of the Muslims of the world. He estimates that 60,000 *Jihadis* from more than sixty countries participated in the war. See General Mirza Aslam Beg, "The Turning Points of History," *National Development and Security*, Vol. 12, No. 48, Summer 2004, pp. 151–55.

4

The United States and the War on Terrorism

This is a war against a country that was traditionally considered remote and peripheral to American interests. But the massive terrorist violence of 9/11 has brought the United States, its NATO, allies and other friendly powers to Afghanistan to clear Afghanistan of their Taliban and Al Qaeda adversaries. Ironically, in the 1980s, the United States for Cold War reasons became a strategic ally of the Afghans and the transnational Islamic forces that had wanted to defeat and expel the Soviet Union from Afghanistan. However, American interest in Afghanistan did not go beyond helping defeat the Soviet aggression. Once the Soviet Union was forced to withdraw and consequently there was a disintegration of its territorial unity, ideology, and political order, Washington left the conflict, which had complex legacies of the Islamic resistance, the Afghan civil war, and multiple regional actors, largely unattended. For the United States, Afghanistan was once again a distant country with leaders who were addicted to the habit of fighting wars and did not want to construct peace.

The problems of stateless Afghanistan as a hub of international terrorism visited the United States in the tragic episodes of 9/11. It was only after tremendous human and material loss that the United States acted to remove the Taliban from the Afghan scene and destroy the sanctuaries that they gave to Al Qaeda members. The tragedy in the United States could have perhaps been averted, if the United States had paid some attention to reconstruction after Moscow pulled out of Afghanistan. In hindsight, the benign neglect of a cold war ally, fatally wounded and unable to cure itself, was a self-defeating policy. A country without state institutions, a political center and a viable economy was allowed to slip into a deadly civil war, which sucked in different elements with different motives from near and far. As Afghanistan became the epicenter of transnational movements, it affected countries and societies that were located around and far beyond its immediate boundaries. Our main argument is that stateless societies driven to despair, poverty, and chaos are both sources of religious extremism and a fertile ground for terrorist networks. Second, modern day terrorism, particularly of a religious nature, is not a problem restricted to a single country. Terrorism has become a global phenomenon with multilayered transnational connections among militants. In this chapter, we look at coalition building at the international level, the regional strategy of the United States on Afghanistan and the military operations to defeat the Taliban and Al Qaeda forces. We will tie up this discussion with American interests in cultivating moderate regimes in Central Asia, Afghanistan, Pakistan, and southwest Asia. We will also evaluate the political gains of the war on terrorism, constraints, future risks, and challenges for American security role in the region.

U.S. POLICY TOWARD AFGHANISTAN

In order to understand the present American policy toward Afghanistan, which is a combination of a war on terror and state reconstruction, we need to briefly examine the various phases of U.S. policy. American policy has neither been consistent nor part of any comprehensive strategic plan for the region. Rather, the policy makers in Washington have always reacted to the events in and around Afghanistan, assessed the relevance of the situation in relation to their own regional and global interests, and have then shaped an appropriate response.[1] Whether their assessment of events, situations, and policy responses were apt or not is open to debate. The first phase of American policy was influenced by the general concern about underdeveloped countries in the post–World War period. The United States as a new and emerging global power after the demise of the old European colonial powers had a great advantage in engaging the postcolonial developing countries. It had a clean image, as its character was not stained like that of the former European colonial powers in the region. The generosity and frankness with which it approached the developing countries was refreshing and the United States was welcomed as a partner for economic and security assistance to eradicate poverty, and to support education, health, and other nation-building activities. The United States approached Afghanistan through its global assistance program in these areas. But how much assistance a country would receive or how deep the relationship would become was never independent of American strategic goals that mainly centered on containing the Soviet influence and curbing the expansion of communism outside the recognized zones of Soviet influence.

In U.S. strategic calculations, Afghanistan was marginal to its interest in containing the former Soviet Union. There was a reasonable understanding of Afghanistan's strategic location, and an attempt, though half-heartedly, was made to win the Afghan rulers over to its side during the first few years of the Cold War. But the tensions between Afghanistan and Pakistan over the border issues forced the United States to make a choice between the two. Pakistan was bigger, had greater potential, and was more relevant to the strategic needs of the Western alliance. This choice reduced Afghanistan as an unimportant periphery, a medieval kingdom, and a landlocked buffer situated between the Soviet Central Asian republics and the new states of south Asia. In the beginning, the United States extended a good amount of assistance in agriculture, education, and infrastructural development to Afghanistan.[2] The United States was somewhat apprehensive about the growing Soviet influence in Afghanistan, but came to recognize the role of the Soviet Union as long as the Soviet Union did not upset the internal political arrangements in Afghanistan or go beyond its borders. The two great powers picked up different development projects and competed for influence peacefully, which suited the foreign aid–dependent Afghanistan and aided it in modernizing itself and in laying down the infrastructure for development. Afghanistan was not apparently drawn into the Cold War rivalry, but for geographical reasons, and due to its experience with the British, it was relatively more open to a wide range of economic and security assistance that Moscow was willing to offer. Washington's close alliance with Pakistan foreclosed the possibility of American arms or extensive economic assistance to Afghanistan. During this phase American relations with Afghanistan were cordial, friendly, and trouble free, but questions about Washington's security assistance to Pakistan remained strong on the mind of the Afghan leaders. The occasional eruption of problems between Afghanistan and Pakistan, and the growing Soviet influence in Kabul, were also responsible for the low-keyed relations between Kabul and Washington.

With the end of monarchy in 1973, Afghanistan began to experience the impact of Soviet influence. Many military officers who were involved in the overthrow of the king had received training in the Soviet military academies, and had strong communist inclinations and political linkages with the newly established communist groups in the country. The new regime led by Sardar Daoud, a member of the royal family himself, became hostage to the pro-Soviet military leaders. Perhaps Daoud was unaware of the connections between the communist groups and the pro-Soviet military officers and how both were managed by the Soviet intelligence. The United States watched these developments with distant interest for two reasons. First, it was in the process of winding down its war in Vietnam and had become engaged with the Soviet Union on reducing strategic arms. Second, its new strategy of propping up regional powers to protect Western interests at that time, like Iran in the region, shaped its policy of benign neglect. The Shah of Iran, being the American frontman for the security of the region, was assigned the responsibility of handling the small bushfire of crises in the neighborhood. Facing no clear dangers, the United States relieved itself of the greater part of the responsibility in the Persian Gulf and its hinterland, which included Afghanistan.[3] Even within this policy framework, the United States was gradually building its security capacity in the Indian Ocean and filling the political and security role that Britain had vacated in this region. Although such a role was cast in the East-West confrontation and was an attempt to ward off any possibility of rival Soviet Union attempting to control the oil resources of the region, the American force structure had multiple tasks capacity, including engaging any hostile regional state.[4]

American policy toward Afghanistan began to take a new shape with the communist coup in April 1978, which had a clear Soviet stamp on it. The United States maintained diplomatic relations with the new regime but kept watching the situation carefully as the Soviet-inspired revolution and reforms provoked a mass resistance in different parts of the country. With communists in power and dependent on Moscow for their survival, their relations with the United States were cool and indifferent, if not completely strained. At this stage, the United States became apprehensive with the increasing number of Soviet advisers guiding and supervising high numbers of departments of the new government in an effort to help shape a socialist future of a primitive, feudal society. Being distant and with very few assets in and around Afghanistan, the United States could just keep observing the developments in the country without a focused, clearly defined policy and a capacity to influence events. The Shah of Iran was facing simmering protests, and Pakistan had a military regime that the Carter administration had decided to isolate due to its pursuit of a nuclear program and overthrow of an elected regime.

Only when the Soviet forces invaded Afghanistan in December 1979 to take control of its politics and security by killing the sitting president and installing a more pliant puppet, Babrak Karmal, did the United States react sharply. It cancelled the participation of its athletes in the summer Olympic games in Moscow scheduled for 1980, and offered Pakistan a modest economic and military assistance package, which the latter turned down, saying it was "peanuts," and declared that it would resist by force any move by the Soviet Union in the direction of the Persian Gulf. This became known as the Carter Doctrine.[5] The U.S. prestige and credibility to maintain security in the region had already suffered a grievous blow with the fall of the Shah of Iran and the success of an anti-American Islamic revolution in that country. The Soviet invasion of Afghanistan spun the American policy in the region into greater chaos. The U.S. policy of isolating countries that had been its allies and stood up with it during the Cold War had in fact weakened its capacity to put up a coherent policy against the former Soviet Union.[6]

The immediate interest of the United States, in the wake of Soviet aggression against Afghanistan, was not that country itself, but ensuring that the Gulf States and its other partners in the region had the political will and capacity to stay with the United States and prevent the Soviet Union from endangering their security.[7] The United States reacted to the Soviet threat by sending out a strong signal to all the regional countries that it was sincere and serious to assist all countries and social movements that were opposed to Soviet presence in Afghanistan. Pakistan was the first country that it approached because even before the United States appeared on the Afghan scene, Pakistan was supporting the Afghan resistance against the communist regime. It had been hosting both refugees as well the Mujahideen leaders without much international publicity.[8] Pakistan had been offering itself as a staging base for attacks by the Mujahideen. Pakistan's military ruler, General Zia ul-Haq, found the United States offer to assist the country and the Afghan Mujahideen as a great political opportunity to stay in power and implement a vision of free and Islamic Afghanistan. General Zia was the chief architect of Pakistan's Afghan policy, and by all evidence, his influence on American policy in Afghanistan was immense.[9] In his view, the Soviet Union had neither the political skills nor the ideological appeal to stabilize Afghanistan and retain it under its influence. The Soviet Union only had a deadly military force that knew how to decimate populations, and the image that it had never withdrawn from the country it occupied.[10] Zia told the Americans that the Soviet Union was vulnerable and hardly had any chance of succeeding, but the struggle to oust it would have to be long, consistent, and collective. The United States' policy makers did not find this logic very convincing, but were willing to do whatever they could to support the Afghan resistance. In their estimation, it was an opportunity to bleed the Soviet Union, destroy its image in the world, portray it as an aggressor against a Third World Islamic country, and make its adventure costly in order to prevent it from going to areas beyond its traditional sphere of influence.[11] In a few years' time, Washington found the ideological fervor rooted in the Islamic concept of *Jihad* or holy war and the national passion to liberate Afghanistan immensely impressive. The Muslim and most of the Third World countries were vehemently opposed to the Soviet war and in varying degrees they supported the resistance movement. This is evident from the number of countries that routinely voted for resolutions annually at the General Assembly session calling for an immediate withdrawal of the Soviet forces and for negotiating a peaceful settlement of the problem.

The U.S. policy had remarkable success in forging a very broad-based international coalition of forces that supported the Afghan Mujahideen resistance.

Its European allies, pro-West Muslim countries, and the wealthy oil-producing Middle Eastern states extended enormous support to Pakistan and the Mujahideen. An important, and now very controversial, aspect of American policy was to indirectly encourage young Muslim fighters across the Middle East, Pakistan, and other Muslim states to join the struggle of the Mujahideen. Of course, this grass-root Islamic resistance movement was not entirely on the behest of the United States; however, the United States was neither averse to it, nor did the United States see any danger in radicalizing Islamic youth. Islam as a religion, Islamic movements, and groups of all shades because of their strong opposition to communism were thought to be natural allies of the West during the Cold War.[12] The same Islamic elements became a partner of the United States, as both had a common interest in defeating the Soviet Union. Freedom from communism was a common and unifying theme between the Islamic radicals and the United States. There is an unending debate on why the United States did not read the danger in the militancy of the Islamic youth and their flocking into Afghanistan, and what consequences their political and military experience would have on the home societies when they returned to them, or why would they not turn their guns on the West when the Soviet Union was gone?[13]

There cannot be and will never be a satisfactory answer to these troubling questions. Because much of this questioning is based on hindsight wisdom and hardly addresses the issue of the great power confrontation in the 1980s and the American need for a broad-based strategic alliance against the former Soviet Union. Moreover, the Mujahideen resistance had nationalistic as well as strong Islamic orientations and would have gone fighting against Moscow even without American support.[14] It is also a question of relative importance of each partner to the common strategy of rolling the Soviet forces out of Afghanistan; did the United States need the Mujahideen more or the vice versa? There are other questions, like why did it not support the moderate elements in Afghanistan? Perhaps they were very few in numbers, had a narrow social support base, or were unable to organize a massive resistance comparable to what the religious groups had. The moderate Afghan groups were at a disadvantageous position in Pakistan because Pakistan had a policy of preference for the groups with strong Islamic orientation. The Islamist Mujahideen flowed into Pakistan with millions of refugees. They had ethnic and religious networks across the border, and received personal political support of Zia, who favored them greatly.[15] Many of the Mujahideen groups welcomed American support and highly valued its extensive assistance through Pakistan. But they were also conscious of the fact that the United States had its own interests in the situation, as it saw its rival superpower in great trouble. There is hardly any evidence that the Afghans during the Jihad against the former Soviet Union considered the

United States as an enemy or as the next target or had any coherent ideology to compete against the American global influence.

The United States and its Afghan and regional allies, notably Pakistan, achieved their central goals—forcing the Soviet Union to make a retreat, leaving a weak communist government to fend off for itself. There is hardly any recognition of the sacrifices that the Afghans made in causing the collapse of the Soviet Union and fall of communism.[16] Once this central goal of American policy was accomplished, Washington, after agreeing on positive/negative symmetry with Moscow over their respective economic and military assistance to their Afghan clients, began to gradually pull itself out of the Afghan war. Indirectly, through Pakistan and on its own using the good will that it had earned with some of the Mujahideen groups, it tried to promote some political understanding among them for a workable political alliance. But it found working with the Mujahideen groups frustrating and was not comfortable with the Islamic ideology of some of them. It is also important to note that the demise of the Soviet Union kicked up a new intellectual and policy discourse on what would be the future security threats for the United States and its Western alliance. Or who will be the new enemies that the United States would be most likely to confront with the end of communism. Real or concocted, there is a lot of controversy that the Islamist groups and countries supporting them slowly began to emerge as the new 'other' in the American security assessment. Afghan Mujahideen, vowing to establish an Islamic state in Afghanistan in the greatly altered world security environment, couldn't win American support for this kind of cause. Had their focus been on political and economic reconstruction or ending internal strife to make Afghanistan a stable and peaceful country and been pragmatic enough to respect and engage the West in their own benefit, the United States might have continued its assistance and political support. Many of the Afghan leaders wasted this important source of international support by taking an unnecessarily anti-Western posture. Another reason for the United States to quit Afghanistan was its ad-hoc, goal-oriented, and pragmatic foreign policy. The Afghan war had served its purpose, now the United States had other issues to attend to and reassess the value of its partnership with the Mujahideen. Reappraisal of the situation in and around Afghanistan suggested that it was time for Washington to leave that country because the multiple confrontations it was facing didn't deserve taking sides or staying engaged with the Mujahideen factions fighting to capture political power.[17]

This turned out to be one of the greatest mistakes of American foreign policy. It is true that Afghanistan's liberation war had deteriorated into a civil strife and it was difficult to stabilize the country with so many centers of powers, warlords, political factions, and creeping intervention of neighboring countries, but these were the very reasons for the United States to stay engaged. The confrontation between the Soviet Union and the Afghan Mujahideen had ruined the country. Afghanistan hardly had any economic, political, or state-based institutional structure left to handle the reconstruction. More than anything, it required peace, solidarity, and unity among the warring factions to restart a new life. The United States and Western powers, despite many irritants, including rhetoric of anti-Americanism of some of the Afghan factions, could have shown some patience and understanding of the troubles of the Afghan society, which was going through cycles of conflict. The United States unfortunately left the country, when the Afghans needed its support the most, in the area of economic reconstruction. It is evident now, after the ouster of the Taliban, economic rehabilitation and support to state and society institutions are vital for rebuilding peace and creating stability in postconflict conditions. The United States and other partners of the Mujahideen resistance did not realize how a stateless society, fragmented and porous to regional influence and intervention from so many opposite directions could menace the security of the entire region, and dangerous anti-American forces could seek a refuge therein and plan and execute a global strategy of terror. It needs to be clarified that the Afghans themselves were never on the front of the anti-American war of Al Qaeda. This organization was not launched as a consequence of war in Afghanistan either, but had emerged with a mission to liberate Islamic lands, specifically Saudi Arabia, Kuwait, and other states in the region after the American-led war to vacate Iraqi aggression against Kuwait. This is a complex issue and it is out of the purview of this chapter to examine it in length. It would suffice to say that the Afghans, because of their camaraderie of the war of resistance, embraced the fugitive Al Qaeda into their fold. More than the memory of their wartime association, there was a mutuality of interest between the Al Qaeda and Taliban leadership. One needed a space, a shelter, and freedom to train forces and plan attacks; the other needed determined fighters and material resources to win the internal war against the Northern Front. Islam and a vision of an Islamic state and a powerful narrative of Muslims as victims facing prosecution, injustice, and oppression were some of the common themes between the two organizations.

Washington has to accept part of the responsibility for how Bin Laden and his associates escaped to Afghanistan, and that the United States was unable to capture him or get his custody when he was still in Sudan or on his way to Afghanistan. The official claim is that Bin Laden was well protected in Sudan, and that it was thought he would be an easy target when he relocated himself in Afghanistan. Sudanese authorities have claimed that they offered to turn over bin Laden to the U.S. authorities, but they declined to take him.[18] The 9/11 Commission Report has found the Sudanese claim without "unreliable evidence."[19]

There is a good amount of evidence to show that the United States tried its best to get bin Laden out of Afghanistan indirectly through Pakistan and directly by using some direct contacts with the Taliban leadership.[20] The efforts did not materialize because of the conditions put forward by the Taliban for delivering bin Laden. First and foremost was the demand of the Taliban for recognition by the United States and membership of the UN, which Washington was not willing to grant for the disputed legitimacy of the Taliban, their treatment of women, minorities, and those who were opposed to their rule. The United States had found evidence of involvement of Al Qaeda and bin Laden in the bombing of two of its naval ships in the port of Aden, and wanted the Taliban to hand bin Laden over for questioning and a possible trial. The Taliban's condition was that whatever evidence the United States had should be placed before them and, if the Taliban was satisfied, it would appoint a committee of Islamic jurists to try bin Laden rather than turn him or his associates over to the U.S. authorities.[21] During the Taliban reign, getting bin Laden became one of the central objectives of U.S. policy. The United States tried several options to get hold of the most wanted man on the U.S. list, which ranged from negotiating a deal with the Taliban to using the good offices of the third parties friendly to both the United States and the Taliban, like Saudi Arabia and Pakistan. The CIA collaborated with Pakistani ISI to train a special commando force to capture him.[22] Before this, the U.S. naval forces present in the Arabian Sea fired scores of cruise missiles on 28 August 1998, at Osama's camp in the eastern part of Afghanistan. The missile attack killed hundreds of trainees (including some Pakistanis) and completely destroyed the camp. But the real target had escaped before the missiles landed.

American relations with the Taliban were frosty most of the time. Washington used some bait to change Taliban's policy on bin Laden, but nothing worked. In a way the United States exhausted all means, which included indirect influence, persuasion, intervention of common friends, threats, isolation, sanctions, and some vague promises to accept the Taliban after they fulfilled certain conditions, expelling, and preferably giving bin Laden over into their custody. The Taliban leadership used many excuses to continue giving protection to bin Laden. These excuses included the Islamic duty to provide secure refuge to fellow Muslims fearing persecution or oppression; Pashtun culture based on social code of Pashtunwali that among other things shelters the fugitives disregard to their nature of their crime; questioning the quality of the evidence against bin Laden and the failure of the United States to place all the evidence on the table; insisting that Taliban government was more qualified to try bin Laden if it had evidence than any other government; and there was no guarantee of a fair trial for bin Laden if he was handed over to the U.S. authorities. The Taliban, true to its character, took a very rigid position; almost all the demands it placed before the third party emissaries were nonnegotiable. The real difficulty was that the Taliban operated on very different premises and assumptions than the traditional diplomacy. As an essentially nonmodern, tribal force functioning under the absolute control of Mullah Omar, the self-designated *Ameer Ul Momineen* (leader of the faithful), a man who never even visited Kabul, the outside powers found it extremely difficult to negotiate with the Taliban on anything. They had neither any political grooming nor understanding of how the world system functioned. Their socialization in the madrasa environment gave them very little and narrow exposure to the world outside their educational institutions. Therefore, the principles of normal diplomacy did not work; nor did polite and persistent pressures from two of the common supporters, Saudi Arabia and Pakistan. The United States did not give up its pursuit of finding Bin Laden and continued to explore all possibilities short of direct military intervention.

The terrorist attacks on 9/11 entirely changed the whole world's perceptions about the Taliban and Afghanistan. It did not take the Western powers much time to dig out evidence that connected the bombers of the World Trade Center with the Al Qaeda leadership present in Afghanistan, and being protected by the Taliban.[23] For the United States, it was not just the destruction of thousands of lives and the loss of billions of dollars but the stark question of how stateless terrorists dealt such a grave blow to its national security and global prestige by targeting symbols of its wealth and power. The 9/11 attacks might be termed as the second Pearl Harbor for the United States. The tragic event had two immediate effects. First, it generated unprecedented sympathy for the United States and its people from all over the world and a global disgust for the ghastly act of terrorism. Second, the terrorist attacks caused an unparalleled upsurge of nationalist sentiment among the American masses. A feeling of deep hurt and anger united the entire nation behind conservative president Bush surrounded by a group of right-wingers who had long entertained a vision of a hostile world. The tragic event offered more than adequate evidence to their worldview in which the security of the United States depended on a willingness to use disproportionate power against the real and "imagined" enemies.[24] The world sympathy and national solidarity in a moment of deep grief gave the American president a free hand to respond to the situation.

REGIONAL ALLIES

The war on terrorism in Afghanistan has many dimensions and involves many sets of players, national, regional, and global. In this section we will examine the role that some of the regional countries have played in assisting U.S. operations, providing basing rights, sharing intelligence, and extending political cooperation. In our view, four of them are greatly relevant in understanding the contribution of regional allies to the U.S.-led war against the Taliban and Al Qaeda. They are: Afghanistan's Northern Front, Pakistan, Iran, and central Asian states.

ALIGNING WITH THE NORTHERN FRONT

Before the dust of the twin towers settled or even the smoke and fire were put out, the Americans began to evolve a comprehensive strategy toward Afghanistan. The policy had multiple prongs that covered the mechanisms to effectively punish and quickly oust the Taliban regime and destroy the Al Qaeda network throughout the world, specifically in Afghanistan where its leaders had found a secure refuge. Having left Afghanistan high and dry in the midst of civil war in the early 1990s, the United States operated with very limited resources. Therefore, the first prong of its plan was to establish a strategic partnership with the Northern Front that consisted of non-Pashtun ethnic minorities. The Front had been fighting against the Taliban for the past several years. Although it was weak and demoralized after the assassination of its charismatic commander Ahmed Shah Masud, the Front had retained tremendous social capacity to mobilize fighters within its communities against the Taliban. The United States had maintained some intelligence links with the Front during its troubled relations with the Taliban but abstained from assisting it in the war. Now the situation had changed. The Front wanted the U.S. partnership to oust the Taliban as much as the United States wanted the territory and militia of the Front to use against the Taliban. It was a perfect marriage of convenience for both of them. They now saw a common end against a common enemy, the Taliban. This book is not the place to go into the detail of the negotiations, the amount of money that changed hands to buy off commanders of the Northern Front, or the role local militia played as an adjunct of the American forces in defeating the Taliban. The Northern Front, having taken beatings repeatedly from the Taliban and squeezed into a narrow band of territory, found the opportunity propitious in having an angry, desperate, and very powerful country in the world on its side. Once it became clear that the United States was committed to changing the regime in Afghanistan and was willing to apply the most lethal force to do the job, the anti-Taliban forces began to attract hordes of fighters with prospects of an assured salary, uniforms, and weapons. The smell of victory against the most hated enemy, the Taliban, forged among them greater unity than could have been possible before 9/11.

There are many questions that need to be addressed about why the United States went all the way to embrace the Northern Front that had some of the warlords within its fold with worse records of atrocities against their opponents. Did the United States explore other options, like creating divisions within the Taliban and using factions within the majority Pashtun community to topple the Taliban? What role did the Northern Front really play? Did the United States contemplate fully the implications of aligning with the regional warlords and using them as proxies against the Taliban for the future political unity and integration of Afghanistan? We think these questions are important to be debated and discussed among the historians and political observers of Afghanistan and policy makers of regional states and Western coalition. We do not wish to be an apologist for U.S. policy in the initial phase of its military action against Afghanistan, but understand the national sentiment and political atmosphere within which the United States took critical decisions regarding Afghanistan. There was a national outrage against the terrorist attacks within the United States and a sense of humiliation. Unlike many other incidents of terrorist violence, there was a visible and identifiable source from where Al Qaeda had operated. Those who had provided protection and sanctuary to Bin Laden and his associates were state functionaries and had control over Afghanistan. In the face of evidence that the Bush administration presented to the media and the world, inaction, delay, or wavering would have caused embarrassment and a tremendous political cost. All accounts of inside stories within the close network of the Bush administration suggest that quick action was consistently on the mind of the President.[25] The CIA and other outfits of the government were eager to win over the Northern Front leaders because it was easier and doable, along with being a strategic necessity for operational purposes. The United States badly needed local partners on the ground, inside Afghanistan with secure rear and firm positions on the front. Besides these qualities, the Northern Front had good intelligence assets, long and valuable operational experience against the Taliban, and more than that, they possessed the will to fight and oust the Taliban militia. In a political sense, the Front made a perfect natural partner of the United States in its war against terrorism and the Taliban.

What other possible options were available for United States? Very few. Exploring and pursuing other options like divisions within the Taliban or cultivating Pashtun factional leaders would have required more time, energy, and political resources. Washington did not entirely ignore these options, as it tried to win over "moderate" Taliban or those who were not ideologically deeply committed with Mullah Omar. But defections were very few and ineffective in causing the collapse of the Taliban from within. It was the lethal use of force from above, the heavy and consistent aerial bombardment, that finally made the Taliban fighters run for life. This was not the kind of war that the Taliban had expected or could be prepared for. With the softening of the Taliban positions and withering away of Taliban forces that were concentrated around Kabul and largely in the northern parts of the country, the United States tried to push through the Pashtun regions by fielding former Mujahideen commander Abdul Haq in Jalalabad and Hamid Karzai in the Kandhar area for causing uprisings against the Taliban at a popular level. None of the missions succeeded beyond limited incursions confined to the immediate tribal networks. The Taliban captured and executed Abdul Haq, while Karzai had a narrow escape and was rescued by the American forces.[26]

The U.S. alignment with the Northern Front factions, though justified on pragmatic and operational grounds, was not without adverse political effects. Although U.S. intervention in Afghanistan was independent of the civil war between the Northern Front (comprising non-Pashtun minorities) and the largely Pashtun Taliban, it has been seen as being on the other side by the Pashtun majority. The post-Taliban power shift in favor of the Northern Front further strengthened the impression that the Pashtuns had lost power, and it was a direct result of the American intervention and war against the Taliban. The United States has tried to correct the ethnic imbalance by facilitating Hamid Karzai, a Pashtun from the Kandhar region, to head the interim administration. It was tactically a smart move and has produced better political effects in terms of rallying some elements of the Pashtun community behind Karzai. A lot has changed since the election of the parliament in September 2005 as Pashtun representatives affiliated with different political groups, including some moderate Taliban, have been elected to the legislature. The electoral process over time will settle the question of political balance in the country.

NEUTRALIZING IRAN

Initiating and firming up a partnership with the Northern Front was just one of the elements of the American strategy. The United States needed the support of the regional states adjacent to Afghanistan for using their air space, bases, and intelligence assets and continuing assistance in many other ways to achieve its ends. Iran, because of its longstanding row with the United States over a number of issues, could not be a direct and visible partner, and Washington made no serious attempt in this regard except seeking some support for search and rescue missions. Tehran had been one of the major players inside Afghanistan supporting the anti-Taliban forces and its opposition to the Taliban for sectarian and political reasons was well known.[27] When the United States initiated attacks against the Taliban regime, Iran did not make an issue out of foreign intervention in Afghanistan and abstained from throwing any wrench in the way of American strategy against the Taliban. The American resolve, the broad-based support its leadership had, and international revulsion against the Taliban were some of the factors that also kept the Iranians from intervening against foreign presence in Afghanistan. The United States did not need to issue threats to neutralize Iran, as Iran had silently prayed and hoped for the removal of the Taliban. Unlike some support in the streets of some of the Muslim countries for the Taliban when the United States launched its attacks, the Iranian streets were empty of such protestors. Iran became neutral in the American war against the Taliban and rather rejoiced the fact that two of its adversaries were fighting among themselves. As we will explore in another section, the long-term effects of American presence in the region on Iran's strategic interests in Afghanistan and beyond will be quite adverse. Iran does not find itself in a happy situation as a weaker adversary; the Taliban has been replaced by a stronger global power, covering Iran's eastern flank from air bases in Afghanistan. But it hardly had any choice, and it very prudently avoided creating any trouble for the U.S. forces.

The United States and Iran have an uneasy relationship in Afghanistan, which is influenced by a host of other factors that are not directly related to the situation in this country. Three issues can be mentioned here. First is the American invasion of Iraq and its political and security consequences. There has been lot of debate on why the Bush administration decided to invade Iraq when the Iraqi regime had nothing to do with the terrorist attacks or Al Qaeda.[28] The allegations that Iraq possessed weapons of mass destruction have proven to be absolutely false. It is not relevant here to explore all the conspiratorial and not so conspiratorial theories that try to explain why the United States invaded Iraq—oil, interest in spreading democracy, domestic political compulsions, establishing American credibility as a global power, and redefining its role in the larger security framework of the Middle East under the new doctrine of preemption. Whatever the U.S. motives, interests, and strategy in the region, Iran has considerable stakes in the futures of both Iraq and Afghanistan.

Iran has in many ways played a complementary role to U.S. policy toward post-Taliban Afghanistan in providing development assistance, opening up alternative trade routes, and working closely with the Karzai government. Iran has a long-term strategic perspective on Afghanistan beyond the U.S. involvement. On security and internal politics issues of Afghanistan, Iran has been lying low and concentrating more on trade and development to sustain its constituency of influence in Afghanistan, independent of U.S. purposes and policy.

BASE FACILITIES IN CENTRAL ASIA

As the American military needed bases from where it could launch its operations, it focused on Uzbekistan, Kyrgyzstan, and Pakistan. We will deal with

Pakistan at the end of this section. Let us first examine briefly the strategic relevance of the two Central Asian states, the former Soviet republics for the American military operations. Both of them have well-developed air bases, stationing facilities for the forces, and proximity to Afghanistan. Both of these two states have had strong interest in getting the Taliban out due to the support the Taliban was providing to the states' religious militia. The Soviet Union in its war against the Afghan Mujahideen had used these bases in its counterinsurgency operations. Moscow itself, wanting American good will, did not object to the use of its "near abroad" periphery. One of the important effects of the new situation in the region was the change in American policy on the question of human rights and democracy, the two conditions it had set for deeper and extensive engagement with Uzbekistan. When the United States sent a request to Uzbekistan for assistance in terms of use of the Khanabad airbase in the southern part of the country, it did not take much time for them to make a choice, because the opportunity offered political support to fight against the Islamic movement and marked an end of criticism against them for human rights violations. In a quid pro quo, the United States provided $500 million security, and repackaged the country as a "stable and moderate force."[29] President Islam Karimov and his regime have one of the worst records of oppression of dissidents, fixing elections, and corruption has used the American connection to his political benefit. Since 9/11, Karimov has declared all his political opponents as "Islamist terrorists," and unfortunately, Washington has embraced this tyrant as a partner, because in its view the strategic interests overweigh interest in supporting democracy in this region.[30]

PARTNERSHIP WITH PAKISTAN

Pakistan once again emerged as the key state in helping the United States end the Taliban rule, the regime Pakistan had supported against persistent international criticism. One of the first calls to world leaders was placed to Pakistan's General Pervez Musharraf, who had been isolated for toppling an elected government in October 1999. Former secretary of state Colin Powell was as blunt as one can be in diplomacy in presenting a list of demands. The demands were extensive and included basing facilities, permission to use airspace, intelligence information, and halting of all support to the Taliban.[31] The central theme of the conversation was that Pakistan had to decide whether it was the United States or with the terrorists, and if it chose the terrorists, it was to "be prepared to be bombed to the Stone Age."[32] Pakistan, which recalculated its interests when the U.S. intervention in Afghanistan appeared imminent, decided to accede to the U.S. demands for unconditional support.

For almost a decade after the departure of the Soviet forces, the United States and Pakistan had found very little to restructure a new partnership and the drift in opposite directions continued on some of the important issues like Pakistan's support to the Taliban, Kashmir insurgency, the nuclear program, and combating religious extremism and religious extremism's fallout in the region. Pakistan had failed to convince the United States about the rationale of its policies on these issues. After getting the former Soviet Union out of Afghanistan it wanted Pakistan to finish the support extended to the Islamist groups there, banish the religiously motivated private militias from crossing national boundaries and close its doors to Islamic activists from other countries who had grown links with like-minded elements in Pakistan during the Afghan war.[33] It was a tall order for the Pakistani state that had developed strong links with these groups to fulfill part of its foreign policy agenda in the region. This factor was no less important in the minds of American policy makers than the nuclear program when they slammed sanctions against Pakistan in the fall of 1990.[34] Three years later, Pakistan was put on the watch list of terrorist states on the question of supporting militants in the Indian-held Kashmir. Nuclear testing in May 1998, which was in response to Indian tests earlier in the month, invoked a new wave of sanctions. A third wave of sanctions came when the military took over power in October 1999. The events of 9/11 presented a new situation to both the countries and also a moment of reflection on what had gone wrong and how they could cooperate to oust the Taliban regime.

Why did Pakistan emerge as central to the American war against the Taliban and Al Qaeda network? It did so for two fundamental reasons. First, it was due to Pakistan's strategic location on the southern fringes of central Asia, covering the southern and eastern flanks of Afghanistan. Furthermore, Pakistan's long coastline along the Arabian Sea placed it at the center of maritime strategy for the hinterland in this direction, as it later became obvious from the American use of airpower from its aircraft career groups in the area. No such operations could be conducted within the exiting international legal regime without the consent and cooperation of Pakistan. Pakistan's airfields, intelligence resources, and the institutional strength of the armed forces were considered essential for defeating the Taliban and routing out the Al Qaeda from the region.[35] The most important consideration in soliciting Pakistan's support was the proximity of its bases from which search, recovery, and other vital operations could be launched. Along with the Karachi port, the air base at Jacobabad has given the U.S. forces a valuable logistical and supply facility because of the short distance between this region and Afghanistan.

The second important reason behind seeking partnership with Pakistan was Islamabad's experience of handling Afghan groups for three decades and the intelligence assets it had acquired over the years. Pakistan's support was crucial in sealing the borders, preventing the Taliban and Al Qaeda fighters from crossing over to the country and taking shelter there. However, the joint watch over the border through deployment of Pakistani troops and American technical means had many loopholes which allowed some of the Al Qaeda operatives to slip through the lines using local contacts in the tribal areas bordering Afghanistan. There were many questions raised about the capacity of Pakistan to control these elements and even face a backlash, which it did two years later during its operations in South Waziristan.[36] The control over the borders required heavy deployment of troops, and for the first time, Pakistan's armed forces had done a splendid job in denying territorial space to the Taliban. Since Pakistan is a strategic backyard of Afghanistan, no movement or military operation has succeeded in Afghanistan without the active support of Pakistan's tribal belt. This belt played a central role in Pakistan's policy of organizing resistance against the Soviet occupation of Afghanistan. Before that Nadir Khan had mobilized Pashtuns in this region and raised a big militia in the late 1920s for removing Amir Habibullah, the Tajik bandit, popularly known as *Bach-a-Saqa* (son of water carrier).[37] This time also, the Pashtun Taliban have received political and social support in Pakistan's tribal region that has partly sustained their resistance against the American forces. For this reason, the post-Taliban regime and the U.S. administration have continued to raise questions about the sincerity of the Pakistani government in expelling or arresting the Taliban and Al Qaeda leaders.[38] Pakistan's position is that it has arrested a large number of Al Qaeda leaders and has handed them over to the American authorities. It asserts that there cannot be better evidence of its commitment to the war on terror than the fact that hundreds of its troops have lost their lives fighting Al Qaeda terrorists. Washington has repeatedly acknowledged Pakistan's contribution in the effort to stabilize Afghanistan. It is easy to trade accusations and raise doubts in difficult situations like along the borders between Afghanistan where neither Afghanistan nor Pakistan established any effective control. The situation is complicated further because during the war of resistance against the former Soviet Union, the Afghan and foreign fighters used the border regions as staging points and thousands of Arab fighters decided to marry local women and eventually settled down there. Blood ties among the local Pashtuns and Arab veterans of the Afghan-Soviet war have created enormous difficulties for the Pakistani government to flush out the foreigners from the region. Their presence, which is much lower than it was at the start of American war in Afghanistan, raises fears about the stability of adjoining provinces of Afghanistan, where American forces have faced tough and persistent resistance from the remnant Taliban elements.

The terrorist attacks on 11 September 2001 presented Pakistan with a difficult political and diplomatic terrain to negotiate. Essentially, it only had two options; to stay an ally and supporter of the Taliban or to join the

American-led international coalition against terrorism. Realistically, there was nothing in between these two alternatives, as even genuine attempts to find a neutral course would have damaged Pakistan's national security interests. Triggered by public anger, humiliation, and the scale of human tragedy, the immediate reaction of the United States left Pakistan with no room for any gray area. So when Pakistan was posed the question of whether it was with the United States or not, Pakistan's military leaders understood the logic of this question, and responded positively.[39]

By calculating risks and pay-offs between the two options, Pakistan made the right decision in supporting the United States in its new war against terrorism. Any delay or margin of error would have taken the initiative away from Islamabad, and perhaps pushed it to the brink of disaster. Had it wavered, tried to hedge out or ride on emotions of nationalism and religious solidarity with the Taliban movement, it might have faced its gravest dangers to its national security. Pakistanis understood the urgency of the situation, intensity of international revulsion against terrorism and global sympathy for the United States, and therefore decided to support the war efforts of the United States against the Taliban. Under the vastly changed circumstances, Pakistan reversed its policy toward the Taliban, the closest allies in Afghanistan, from collaboration with them to joining an international coalition against them. It was not a moral or religious issue but one that related to reassessment of national security interests.

Reversing its policy toward the Taliban and siding with the United States to destroy the Taliban's regime was a bold but at the same time a controversial step at the popular level for Pakistan. The change may have long-term effects on Pakistan's internal as well as regional security environment. The question is what will Pakistan gain or lose by such an abrupt and fundamental shift in its policy from an ally of the Taliban to their adversary? Apart from the heavy weight of international circumstances, Pakistan acted according to the old maxim "There are no permanent friends and enemies. Only national interests are permanent." What are then Pakistan's interests in Afghanistan? It has a basket of interests. Many governments during the past twenty-five years have added new items, and have taken out some of them with the changing circumstances. I believe that with the American entry into Afghanistan, the size and shape of the basket and the items in it have changed fundamentally. The real and substantive change is between the old policy that rested in carving Afghanistan out as sphere of influence with strong security and political ties with Islamabad to a new policy of neutrality in the internal affairs of Afghanistan and support to international measures in reconstructing the Afghan state. Pakistan's geopolitical location and ties with the Afghan tribes, ethnic groups, and historically with so many different factions and parties during the Afghan war are such that it can be a spoiler as well as a friendly supporter. Under the old policy it put its weight behind the Taliban movement by extending considerable economic, military, and political support in its attempt to secure a strategic advantage over its regional rivals that were supporting their own favorite groups in this complex and confused contestation of power. Some would argue that Pakistan's support was crucial for the military success of the Taliban against their opponents. At the end of the day, however, Pakistan gained very little. By helping the Taliban it alienated other ethnic and regional groups that began to see Pakistan as an adversary fueling internal strife and guilty of staging intervention through the Taliban that included big contingents of religious militants. The country remained unstable and in perpetual conditions of war. This ruined Pakistan's dream of opening up to Central Asia. The leaders in these states found the nature of Taliban regime, its fanaticism, and policy of giving sanctuaries to militants from other Islamic countries to train themselves, hide, and plan attacks against their targets quite alarming. The Central Asian states accused Pakistan for its support to the Taliban, which they feared could trigger unrest and further fan the forces of militant political Islam in their territories at a difficult stage of political transition and state formation. These states more or less developed a sentiment of passive hostility toward Pakistan for its support to the Taliban. The United States, Western countries, and Pakistan's close ally, China, also felt offended due to Pakistan's failure to influence policies of the Taliban on any issue. Pakistan's post-Soviet policy toward Afghanistan was a failure.

One of the more stubborn and negative effects of Pakistan's support to the Taliban was their nexus with the sectarian terrorists in Pakistan. With sanctuaries and training facilities in Afghanistan the Taliban caused tremendous damage to intersect harmony in the society. It is an overstated fact that Pakistan has been a victim of ethnic and sectarian terrorism for about quarter of a century. But Pakistan must take part of the blame for its own policies that created a social environment conducive to the growth of ethnic and religious violence. Long years of military rule, absence of genuine mass-based political leadership and expedient domestic and foreign policy agenda, were responsible for the rise of violent ethnic and religious groups. The ouster of the Taliban and reengagement with the international coalition against terrorism provided Pakistan with a fresh opportunity to combat terrorism within the country. Pakistan continues to face backlash from the extremist elements on the outer fringes of the religious right for turning off support to the Taliban. But it is better to deal with this menace now when it has sympathy and support of the international community than to fight this problem later alone. Pakistan, in our view, made a bad policy choice in opting for the Taliban. The geopolitical assumptions that inspired the shift in Pakistan's Afghan policy were not thoroughly thought out. There were better alternatives to the Taliban but its policy makers were stuck in their alignment with the Pashtun groups. This policy increased Pakistan's political, diplomatic, and long-term security costs. Presented with difficult challenges, and narrow choices under a very compulsive international environment, Pakistan changed its course on Afghanistan, abandoning the Taliban in the lurch.

The Taliban have a social support base in the border regions among the Pashtuns on the Pakistani side and even in the rest of Pakistan through the madrasa and mullah networks. The groups sympathetic to the Taliban staged a few big demonstrations in the wake of American military strikes. However, these groups failed to keep on the momentum of Friday protests or pressurize the military government to change its policy of giving support to the U.S. forces in Afghanistan. The crowds of protestors outside the mosques and in the streets of major towns began to thin out every successive week. But there has been a political backlash in the massive popularity of *Mutahida Majlis-e-Amal* (joint action council) or MMA, a coalition of six religious political parties representing all religious sects and denominations. The alliance won largely in the Pashtun territories for its support to the Taliban and opposition to the American war.[40] There is a strong view in Pakistan and outside that the electoral performance of the MMA in the provinces of Balochistan and Frontier in the October 2002 elections was mainly due to pro-Taliban sentiments among the Pashtuns. This is a contestable issue, but nonetheless, the American war in Afghanistan was one of the important situational factors in determining MMA's electoral victory.[41]

Many would argue that Pakistan hardly had any choice, when its leadership was posed with a straight question: are you with us or with them? Ditching the Taliban meant making a u-turn on Pakistan's Afghan policy that it had pursued for a quarter of a century.[42] The policy in brief was meant to bring Afghanistan into Pakistan's sphere of influence and use it for furthering Pakistan's economic and political interests into the Central Asian region. Some of the former military leaders of Pakistan have described this policy in terms of seeking a strategic depth, which in the opinion of this scribe is ambiguous, empty of any meaning, except if it is interpreted in terms of a high degree of influence over the government there. That had been a declared goal of Pakistan's policy, but the experience of dealing with the Afghan resistance groups, the *Mujahideen* government of Professor Burhanuddin Rabbani and later that of the Taliban suggested how independent the Afghans have been. The Afghan leaders, during the anti-Soviet war and afterwards, wanted Pakistan to be a supporter, friend, and facilitator, not a bully around the block or a king-maker, playing one group or faction against another. Pakistan of course has a different narrative of its engagement with Afghanistan, but our impression is that prominent Afghan leaders have never been comfortable with Pakistan's approach toward its country, particularly when it came to handling the issues of stability, peace, and reconciliation.[43]

The unease of all types of Afghan leaders, traditional as well as those who rose to prominence during the war of resistance against the Soviet Union, was quite visible about Pakistan's assistance to the Taliban. Such a discomfort was not confined to the Afghans alone; Pakistan also failed to convince the rest of the world that the Taliban were good guys and that they had reasonable success in stabilizing and reunifying the country. These values could be higher on the agenda of Taliban or Pakistan, but the world was more interested in humane conduct of politics, and the Afghan groups were more concerned with national reconciliation. Taliban's human rights record and treatment of women became international issues and the world looked at the Taliban as primitive, brutal, and even uncivilized in their political dealings with the opponents and enforcement of their interpretation of Islam in the Afghan society.[44] Pakistan's policy on Afghanistan had met virtually a dead end. But those in Pakistan addicted to the lost causes wanted to hold on to that policy as long as they could. Their definition of Pakistan's interests in Afghanistan was essentially geopolitical, and essentially security driven, which they did not want to change.[45] It never occurred to them that a peaceful Afghanistan, so dependent on transit routes and economy of the larger parts of the country and were so integrated with the Pakistani market, that they would have no choice but to stay friendly with Pakistan, no matter which group or faction ruled Afghanistan. This fundamental fact of Afghanistan's political economy and geopolitics has persistently escaped the analysis and attention of decision makers in the Foreign Office and the ISI.

The moment of truth arrived with the straight talk from Washington immediately in the aftermath of the terrorist attacks in New York and Washington, D.C. Pakistan had no escape from compulsory retirement from its policy of interference in Afghanistan in the name of security and other compulsions. It was a wise, rational, and pragmatic decision to change sides from the Taliban to the international coalition against terrorism led by the United States. It might have been a difficult decision, but could Pakistan stay neutral in the war or risk being with the Taliban that had no chance of surviving? The answer is categorically no. Pakistan exhausted its moral responsibility to the Taliban by conveying to them at the last moment that they could perhaps procure their survival by surrendering Osama bin Laden and Al Qaeda for their involvement in the terrorist attacks. True to their image of rigidity, the top Taliban leaders refused to budge.[46] A combination of fatalism, tribal inflexibility, and ignorance of the destructive nature of modern warfare prevented them from understanding what was in the offing for them.

The decision to fight a common war against terrorism brought Pakistan back to the center stage. For the second time in twenty years it became a frontline state, this time, against international terrorism. Washington also realized that the nature of war against international terrorism required strategic partnership with countries like Pakistan that are close to the sources of trouble in all directions. A big embrace by the United States for the third time was based on sound judgment of Pakistan's strategic environment, its character as a potentially moderate and progressive Islamic country but troubled by the legacy of the Afghan conflict. Pakistan was willing and quite relevant to the American strategy of fighting new threats, like militancy and terrorism of some of the Islamic groups operating from its territory. The United States was equally keen to revive the old relationship with Pakistan because its earlier policy of imposing sanctions against Pakistan for well over a decade had undermined its leverage and diminished its influence with the successive civilian and military governments in Islamabad.

Pakistan made virtue out of necessity in becoming part of the American-led international campaign against terrorism in Afghanistan, which is a euphemism for physically eliminating the Taliban and Al Qaeda. Aligning with the United States for the third time has served Pakistan's interests well. It is no longer as isolated as it was before 9/11. All the sanctions that stood against Pakistan for more than a decade have been lifted, and now Pakistan is receiving large-scale economic assistance to implement its reform agenda.[47] The rescheduling of debts could not be possible without the support of the United States and other Western countries that are sympathetic toward Pakistan for the risks it has taken in distancing itself from the forces of religious extremism. The United States has also responded positively to Islamabad's long-standing request for the purchase of F-16 fighter-bombers.[48] This is a reconfirmation of a new strategic partnership between the two countries. Washington has repeatedly acknowledged the role Pakistan has played in ending the Taliban regime in Afghanistan and extending extensive support in stabilizing the situation there.[49] But on occasion, more frequently during the past year, the opinion has been that Pakistan has to do more for preventing the Taliban and its foreign supporters hiding in the border regions from crossing over to Afghanistan.[50]

MILITARY OPERATIONS

Once the United States began to mobilize forces and started building up an international coalition and equipped itself with the legal authority from the UN, the question of how and when the Taliban regime would be removed was no longer a speculative question. No rational person looking at the combination of forces that were zeroing in and around Afghanistan could give even a slight chance for the survival of the Taliban regime. Under the psychological pressure of the coming war, the Taliban regime had started melting down on the margins. The commanders in remote areas always had fluid loyalties and preferred to go with the more powerful and resourceful patrons. The threat of American war also produced a new wave of refugees from Pashtun areas into Pakistan that contributed to the disintegration of the popular support base for the Taliban.[51] The cities, towns, and villages began to wear a deserted look. Rhetoric, Islamic and nationalistic sentiments of the Taliban and its supporters failed to maintain political coherence of its constituency inside Afghanistan and across the border into Pakistan in the face of clear and imminent danger. There were serious doubts if the Taliban forces could stay on the ground and engage the United States in conventional military encounters. This time around, the invading forces had the most advanced weapons, more lethal than ever used and a political determination to wipe out the Taliban. A few years later, Navy Vice Admiral Eric T. Olson, speaking on the role of the Special Operation Command said it "used nearly every tool in its toolbox to remove the Taliban from power and render al Qaeda less effective."[52] It is evident from the wide array of forces that Washington gathered around Afghanistan.

The structure of forces that the United States assembled in the Arabian Sea and around the region was awesome. In addition to task forces, fifty that had been based routinely in the region with fifteen to thirty-five ships, United States deployed four carrier forces. More than 30,000 soldiers, sailors, airmen, and marines, and about 300 military aircraft of various types were estimated to be in the region, giving the U.S. leaders multiple choices. The military buildup was paced up because the president wanted to send a political message home that it was prepared and willing to face the new challenges and deal with the post-9/11 situation. In the early phases of deployments, the United States moved two carrier battle groups— one led by the USS Carl Vinson and the other by the U.S. closer to Pakistan's coast from where they conducted air strikes. Each carrier had seventy-five aircrafts aboard, including F/A-18 Hornets and F-14 Tomcats. Numerous ships in these groups were equipped with Tomahawk cruise missiles. The third carrier, USS Theodore Roosevelt, which left Norfolk, Virginia, in September also moved into the Indian Ocean after completing multinational exercises near Egypt. It had fourteen warships and 15,000 sailors and marines. The fourth carrier, USS Kitty Hawk, came from the Pacific. B-52 and B-1 bombers as well as tanker refueling aircraft, U-2 reconnaissance planes, and RC-135 surveillance aircrafts were stationed in the region along with air force ground support personnel. The United State used these forces in combination with the staging facilities, and logistical and intelligence support from the neighboring states, like Pakistan, that declared open support to America's war against the Taliban.[53]

One of the criticisms of American strategy in Afghanistan is that it missed the opportunity of capturing or killing Osama bin Laden when he was assumed to be hiding in the Tora Bora caves and tunnels during late 2001. The reason for this failure was that this job was "outsourced" to the local

Afghan warlords and their fighters. Presidential candidate Senator John
Kerry repeated this allegation several times close to the November 2004
elections to establish the incompetence of the Bush administration.[54]
Tommy Franks, the former commander in chief of the Central Command at
that time has refuted this claim by saying that there was no credible evidence to suggest that American forces had surrounded bin Laden there. But
the General does admit to the fact that most of the fighting on the ground,
killing, and capturing of the Taliban and Al Qaeda was done by the Afghans
who knew the terrain, the area, and were familiar with the complex tunnel
system that had been under use of the Mujahideen.[55]

FALTERING WAR ON TERRORISM

Overthrowing the Taliban was perhaps the easiest part of the American war
in Afghanistan. Consolidation, recovery, and reconstruction of the country
which are hinged on internal peace and security have proved to be very difficult tasks. And this is a war that the world community cannot afford to
lose because of its wider ramifications for the security of the entire region.
But the progress on rebuilding institutions of Afghan state, ensuring security beyond Kabul, and extending the authority of the state to the hinter-
lands has been very slow.

The last couple of years and particularly 2006 have not been good for
Afghanistan, its people, or the countries fighting a counterinsurgency war
against the Taliban. By all accounts, the year witnessed a remarkable come-
back of the Taliban, or whoever the insurgents in the southern and eastern
parts of Afghanistan are. There are two emerging trends in the Afghan war.
First is coming on to the scene of the suicide bomber, blowing himself up
in crowded places or very close to the Afghan and NATO forces in the region.[56] Hitherto, it was thought that suicide bombing was a problem
unique to the Middle East and Sri Lanka. It is no longer true. The suicide
bomber has become the most dangerous weapon of our time, and it is very
much in Afghanistan and Pakistan as well.

The second important development is the mounting of conventional attacks by the Taliban forces, which it carried out in early September at large
human costs to themselves.[57] By any indication, the Taliban has a big presence, and it is better armed and organized than in any previous year.[58] Ob-
viously, the International Security Assistance Force, and now NATO having
taken control of command and operations have failed to achieve their objectives of stability, security, and reconstruction of this tragic country.[59]
There is no, and cannot be any, better evidence of their failure in
Afghanistan than the rise of the Taliban forces, emergence of Afghanistan as
a narcotics state, and persistence of the warlord phenomenon.

Let us examine in some detail why NATO is failing and the Taliban appears to be succeeding in at least persisting despite the regularity and lethality of attacks. The first problem of the United States is that leading the war in Afghanistan, and that of NATO is that they do not seem to be recognizing or openly admitting the identity of the insurgents in Afghanistan. They continue to label them as Taliban. This name and the images associated with Taliban invoke international sympathy for the U.S. and NATO forces in their respective countries because of the popular perceptions of the Taliban as "Islamic" militants, medieval in thinking and hostile to the West and modernity. The Taliban is very important and perhaps a critical element in the insurgency, but the Taliban is neither exclusively Taliban in character, nor is it entirely motivated by religious factors.

Behind the Taliban façade is Pashtun ethnicity,[60] and if one wants to learn from Afghanistan's three wars against two great powers, Britain and the former Soviet Union, it is Afghan nationalism and its conventional resistance to the presence of foreign forces. In these wars, the Pashtun took up the flag of Afghan nationalism, mobilized resistance, and paid the heaviest price in human and material loss. One may argue that there are Pashtuns and other Afghans from other nationalities who are on the side of international forces in their country. But there were also Afghans with the former Soviet Union and quite a few with Britain as well. This is a dangerous symptom of political polarization and the ethnic divide in the country.

The leaders of Northern ethnic minorities, President Hamid Karzai and his allies, are very keen to have the international security forces do the tough job of security, reconstruction, and stability in their country. And they have a primary political interest in the defeat of the insurgency in the Pashtun regions. But unfortunately, this is very unlikely and does not seem to be happening, and may not happen until the United States and NATO do some serious rethinking about reconstruction, national reconciliation, and dialogue among different contending forces, including the Taliban, which would require a major course correction.

In the annual NATO summit meeting in Riga, Latvia, in November 2006, and before it, in many of the statements of commanders dealing with Afghanistan, three dominant themes have dominated their deliberations. First, Afghanistan is a very important country and the security of the world and surrounding regions in the new century would depend on how this country is rebuilt, made secure, and stabilized. One cannot disagree with this prognosis of Afghanistan and the likely implications of failure of the international coalition. The second important subject of discussion is that NATO needs more forces on the ground to combat the surging tide of the Taliban. NATO already has 32,000 troops under its command. In addition, the United States operates 11,000 troops outside the NATO command for logistics and antiterrorism purposes. It seems, for good reason, some of the

NATO countries are not willing to send more troops to Afghanistan because there is a high risk of combat there, and so far the results of military operations are not too positive or visible.

Facing reluctance on the part of member countries to the idea of more troops, NATO commanders have sought decreasing restrictions on the deployment of troops to combat zones in the south and east of the country. They have secured an agreement in the Riga meeting on calling troops from other countries present in Afghanistan into combat situation from areas of their regular deployment.[61] In emergencies and in volatile areas, the U.S, British, and Netherlands forces have done most of the fighting. That may give the commanders some flexibility and increase their troop strength to an optimal level, but that hardly presents a long-term or realistic solution to the growing insurgency.

NATO and the United States need to focus on a three-pronged strategy to stabilize Afghanistan. First and foremost they need to address the issue of Pashtun alienation. There has been good progress on Pashtun representation in the power structure since the parliamentary elections, but there is more that needs to be done. The perception of the power shift in favor of Tajiks and other groups persists among the Pashtuns, and that is not a good political sign. Secondly, they must concentrate, with greater commitment, on reconstruction programs and revival of the legal economy. Unfortunately, drug production and trafficking have increased at alarming rates, providing the insurgents with resources and local support for the protection they provide to the poppy cultivators.[62] This also demonstrates failure of the international agencies in providing alternative sources of livelihood to people who seem to have fallen back on the old practice of drug production. Third, and in our view the most important and effective way of stabilizing Afghanistan, would be peace talks and peace agreements with the Pashtun tribal leaders and with those Taliban who are willing to come to the negotiating table.

The American-led war in Iraq, the rise of insurgency, and the pattern of conflict in Iraq have demonstrative political and psychological effects on the situation in Afghanistan. As the United States approaches the endgame in Iraq, it must focus on Afghanistan, wiser with the lessons learned in the course of the Iraq tragedy. One of the lessons that one can learn from Iraq, which now teeters on the brink of disintegration, is that different social groups locked in a power struggle need outside help to evolve institutions and political consensus to live in harmony. Afghanistan has also become divided along ethnic lines, and may face the same consequences, if the U.S and NATO forces fail in their avowed mission of nation and state building.

WHAT WENT WRONG?

The twin strategy of war and reconstruction in Afghanistan has failed to achieve any remarkable success. The country is sliding fast into chaos and disorder, particularly its southern and eastern periphery. If other areas are calm, it is not because the state has extended its writ, but because the state has surrendered its authority to the local warlords. There is general despondency, disappointment, and frustration among the population. Their grief and anger is widely shared by the international community and friends of Afghanistan throughout the world. After three bouts of deadly war, the Afghans thought they would have a better and peaceful future with economic opportunities to reconstruct their individual and collective lives.

Against the hope that international intervention and political reconstruction would end the war, the Taliban has reemerged as a formidable force, and the warlords continue to stay put and strong, forcing President Hamid Karzai to make compromises. The Pashtun regions remain unstable and out of the control of the government. The local farmers and international drug traffickers have found the absence of the Afghan state and weak political and security arrangements to their benefit in reviving poppy cultivation on an unprecedented scale. Afghanistan unfortunately has become a narcotics state—a development that has taken place in the presence of NATO, ISAF, and U.S. forces. The situation inside Afghanistan is not very hopeful and it is likely to get worse. The numbers of those optimistic about the future of the current government or about the ability of the international coalition of forces to do better in the coming months and years is on the decline. Let us examine in detail what went wrong in Afghanistan.

First, the U.S strategy toward Afghanistan was shaped hurriedly in an atmosphere of anger and thus it became centered on ousting the Taliban, whose ideological makeup, ruling style, and leadership had been widely demonized in the Western media. The presence of Al Qaeda and Osama bin Laden and their operation from sanctuaries in Afghanistan presented good justification for war to show results to the angry and highly demoralized people of the United States after the terrorist attacks of 9/11. We believe the Taliban was misunderstood as a religious force in the image of extremist Islamic political movements.[63] They were essentially Pashtuns in terms of ethnicity and had among their ranks all kinds of Pashtuns, not just those motivated by religion. The Pashtuns of all political colors and categories who represent the majority of the population of Afghanistan were frustrated over the way Tajiks captured power in Kabul after the fall of the communist regime in 1992. They found themselves out of power, divided in small factions, and controlled by large numbers of gun-toting warlords. The rise of the Taliban presented them an opportunity to reclaim the country from the Tajik rule. The United States and its Afghan informers and experts were wrong in presenting the Afghan civil war merely in religious terms, which in fact was ethnic in orientation, structure of forces, and social bases of support. Religion and nationalism are two sides of the Afghan identity, which is historically associated with Pashtun national ethos.

The focus of an antiterrorist military campaign in Afghanistan on the Pashtun regions has alienated most of them due to the collateral damage it has caused, providing a fresh opportunity for the Taliban to recruit fighters and continue to seek support from the local populations.[64] The neo-Taliban forces are no different in terms of social composition; they are essentially Pashtuns inspired by their glorious tradition of resistance against foreign forces and those who cooperate with them. Today's conflict in Afghanistan is no different in its essential structure than the one during the Soviet war in the popular Pashtun imagination; foreign forces occupying the country, supporting a regime constructed by it. The present Taliban force is built around Afghan nationalism and its driving force is Pashtun ethnicity more than it was before the American war.

The second major mistake the United States made in Afghanistan was to rely on ethnic minorities who had suffered the most at the hands of the Taliban. The logic of war, not the logic of political reconstruction, shaped the U.S. choices for allies in Afghanistan. In targeting the Pashtun Taliban and removing it from power, the United States helped the Tajiks, Uzbeks, and to a lesser extent, Hazaras, to capture primary institutions of the post-Taliban power structure—police, intelligence agencies, armed forces, and reconstruction agencies with enormous amounts of foreign funds. The coalition forces in a way have become a partisan force, not a neutral one in the eyes of the general Pashtun population.

The Afghan civil war during the Taliban rule had another dimension, which is of the warlords who belonged to all ends of ethnic and political fragmentation. The warlords humiliated, coerced, and murdered tens of thousands of Afghans, and most of them had narrow support bases in their immediate ethnic or tribal communities. The United States, by coopting them as allies against the Taliban, rehabilitated and empowered them with money, weapons, and a dignified space in the new political structure. Most of them have committed untold atrocities against their political and ethnic rivals and could be put before the international criminal tribunal for their crimes against humanity. All of them have been spared for the 'good' work they have done for the U.S. and ISAF forces.

The third major mistake the United States has made is the refusal to negotiate with the Taliban. Except occasional hints and suggestions by President Karzai and American spokespersons that they would welcome a moderate Taliban, which in itself is a questionable construct, there have been no concerted or serious efforts toward that end. The conservative American leaders have a tendency of thinking and speaking through the barrel of gun. This has not worked in Iraq and it is not working in Afghanistan either. If the interest is in rebuilding Afghanistan as a viable state and ending the insurgency, military operations should be considered a matter of last resort and not a first-choice strategy, as appears to be the case. The United States and its Afghan allies need to reconsider their strategy and focus more on negotiating local and regional political settlements with an open mind to include the Taliban in the process of national reconciliation. Its atrocities and bloodletting were no worse than some of the warlords in power in and around Kabul.

NOTES

1. See the following works: John K. Cooley, *Unholy Wars: Afghanistan, America and International Terrorism* (London: Pluto Press, 1999). Chapter one (pp. 9–28) of this book deals with Carter and Brezhnev's decision-making process regarding Afghanistan while chapter 3 (pp. 47–64) deals with how the United States and Ziaul Haq worked together to combat Soviet intervention in Afghanistan. William Watts, *The US and Asia: Changing Attitudes and Policies* (Boston: Lexington Books, 1982), pp. 273–92 deal with the early days of U.S. policy toward Soviet intervention in Afghanistan. Norman A. Graebner, *America as a World Power: A Realist Reappraisal from Wilson to Reagan* (Wilmington, Delaware: Scholarly Resources Inc., 1984) deals with the Carter and Reagan administrations' response to the Soviet invasion of Afghanistan. On 3 February 1980 at Islamabad, both Zbigniew Brzezinski and Assistant Secretary of State Warren Christopher agreed with Zia that the Soviet intervention in Afghanistan constituted 'a serious threat to the peace and security of Pakistan, the region and the world.' *US-Pakistan Joint Statement on the Conclusion of Talks between Ziaul Haq and Zbigniew Brzensinski*, 3 February 1980, in K. Arif (ed.), *Pakistan's Foreign Policy: India Perspectives* (Lahore: Vanguard Books Ltd., 1984), p. 380.

2. See details in Richard P. Cronin, "Afghanistan: Challenges and Options for Reconstructing a Stable and Moderate State," *Congressional Research Service*, 24 April 2002; Robert J. McMahon, "United States Cold War Strategy in South Asia: Making a Military Commitment to Pakistan, 1947–1954," *The Journal of American History*, Vol. 75, No. 3 (December 1988); Shirin Tahir-Kheli, *The United States and Pakistan* (New York: Praeger, 1982).

3. Hafeez Malik, *Soviet-American Relations with Pakistan, Iran and Afghanistan* (London/New York: MacMillan Press, 1987).

4. Rasul Bakhsh Rais, *Indian Ocean and the Superpowers: Economic, Political and Security Perspectives* (London: Groom Helm, 1986), pp. 94–103.

5. On 31 January 1980, in his annual State of the Union address, President Carter promulgated the Carter Doctrine which was as follows: "An attempt by an outside force to gain control of the Persian Gulf region will be regarded as an assault on the vital interests of the US. Such an assault would be repelled by any means necessary including military force." *Newsweek*, 4 February 1980.

6. For a critique of American policy after the fall of Shah, see Samuel Huntington, "Renewed Hostility," in Joseph S. Nye, Jr. (ed.), *The Making of America's Soviet Policy* (New Haven & London: Yale University Press, 1984), pp. 265–89.

7. On the Carter Doctrine, see Rasul Bakhsh Rais, *The Indian Ocean and the Superpowers* (London & Sydney: Croom Helm, 1986), p. 53.

8. For evidence that Pakistan was providing support to the Afghans well before the entry of the United States, see Sajjad Hyder, *Foreign Policy of Pakistan: Reflections of an Ambassador* (Lahore: Progressive Publishers, 1987).

9. For Zia's influence on the American policy in Afghanistan, see Frederick Grare, *Pakistan and the Afghan Conflict: 1979–1985* (Karachi: Oxford University Press, 2003). Also See Anthony H. Cordesman, *The Lessons of Afghanistan* (Islamabad: Vanguard, 2003).

10. Many in Pakistan and outside had thought that what Pakistan and the Mujahideen were doing was futile. The Soviet Union had not withdrawn from eastern and central Europe and had repressed the Hungarian and Czechoslovakian rebellions very brutally.

11. The United States didn't believe that the Soviet forces could be pushed out.

12. With the Soviet intervention of Afghanistan, the United States wanted OIC to highlight the anti-Islamic nature of the Soviet invasion. The United States suggested to various Islamic countries and NATO allies to create an international Islamic contingent which would be capable of replacing the Red Army. Zbigniew Brzezinski, *Power and Principle: Memoirs of the National Security Adviser, 1977–1981* (London: Weidenfeld and Nicolson, 1983), p. 434.

13. Charles C. Cogan, "Partners in Time, the CIA and Afghanistan," *World Policy Journal*, Vol. 10, No. 2, Summer 1993, pp. 364–78. Cogan was chief of the Near East and South Asia division of the CIA's Directorate of Operations.

14. Author's interviews with the ISI officials. Islamabad, October 2004.

15. On Zia's policy of supporting the Islamist Mujahideen, see Agha Shahi, *Pakistan's Security & Foreign Policy* (Lahore: Progressive Publishers, 1988); Abdul Sattar, "From Jihad to Civil War," in *Afghanistan: Past, Present and Future* (Islamabad: Institute of Regional Studies, 1997), pp. 460–91.

16. Marvin G. Weinbaum, "War and Peace in Afghanistan: The Pakistan Role," *The Middle East Journal*, Vol. 15, No. 1, pp. 71–85.

17. Andrew C. Winner, "The U.S. Balancing Act in South Asia," *IPRI Journal*, Vol. 1, No. 1, pp. 76–85.

18. Sudan offered handing over bin Laden to the United States. See *The Dawn* for 18 August 2005.

19. *9/11 Commission Report: Final Report of the National Commission on Terrorist Attacks upon the US* op. cit.

20. Author's interview with a former director general of Inter-Services Intelligence of Pakistan, Lahore, 26 October 2005.

21. The Taliban demanded recognition of its government and a seat in the UN General Assembly as two primary conditions. But the Americans and Pakistanis working as a go-between were not really sure if the Taliban would live up to its commitments on delivering Osama to them.

22. Author's interview with a former director general of the ISI, Lahore, January 2005.

23. *The 9/11 Commission Report*, op. cit., pp. 108–214.

24. Jonathan Monten, "The Roots of the Bush Doctrine: Power, Nationalism, and Democracy Promotion in U.S. Strategy," *International Security*, Vol. 29, No. 4 (Spring 2005), pp. 112–56; John Mickletwait and Adrian Wooldridge, *The Right Nation: Conservative Power in America* (New York: Penguin Press, 2004).

25. There is a lot of interesting debate in Bob Woodward, *Bush at War*, op. cit. (New York: Simon & Schuster, 2002).

26. *The Guardian*, 29 October 2001 (www.guardian.co.uk).

27. Marvin Weinbaum, *Afghanistan and Its Neighbors: An Ever Dangerous Neighborhood* (Washington, D.C.: United States Institute of Peace, June 2006), p. 12.

28. Richard N. Haass, "Regime Change and Its Limits," *Foreign Affairs*, Vol. 84, No. 4 (July/August, 2005), pp. 66–78; Larry Diamond, *Squandered Victory: The American Occupation and Bungled Effort to Bring Democracy to Iraq* (New York: Times Books, 2005).

29. "Violence in Central Asia" (editorial), *The New York Times* (www.nytimes.com), 19 May 2005.

30. See a report by Steven Lee Myers and Yola Monakhov, "Uzbekistan Shaken by Unrest, Violence, and Uncertainty," *The New York Times* (on the web), 16 May 2005.

31. Bob Woodward, *Bush at War*, op. cit., p. 59.

32. Pervez Musharraf, *In the Line of Fire: A Memoir* (London: Simon & Schuster, 2006), p. 2001; Keith Jones, "Pakistan's Military Regime Rallies to U.S. War Coalition," in *IPRI Factfile*, Vol. IV, No. 28, March 2002, pp. 4–7. According to Jones, Washington demanded to know whether Pakistan was 'friend or foe' and threatened it with all measures "short of war" if Islamabad did not assist the United States in confronting Afghanistan, (p. 5).

33. Keneth Katzman, *Afghanistan: Current Issues and U.S. Policy Concern* (Washington, D.C.: Library of Congress, Congressional Research Service, Report No. RL30588, 13 June 2002).

34. Dianne E. Rennack, *India and Pakistan: Current Economic Sanctions* (Washington, D.C.: Library of Congress, Congressional Research Service Report No. RS20995, date NA).

35. Lee Feinstein, et al, *A New Equation: U.S. Policy toward India and Pakistan after September 11* (Washington, D.C.: Carnegie Endowment for Peace, Working Paper No. 27, May 2002).

36. Moonis Ahmar, "Tribal Militancy in Waziristan and the War Within," *Dawn*, 31 March 2007.

37. Harvey H. Smith, et al, *Area Handbook of Afghanistan* (Washington, D.C.: U.S. Government Printing Office, 1969), pp. 52–53; Louis Dupree, *Afghanistan* (Princeton: Princeton University Press, 1973).

38. Khalid Hassan, "Qaeda Has Safe Haven in Pakistan to attack U.S.," (A summary of U.S. National Intelligence Estimates), *Dawn*, 18 July 2007.

39. Woodward, *Bush at War*, Op. Cit.

40. Mohammad Waseem, *Democratization in Pakistan: A Study of the 2002 Elections* (Karachi: Oxford University Press, 2006), p. 156.

41. Sarwar Bari & Dr. Farzana Bari, "Making the Myth of MMA," *The News*, Islamabad, 22 October 2002. According to the authors, a stark split in the voters' choice of political parties for the national and provincial seats indicated an ideological crisis in the country. If MMA's success was due to its anti-Afghan policy, then Punjab and Sindh did not mandate against Pakistan's pro-U.S. foreign policy. MMA's success in NWFP and Balochistan can be explained partly due to the Afghan factor and partly due to the fragmentation of liberal parties, and failure of the civil society to mobilize voters around a liberal agenda in these two provinces.

42. "A Convincing Case" (editorial), *The News* (Rawalpindi), 20 September 2001.

43. Author's interviews with Afghan intellectuals, Kabul, August, 2005.

44. Kenneth Cooper, "Kabul Women under Virtual House Arrest," *Washington Post*, 7 October 1996.

45. You may find glimpses of this thinking in the writings of General Mirza Aslam Beg, *National Security: Taliban and Beyond* (Islamabad: Foundation for Research on International Environment, National Development and Security, date, n.a.) Also see Aslam Beg, "Security Imperatives of Pakistan and Afghanistan," *National Development & Security*, Vol. X, No. 39, Spring 2002, pp. 152–160. Aslam Beg, "Afghan Turmoil & Regional Security Implications," *National Development & Security*, Vol. XI, No. 41, Autumn 2002, pp. 1–23.

46. Pakistan sent the director general of the ISI to persuade the Taliban leaders in Kandhar and tell them what was in store for them if they didn't oblige the United States. On 12 January 2002, in his address to the nation, Musharraf stated that he had 'dispatched a number of delegations to meet Mullah Omar. According to Musharraf, through these delegations, "I continued to advise them [the Taliban leaders] tolerance and balance." Musharraf's Address to the Nation, 12 January 2002 in *Foreign Affairs Pakistan*, Vol. 29, No. 1, Jan/Feb 2002, p. 11.

47. Shahid Javed Burki, "Will Aid Flow to Pakistan," *Dawn* (Karachi), 23 April 2002.

48. Mohammad Munir, "Imperatives of Bush's Visit to South Asia," *Pakistan Observer*, 11 March 2006.

49. Susanna Price, "Analysis: Pakistan's Role in U.S. Plans," 15 September 2001, http://news.bbc.co.uk/hi/English/world/south_asia/.

50. On 4 March 2006, in the Bush–Musharraf talks held at Islamabad, Bush urged Musharraf to intensify operations against the Al Qaeda and Taliban terrorists who were hiding in Pakistan's tribal areas. According to Kemal, during the talks, Bush fell for Afghanistan's (President Karzai's) "line," which the U.S. commanders in Afghanistan also reinforced. Bush insisted that "Pakistan was lax in hunting the Taliban fugitives on its soil." On this occasion, Bush stated: "a part of my mission today was to determine whether or not (President Musharraf) was as committed as he has been in the past to bringing these terrorists to justice." Anwar Kemal, "Ties Strengthened, Made More Meaningful," *Dawn*, Karachi, 24 March 2006. Pakistani opposition was strongly critical of Bush's visit to Pakistan because Bush wanted Pakistan to do more in combating terrorism. See for example, Shahzad Raza 'Oppostion Describes Bush Visit to Pakistan as Disappointing', *Daily Times* (Lahore), 5 March 2006. According to a *New York Times* editorial, during his trip to Pakistan, Bush tried to persuade Musharraf "to defy nationalist and Islamic objections and move more aggressively against Pakistan-based terrorists." This was so because the Bush administration supposed that both Osama bin Laden and Taliban leader Mullah Omar were operating from Pakistani soil. Editorial, *The New York Times*, 7 March 2006.

51. See Sanam Noor, "Afghan Refugees after 9/11," *Pakistan Horizon*, Vol. 59, No.1, January 2006, pp. 59–78.

52. Samantha L. Quigley, "Special Operations Makes Mark on Global War on Terrorism," American Forces Information Service, http://www.defenselink.mil, 23 January 2006.

53. "International Contributions to the War against Terrorism," 7 June 2002, http://www.defenselink.mil. K. Alan Kronstadt, "Pakistan-US Anti-Terrorism Coop-

eration," Congressional Research Service, The Library of Congress, updated 23 March 2003 in "Pakistan's War on Terror," *IPRI Factfile*, Vol. 8, No.2, February 2006, pp. 25–30.

54. Senator John Kerry accused Bush of missing an opportunity of apprehending Osama near Tora Bora. See transcript of First Presidential Debate, Friday, 1 October 2004. *The Green Papers Commentary*, http://www.thegreenpapers.com/PCom/?2004 1001-0 (accessed on 11 May 2007).

55. Tommy Franks, "War of Words," *The New York Times*, October 19, 2004.

56. See U.S. Department of State, *Country Report on Terrorism*, http://www.state .gov/s/ct/rls/crt/2006/82734.htm (accessed on May 2, 2007). The U.S. and NATO forces killed over 2,000 Taliban and other antigovernment elements.

57. Darren Ennis, "West Won't Win Afghan War: Former UN Envoy," *Dawn*, October 19, 2007.

58. Rory Stewart, "Where Less Is More," *The New York Times*, 23 July 2007.

59. "NATO plan to Operate in Southern Afghanistan" *Dawn*, 9 December 2005.

60. "The Afghan Mess," (editorial), *Dawn*, 18 January 2006.

61. See "Riga Summit Declaration" issued by the Heads of States and Government participating in the meeting of the North Atlantic Council in Riga on 29 November 2006. http://www.nato.int/docu/pr/2006/p06-150e.htm (accessed on 7 May 2007).

62. Ahmad Rashid, "Nato's Afghanistan Troop Dilemma," http://news.bbc.co .uk/2/hi/south_asia/4526150.stm (accessed on 27 January 2006).

63. Neamatollah Nojumi and Ahmad Rashid overlook this Pashtun character of the Taliban and emphasize their connections with Pakistan and religious roots in the madrasas. See Neamatollah Nojumi, *The Rise of the Taliban in Afghanistan: Mass Mobilization, Civil War, and the Future of the Region* (New York: Palgrave, 2002), pp. 119–134; Ahmed Rashid, *Taliban: Islam, Oil and the New Great Game in Central Asia* (London: I.B. Tauris Publishers, 2002), pp. 82–104.

64. Some 2,000 university students chanted anti-U.S. and anti-Karzai slogans. More than 4,000, including 1,000 civilians, died in 2006, which was the worst year of fighting. "Killings by Western Troops: Afghans Protest for Fourth Day," *Daily Times*, 3 May 2007.

5

Restructuring a New Afghan State

The state and society in Afghanistan have been devastated by wars for the past quarter of a century, and hence, present a challenge to the world community. As observed earlier, the risks and collateral costs of benignly neglecting stateless societies are greater than the costs of their rehabilitation and reconstruction. Postconflict reconstruction is a multidimensional enterprise, involving human resettlement, disarming the warlords, creating state institutions, reviving the economy, providing security in the critical years of national recovery, and putting in place pragmatic and acceptable political arrangements. We are familiar with postconflict reconstruction strategies and we can borrow from successes and failures in other parts of the world, but each conflict situation is unique because of the social structure of conflict, the geopolitics of the region, and the character of the forces involved.[1] We will try to explain the models of national reconstruction as applied to Afghanistan. Rehabilitation of Afghanistan as a normal functioning state has a wide interest among the regional states and world powers, as a unified, peaceful, and stable Afghanistan would contribute to regional stability and security. Contrarily, Afghanistan in turmoil would become a focal point of rivalries, external intervention, and spill over ethnic problems to the neighboring states.

RECONSTRUCTING A FAILED STATE

The idea of reconstruction may not adequately explain the situation of Afghanistan because it can give the impression that the institutions, political structures, processes, and the relationship between the state and society of the prewar period could be revived or rebuilt. Afghanistan as a state and society was still on the margins of the modern world when the communists took over power and sparked the conflict. The economy and state institutions, in Afghanistan, were developing but still lagged far behind any threshold of modernity. It was partly the impatience of intelligentsia and the bureaucratic elite of pulling Afghanistan out of its medieval, archaic economy and power relations that some of them organized to first overthrow the monarchy, and later bring about the socialist revolution in 1978. The nature of the revolution, the flunky character of the revolutionaries, and the oppressive order they created to modernize Afghanistan in their own image of a socialist paradise caused most of the accomplishments of the country to wither away. Therefore, the world community and the post-Taliban Afghan leaders had very little to salvage from the debris of the conflict.

The defeat and departure of the Taliban provided a fresh opportunity to rethink about Afghanistan in terms of its history, heritage of conflict, balance of ethnic groups, as well as its future. Beginning with what was on the ground, the broad coalition of countries and Afghan elites quickly formulated a framework, like an architectural design, to rebuild new Afghanistan. Because the multilayered and multidimensional war had destroyed the old structures of power and institutions, the planners had the flexibility and freedom to try something very different and the option to not dig anything out of the ruins.

If we closely look at the framework of rebuilding Afghanistan, it seems to have been greatly influenced by liberalism. The underlying assumption is that laying the foundation of the new state and society on liberal institutions will rehabilitate Afghanistan as a normal, peaceful society. In doing so, the framework has heavily borrowed from the modernization theory.[2] In the case of Afghanistan, like many other postconflict societies, reconstruction has become synonymous with modernization and development. The reconstruction priorities and the set of immediate and long-term objectives would vary from one country to another, and they thus do in the case of Afghanistan, which that has some of the most stubborn structures of conflict.

Peace and security have been, and continue to remain after five years, the primary objectives. Without a stable and secure environment the reconstruction projects would not commence, take off, or be completed, in time to earn the trust and confidence of the people. This has also been a means to the larger objective of denying Afghanistan as a safe haven to transnational militants. Therefore one has to understand that the driving force behind reconstruction and the liberal framework being applied to Afghanistan is a strategic one: that Afghanistan does not relapse back to statelessness, which would create a vacuum of authority, power, and institutions in which the militants could take refuge and operate from there against other states.

The international coalition of forces undertook the primary task of defeating the Taliban and restoring peace and security in Afghanistan. The intervention authorized by the United Nations was for bringing about a change in the regime for its suspected links with the Al Qaeda and its refusal to hand over Osama bin Laden and his associates. Changing the regime meant replacement, but with a broader political vision for Afghanistan, which included reconstruction of the state, jumpstarting of the economy, and redefining relations between state and society.

Seen in this light, the reconstruction of Afghanistan presents an ambitious and long-term plan of political development with a modernist ethos. Undoubtedly, the reconstruction project of Afghanistan has Western ideological markings with pragmatic sensitivities of social structures, traditional leadership patterns, and communal and regional interests of different stakeholders. Even though the coalition partners in the enterprise of rebuilding Afghanistan have not been able to strike any balance among the different lines of conflicting interests, they are at least aware of them and have attempted to channel the varying interests in their conception of the new Afghanistan.

In every postconflict reconstruction project, political and economic ideas, institutions, leadership patterns, governing coalitions, and resources, have played a vital role.[3] These are essentially the elements that define reconstruction and also determine the outcome of the efforts of rebuilding the state and reviving the society. What are the ideas that have shaped post-conflict reconstruction in Afghanistan? What types of political institutions have been introduced in the conservative traditional society of Afghanistan? What is the quality of leadership and does its social support base carry forward the agenda of reconstruction? And finally, are the resources adequate to meet the needs of Afghanistan? Let us try to answer these questions first, and then examine the challenges facing the postconflict reconstruction.

The vision behind the reconstruction model as applied to Afghanistan is liberal and modernist as indicated earlier. But it needs to be spelled out in what sense is the postconflict vision modernist? Before we do this, we must mention that modernization has been an Afghan dream; an ideal that its elites have pursued several times, but for various reasons it has failed to materialize or stay consistent in their objective of changing Afghanistan's social and political landscape.[4] I wish to argue that the reconstruction project with all the flaws that one might discover is not inconsistent with Afghan aspirations if we see it, on the surface, in terms of economic opportunity, social services, and development of infrastructure. The ideas of modernization draped in reconstruction and their relevance to non-Western societies have been greatly refined on the basis of the vast experience of societies with different cultures that have successfully rebuilt.

First and foremost is the idea of a functional state, one which has legitimacy not as a result of the use of force and coercion but in the trust of people ascertainable through an electoral procedure. That can be the starting point in Afghanistan. Trust and legitimacy of a government are functions of a broad-based representation of social groups, multiple interests, political factions, and people at large. As we have seen in the case of many postcolonial states, getting to this starting point or moving straight forward has not been an easy task. There could not be better political tools to construct legitimacy and representation than through the processes that were set in motion during and after the Bonn Agreement in December 2002.

Second, associated with the idea of effective statehood are other ideas like accountability of those who exercise power, transparency of their actions, and a good degree of commitment to the rule of law. In postconflict situations like Afghanistan, the planners have an opportunity to make a fresh start in institution building. Afghanistan's new political experience is largely shaped by the liberal democratic enterprise. We are discussing the ethos and strategic vision here; it is another matter how Afghanistan is developing itself on these ideological foundations. One may question the pace, and even the seriousness and sincerity of some of the domestic players, but at least a direction has been set.

The attention to civil society organization and allocating resources to them and empowering them to undertake social development and infrastructural work in different areas of Afghanistan is quite remarkable.[5] Parallel to the development of the new state apparatus, the civil society institutions are a new phenomenon, which has come to Afghanistan as a part of the broader liberal vision of social and political development. The founding of the new state and growth of the civil society should reinforce each other. We know the pitfalls of overloading the postcolonial state with multiple tasks of development and political and economic ramifications of state-centered approaches. There is always a risk, as we learned from the experience of many Third World states, of giving too much power and resources to the bureaucracy and oligarchic elites. The concentration of power in them, in many instances, has stunted the growth of democracy and liberal institutions.[6] Building the state and society from the ruins in Afghanistan has made a difference in selecting appropriate institutions and establishing a balance among them. The balance between the state and civil society is vital to the development of democracy in Afghanistan and other developing societies. If we borrow from the experience of Western societies, the state and civil society cannot be viewed as rivals but rather partners that are mutually interdependent and draw energies from each other.

In the postreconstruction process, the role of foreign agency is important, as it is in Afghanistan for several reasons. First, foreign actors are equipped with a vast experience of development, have material and managerial resources, and therefore in reconstruction they make lesser mistakes than would be the case of those who are conceiving and implementing reconstruction for the first time. Secondly, they have political neutrality, which is often difficult to maintain among competing indigenous social and political forces. This gives them the capacity to manage rivalries, balance competing interests, and push elites in one direction. Finally, they come with material resources that the local communities need, and that gives them power and real influence over how these resources would be distributed. Foreign agencies are loath to delegating too much responsibility to local elements in the absence of effective mechanism of accountability. They generally function within their own frameworks, not that they are ideal, but they are the ones they know of and have practiced elsewhere.

No matter how experienced and powerful the foreign managers of development and modernization are, they cannot operate without the cooperation and support of local elites and the communities whose interests they are supposed to serve. Reconstruction and development are joint, collective, and cooperative endeavors. The issue of local ownership is extremely important because without this sense local leaders and communities would become detached and alienated and would have a feeling of powerlessness. It is not easy though to gel foreign ideas of development with local social conditions and to make local actors adopt them or act on them with a great degree of commitment. It is a difficult task to start with foreign ideas; however, if the programs bring concrete and visible results, the local communities don't look at what shapes the process but focus on the benefits that derive on individual and collective levels.

THE BONN PROCESS

The Bonn Agreement brokered by the United Nations on 5 December 2001 in the wake of the Taliban's removal from power set a political process in motion for rebuilding the Afghan state and its vital institutions.[7] However, reconstruction had to be done in a gradual fashion due to the existence of so many other urgencies such as the unfinished business of war against the Taliban, warlords controlling the periphery, militias, and economic and state collapse. The Bonn meeting and agreement among the delegates, representing mainly the anti-Taliban and anti-Mujahideen groups, on the future shape of power arrangements and transitional measures was the starting point in terms of state and nation building, and the political process in Afghanistan.

The Bonn Agreement captured the spirit and essence of liberal ideas in committing to "the right of the people of Afghanistan to freely determine their own political future in accordance with principles of Islam, democracy, pluralism and social justice."[8] It is questionable though, whether or not liberal political ideas could be rooted in the tribal, feudal society of Afghanistan, but liberal political ideas have emerged as the guidepost to show the way and provide some unity of thought and action to state builders. Afghanistan's own history and past political experience did not contribute much to conceptualizing the future state. Therefore, both by necessity and by the ideological biases of foreign actors involved in helping negotiate the Bonn Agreement, the Afghans and their supporters could not escape the embrace of democracy, pluralism, and peoples' rights as defining political ideas.

But the real purpose of the Bonn Agreement was not to settle a debate about democracy in Islamic societies but was determining what type of new Afghan state was to be reconstructed, what framework should guide the creation of the new state, how transitional power issues were to be solved, and to select the actors which would be entrusted with the responsibility to move the process forward. Before we go any further, two points need to be made clear about the actors and the political arrangements that the Bonn Agreement envisaged. First, the Afghan groups that had fought against the Taliban occupied most of the space in the Bonn deliberations. Their fears, aspirations, and concerns were accommodated within the political and security vision of the United Nations and the United States. The United States, which actually conducted the war against the Taliban, carefully selected the delegates, the interim and transitional authorities, and the sequences of political transitions. It would be apt to say that the victors were presented, and the vanquished were nowhere in sight or thought of in the future power relations in the country.[9]

The second but closely related to the first was the objective of giving legitimacy to the Afghan individuals, groups, and external powers for restructuring and rehabilitating the Afghan state and society. As an initial step, the Bonn Accords set a very ambitious, time-bound, sequential political agenda for Afghanistan. The first and immediate question was the formation of an interim government, which would be representative of all social groups (including women), to be in place before a permanent structure could be created. The delegates at Bonn with some prodding, pushing, and gentle influence selected Hamid Karzai to be the head of the interim council that would rule the country for six months and facilitate the next steps. Karzai was an obvious choice for two reasons. He symbolically represented the Pashtun majority, and second, he was a leader with whom the United States could do business because of a history of a close relationship with him. Many of the prominent members who attended the Bonn meeting and signed the Accords secured cabinet positions in the interim authority. The composition of the ruling council gave a de facto recognition to the power of the Panjshiri Tajiks who controlled and commanded the militia that took over Kabul from the retreating Taliban. They got the most powerful ministries—defense, interior and, the foreign affairs.

The power-sharing arrangements created two lasting impressions about haves and have-nots in the post-Taliban governance that did not help the cause of national solidarity or reconciliation. First was the widely held perception among the Pashtuns that the Tajiks had gotten the lion's share, which their smaller demographic strength did not justify. Second, the Pashtuns perceived President Karzai as more of a symbolic head of the state than a real one and did not truly represent the Pashtun interests. The leaders of the Northern Front by displaying arrogance and showing defiance to Hamid Karzai gave enough evidence to the popular theories in Afghanistan about who had the real power.

The next move as outlined in the Bonn Agreement was to convene an emergency *Loya Jirga* that met in June 2002. The Jirga provided a fresh opportunity to Karzai and his foreign backers to address the issue of growing Pashtun resentment over underrepresentation in the new power structure. There was some realization that without adequate Pashtun representation, Karzai would remain weak, dependent on the Northern Front, and unable to create a constituency of support among peoples of his social group. Karzai's attempts to create a balance only partly succeeded, leaving the power of the Northern Front intact, a force that could menacingly undermine authority of the president.[10] This partial success was also due to an increasing rift within the Panjshiri group over who had better credentials and claim to lead them. Ahmed Zia Masud, the brother of the slain charismatic leader of Tajiks, Ahmed Shah Masud, challenged Mohammed Fahim and Yunus Qanooni for factional leadership and began to drift closer to Karzai.

One of the most fundamental accomplishments of post-Taliban Afghanistan and the international coalition assisting reconstruction of the country is the framing of a new constitution. The Bonn Agreement provided for convening of a constitutional *Loya Jirga* to debate, review, and adopt a new constitution that would be drafted by a commission and be approved by another commission. It unnecessarily took more time for the drafting commission to prepare the draft constitution that was then placed before the constitutional Loya Jirga that was selected through the United Nations through consultation with local groups throughout the country. The *Jirga* acting as a constitutional convention or a constituent assembly debated the draft for more than three weeks, from 13 December 2003 to 4 January 2004, before adopting it after minor changes.

The constitution in essence has created a presidential form of government, a system that has no historical precedent in Afghanistan in terms of distribution of power among different organs of the state. The constitutions of communist regimes had an institution of presidency but that was fashioned in the image of the former Soviet Union and borrowed heavily from the political experience of other socialist countries. In the new constitution, the president is elected directly on a national basis. Unlike the U.S. Constitution, it doesn't give any weight to the provinces. This is primarily because of the unitary system and a general political sentiment, at least among the Pashtun, against federalism. It is questionable whether electing the president through popular vote in an ethnically pluralistic society with vastly unequal demographic strengths would make the presidency a national institution. As is reflected in the electoral contest for the first president of Afghanistan, the voting pattern reflected ethnic loyalties.

The constitution gives the president vast executive powers and there is hardly any institution that can effectively balance that power. The *Wolesi Jirga* or lower house of the parliament can impeach the president, but has few levers to place checks on the presidency.

The constitution has created a bicameral legislature, *Wolesi Jirga* (Lower House), and the *Meshrano Jirga* (Upper House). All the members of the Wolesi Jirga are elected, which is common practice for the lower houses in democracies. The Meshrano Jirga has both elected as well as appointed members.[11] The 1964 Afghanistan Constitution had also established two houses for the legislature. The Wolesi Jirga has greater powers in proposing and passing the budget, ratifying treaties, and making laws than Meshrano Jirga, which doesn't have power to initiate legislation but to approve it. It is not clear who the Meshrano Jirga represents. If we go by the historical evolution of democracies in the Western world, the upper houses were meant to represent the aristocratic classes, and in federations, the states. Afghanistan has neither the old Afghan aristocracy nor the ancient regime. They have dissipated since the communist rule that targeted them the most brutally. The constitution does not recognize ethnic identities or their regional homelands. It is also not clear how effective a check the Meshrano Jirga can be on the lower house on legislative and budgetary issues.

The constitution does not establish separate Islamic courts like Pakistan or some other Islamic countries. The drafting and review commissions probably wanted to distance new Afghanistan from the Taliban heritage and identity that the country had earned during those troubled years. Rather, it has a regular pattern of court systems, including High Courts, Appeals Courts, and the Supreme Court.

The gender issue in Afghanistan became internationalized with the widely reported abuse and violence against women, in the Afghan society, which had been abetted or ignored during the Taliban regime. International powers behind the drafting of the constitution wanted to make a difference at least in providing some institutional mechanism for the representation of women in the power structure. They have attempted to ensure this by providing for equality of women under the constitution and securing 25 percent of seats of the *Wolesi Jirga* for women. Each of the thirty-four provinces of

Afghanistan will have two elected seats reserved for women. For the Meshrano Jirga, the presidential appointees shall have 50 percent women.

Constitutions provide a legal structure, fundamental rules of the political game, and establish a framework for a political process. In this sense, the new Afghan Constitution represents a historical milestone. Many developing countries have started their political journeys with procedural democracies—constitutions, elections, some freedom of speech, and political parties. The substantive democracies would grow out of political experience and how different social classes adjust themselves to the political game and how sincerely they commit themselves to the rules of the game. Afghanistan's democratic journey has just started. Its social characteristics, culture, values, and quality of competing groups and individuals would finally determine the stability and quality of its new political experience. The country while at war and under international supervision, has conducted elections for the president and the parliament, provincial, and local councils. Let us turn to this perhaps more complex and difficult part of the political transitions that Afghanistan has made.

PRESIDENTIAL ELECTIONS

October 9, 2004 was a historic day in the troubled political history of Afghanistan. Millions of Afghan men, women, old, and young in towns as well as in remote rural areas cast their ballots for the first time in a direct election to choose the president among eighteen candidates who belonged to different ethnic groups and clans that make up the country. Being a first democratic, participatory exercise after a quarter of a century of war and in a climate of fear and insecurity, it couldn't be perfect. But the very fact that millions of Afghans came out to vote, defying the inclement weather and threats of terrorist disruption, was a major success and a milestone in the democratic journey and political rehabilitation of Afghanistan.[12] The elections, like anywhere else, have a supreme political purpose in constituting a representative government, conferring legitimacy on the existing one and transferring it to a new one. Implanting the seed of democracy in a soil that has had a barren political landscape required careful planning, hard work, and more importantly followed carefully the sequences of political reconstruction, which started with the Bonn agreement in December 2001. The earlier steps toward reorganizing the Afghan state and building its institutions were no less significant. It included first the agreement among the Afghan factions on an interim government and how the factions would share power. The second landmark was the selection of the members of the *Loya Jirga* and its meeting to ratify the new constitution in 2003. And the third was the preparation for the presidential election, which required the registration of voters and issuing them identity cards for recognition on polling day. The October election was a culmination of that process.

There was widespread fear about the surge in Taliban attacks close to the elections or on the polling day.[13] There were a few sporadic acts of violence but the Taliban failed to prevent the Afghans from participating in the elections; however, due to insecurity, voter turnout was lower in some provinces where the Taliban had domination. The Afghan official sources counted thirty-six attacks that were mostly unsuccessful. There are three reasons that might explain why the polling was relatively peaceful. First, the Taliban was not a cohesive force, as it appeared to be two years after the elections. They were scattered and their command lines were weak because their leaders were constantly under threat of attack by the American and other coalition forces. Second, the international coalition forces were present and visible all over the country that assured people of their safety on the polling day. Thirdly, war weariness among the people of Afghanistan was also a major factor, as they wanted to redirect their energies to exploring a peaceful, democratic alternative. Many of the Afghans with first time experience appeared to be eager to vote hoping that the process would bring about stability, order, and peace.

The elections in Afghanistan like any other in the developing world were not without controversy nor was its outcome uncontested by some candidates. The systems that organizers of elections devised to safeguard against multiple polling did not work everywhere and all the time. The indelible ink used as a marker on ballots was found defective and washable. The control over the distribution of voter registration cards were lax; this enabled some to cast votes more than once. The supporters of candidates at local levels pushed such votes to win plurality. These flaws tarnished the clean image of the elections but didn't prove to be politically fatal. Some of the fifteen candidates in the race cried foul over the ink issue and called for fresh elections in view of the irregularities but did not find any support for this call among the people who braved threats to line up and cast their ballots at tremendous personal risk or among the independent observers who monitored the electoral process.[14] The Organization for Security and Cooperation in Europe that sent about forty electoral experts, and the Free and Fair Elections Foundation of Afghanistan that deployed 2,300 monitors observed that there was a "fairly democratic environment" in the polling centers.[15] The high voter turnout, more than expected, and general enthusiasm among the ordinary Afghans shown on the polling day further discouraged rival candidates of Hamid Karzai, who was expected to win with a wide margin, not to push the controversy too far. It was partly due to effective political management by the coalition forces in Afghanistan that the discontented candidates took a retreat on the issue of unfairness of the elections and sought out a way in having an independent body to investigate the matter. The United States presented the Afghan elections as a symbol of its foreign policy success and didn't want to see its legitimacy undermined by allegations of fraud and improper voting. Afghanistan is the first showcase of nation building and flexing of American power around the world in the twenty-first century. For this reason alone, the United States moved fast to settle the question of validity through negotiation, bargaining, positive incentives, and implied threats to the losers. U.S. Ambassador Dr. Zalamay Khalilzad was firm, and perhaps not so polite to Mr. Yunus Qanooni in suggesting to him that he "could best help his own political future by not appearing to thwart the will of the Afghans."[16] Dr. Khalilzad was more than an ambassador in rebuilding the post-Taliban Afghanistan. Behind the position of a diplomat, he was a political negotiator among feuding Afghan personalities, stage manager of political affairs, and a crucial link with strong Afghan sensitivity to the U.S. and Western world. He was one of the major players in the nation-building project and has impeccable credentials in terms of knowledge about the country, training, and experience. Using the right connections and the right attitude he succeeded in diffusing the electoral controversy and forging an agreement on an independent report.

The elections were a watershed in Afghanistan's troubled political history. They marked a clear departure from the old tradition of getting to power through bullet and conquest that was amply reflected in the attitude of the Mujahideen, Taliban, and the warlords. The ballot box offered a new opportunity to pursue power, including the former commanders of the *Mujahideen* and some of the former warlords. In the barren political soil of Afghanistan procedural democracy is a fresh seed that was planted and is being protected by a very large coalition of international forces with a hope that it will grow, gain strength, and adapt to the social climate of the country. Once it takes root, it will definitely influence similar changes in the neighborhood in central and southwest Asian region. From that standpoint alone, it is a brave experiment in nation building on democratic lines. Afghanistan is therefore one place where the interests of the West and modernist Muslims all over the world converge. Democracy, rights of men and women, social and political equality, and internal peace and stability are some of the salient values that they share together.

Afghanistan's electoral process was a step forward to reestablish legitimacy and authority of the central state. Since the collapse of the state institutions during the civil war, the warlords fragmented the country into their separate regional fiefdoms. Political transitions have created a new political environment for the rehabilitation of the Afghan state. The central authority of the Afghan state and the warlords couldn't and will never coexist because the two are an antithesis of each other. Warlords flourished under conditions of statelessness and they have had a vested interest in keeping the central state limited to few functions with limited territorial jurisdiction. The extension of the

state or its expansion in terms of institutional effectiveness and coercive capacities would diminish their standing, and eventually take away their fiefdoms and reintegrate them into the national state. The state, on the other
hand, wouldn't succeed in restructuring itself in the postconflict phase or
grow in legitimacy and effectiveness in the presence of the warlords, who have
a vested interest in denying and undermining sovereign control of the state,
its leadership, and governing agencies.

The elections have strengthened the process of this important political
change. The procedural democracy might be slow, fragmented, or even reversed in certain areas for some time, but the very dynamics of political participation and involvement of ordinary people, if consistent and supported
by external powers through availability of resources and commitment to
build state institutions, would gradually erode and end the influence of
warlords holding sway over the larger periphery of the country. The process
of participation with growing credibility would provide them the incentive
for exploring peaceful and constitutional means to access power. This conversion is not unusual if we look at other instances of postconflict political
reconstruction. In the Afghan elections, the former powerful warlords, Abdul Rashid Dostam, Yunis Qanooni, and Muhammad Mohaqeq contested
presidential elections. The social constraints, tribal political culture, and the
stubborn legacy of the long conflict do pose a barrier in the way of democratic Afghanistan, but the only way to demolish these barriers is more democracy, functional and effective state institutions, and popular legitimacy
of the rulers on the top.

Elections were also important from the point of state and nation building, the twin processes that the conflict pushed back by decades of war. One
of the central questions that the Afghans and their foreign supporters faced
while getting the Taliban out was how to recreate an Afghan state that will
give a sense of ownership to all ethnic communities, create harmony
among them, and reintegrate them into nation. The only answer to this
question could be a new constitution, national elections, popular participation, and a new form of political authority that would emerge through an
electoral process. It can only be achieved on the basis of political pluralism
and through shared institutions. Elections have set this process in motion.

Since elections have been conducted for the first time for all tiers of government, the election only marks the path and points a direction of state
and national building. The direction is right because elections and popular
participations have proved an effective instrument of gelling common nationhood and effective statehood in postconflict societies. Why would the
consequences of the same process be different in Afghanistan? Unfortunately, very faulty arguments like "the West is unique," or "Islam is incompatible with democracy," or the tribal societies are best governed by oli-
garchies, have underestimated the energies of these societies to change,

adapt, and modernize. In fact, this type of cynicism is more about the transformative effects of democracy than the societies in question. The theme that democracy is a universal value shouldn't be left for political rhetoric alone but should be placed on the agenda of global change. All non-Western, traditional societies deserve the benefit of Western political experience in bringing about social, economic, and political changes. Postconflict reconstruction in Afghanistan or in other places with similar situations presents many challenges but also offers opportunities to make a fresh start in sowing the seeds of democracy.[17]

The presidential elections in Afghanistan were a big success if we measure them by the usual standard of enthusiasm, voter turnout, and in the specific conditions of Afghanistan, largely free of violence. For a country known for its bloody past, violence, terrorism, and warlords, elections were a new form of politics that was never tried as a means of forming a government or determining the legitimacy of its rulers. The reason for not trying the democratic route to development or resolving political conflict in Afghanistan and other developing countries is an absurd view based on the notion that the cultural, social, and economic conditions of these countries don't permit such an experience.[18] We understand democratic development is a long and difficult process and it takes a lot of time, commitment, and social energy to move along that path. But that is the only civilized method to organize political power and give people a sense of ownership of the political system. There is no better guarantee of peace, stability, and political certainty except a system based on popular legitimacy. It may be a new experience for the Afghans, but like other nations that started their political life with democracy earlier, they would learn their own political lessons and over time remove the flaws, imperfections, and problems that may come up on its way of democratic journey. What is remarkable about Afghanistan is that their new leaders, some with the troubled past of warlordism, have embraced the idea of elections. That itself is a revolutionary thing in Afghanistan.

There are important reasons why the elections were so successful and why they give us hope that Afghanistan is on the path of recovering its lost state and nationhood. First and foremost is the fact that the people of Afghanistan are weary of warlords, conflict, violence, and a life of insecurity and fear that dominated their minds and existence for well over a quarter of a century. The society has exhausted its energies and there is a new realization that it can and must charter a new course, away from the old factional leaders and their rivalries. The elections offered them a credible opportunity to bring their country out of that phase by electing their leader through peaceful and democratic means.[19] There are also some other reasons for the successful conduct of the elections. The role of the United States, which is a major player in Afghan politics and security, was crucial.

In an elections year, just a month before the presidential elections, the incumbent president George W. Bush wanted to project elections in Afghanistan as an American success story in nation building.[20] The American forces along with ISAF were more vigilant, active, and present than before to deter and prevent the Taliban elements from disrupting polling. Show of strength and movement of troops even to very remote areas was one of the major factors in maintaining peace. The United States put considerable pressure on Pakistan to seal the border, deploy more troops, and make sure that the Taliban movement across the lengthy border was effectively checked.[21]

ETHNICITY AND ELECTIONS

The voting results of the presidential election in Afghanistan closely resemble the ethnic patchwork of the country. The ethnic groups have voted largely for the candidate from their own communities—Pashtuns voted for Karzai, Uzbeks for Abdul Rashid Dostam, Tajiks for Yunis Qanooni, and Hazaras for warlord Mohammad Mohaqeq.[22] Karzai received more than 55 percent of votes; this roughly corresponds to the size of the Pashtun ethnic group. However, some estimates put the figure of Pashtuns as low as 40 percent. Demography like political power has been a contested issue and will remain so until a census is held. If we accept the 40 percent share of Pashtuns in the Afghan population, then it seems that Karzai has also received some votes from other ethnic groups, but the number is not too significant.

Afghanistan's ethnic fault lines are too obvious to be ignored. Rhetorically Pashtuns and other leaders from other ethnic groups present themselves first as Afghans before anything else, but the political fact of ethnic divisions and the question of empowerment, representation, and a share in the allocation of resources remains troublesome. As we have seen in the case of other countries, well-intentioned statements of national solidarity and unity are poor substitutes for an effective policy of addressing grievances and addressing genuine interests of each community. For a very long time to come, ethnic groups might go along with the leaders from their own community in electing representatives for the parliament or for making choices about who to vote for in the presidential races. One cannot wish this pattern away in a less integrated society, or in the preliminary stages of state and nation building that Afghanistan represents.

Over time the pattern of ethnic bloc voting will change because the requirements of majority or plurality for a presidential candidate to be elected, or for leadership in the parliament, will change. Out of political necessity, different groups and subgroups will have to form electoral and ruling coalitions to stay afloat in the rough political sea of Afghanistan. Democracy in practice perforce forges alliances among different groups and brings them together. It will therefore be a function of consistency of democratic experience and its quality, and how quickly it sinks roots in the political culture of Afghanistan that ethnicity will become diffused.

PARLIAMENTARY ELECTIONS

According to the Bonn Accords, the parliamentary elections were to be conducted at the same time as the presidential elections. However, they were held roughly one year later on 18 September 2005. The parliamentary elections like the presidential elections were well contested. In terms of the sheer number of candidates contesting, the elections created a lot of excitement. The electoral law established multimember constituencies and allowed single-nontransferable voting. This generated a lot of hope even among candidates with an insignificant support base to contest. This is evident from the fact that roughly 6,000 candidates were in the running for 390 parliamentary (Wolesi Jirga) and 217 provincial council seats.[23]

From the planning stage to the eve of elections, wild hopes and expectations existed about the type of mandate, majority, consensus, or support for the political agenda and reconstruction would emerge. Clearly Karzai, his political associates, and foreign powers backing him wanted to strengthen him through a legislative majority. How could this be possible without any party symbols, party manifestos, and party leadership collectively mobilizing voters and canvassing according to their vision of Afghanistan? The reason that nothing of this sort happened is due to the electoral law that prevented candidates from using party platforms and names. The planners and perhaps President Karzai himself, in enacting the law, vainly hoped to keep the Mujahideen parties that had local political infrastructure out of the parliament.[24]

Elections have dynamics of their own and short of rigging them they seldom follow the pattern set by those in power. In a country that had no history of party-based free elections, and where social and kinship networks dominate social and political choices of individuals and families, this kind of election could only give popular legitimacy to individual candidates with some local influence.[25] It is evident from the electoral results that smaller local communities voted for their candidates along narrow tribal, ethnic, and sectarian lines. In the cultural climate of Afghanistan, like other tribal and feudal societies, voting patterns manifest social solidarities. Theories of voting behavior of democratic societies, where ideology, party loyalty, and calculations of self-interest matter, would not apply to Afghanistan, at least in the initial decades of democratic development.

Parliamentary elections produced mixed political results without a clear or significant mandate for any major political player. President Karzai did not get the numbers that he hoped and worked for. Nor have his political opponents been able to gather enough support to create major obstacles in his way. In essence, both the houses of parliament are politically fragmented and demonstrate a "personalistic political process."[26] Influencing individuals, groups, or voting blocs in the parliament that form around strong leaders would require the accommodation and inclusion of traditional politics of patronage in networks of power. In the absence of political parties, individuals and small groups negotiate and influence legislative agendas.

Even in socially fragmented and politically divided societies, legislative caucuses or blocs eventually do emerge, and it seems to be happening in Afghanistan as well. But the common ground on which they meet is wobbly without political parties or common ideologies disciplining the members and holding them together. Often they reach temporary agreements and form alliances around issues and consequently, when the issues are resolved or disappear, the political bonding loosens up. The members of the Afghan parliament have weak and shifty solidarities. This is usually the outcome of partyless elections and not allowing parliamentary parties to emerge.

The Afghan parliamentarians are prominent persons with a strong social presence in their localities. However there are many factors that have contributed to their electoral success. The most important of all is the multi-member constituency. Candidates receiving even less than 2.5 percent votes have won because of too many candidates fragmenting the votes. Anybody with some degree of local influence could get elected without the majority voting for them. These influential men belong to one of the following political and social categories: former commanders of local militias, members of the defunct Peoples Democratic Party, warlords, tribal chiefs, royalists, and urban professionals.[27]

One of the most positive outcomes of the Bonn process and parliamentary elections is the representation of women in the formal legislative institutions. They occupy one quarter of the seats in the Wolesi Jirga. They have representation, some voice, and a place in the emerging power structure of Afghanistan, which is unparalleled in the history of Afghanistan. Women of Afghanistan did not fare well during or before the war except in a few urban areas where they had the opportunity of obtaining an education and even choosing a career.[28] This and other concessions to Afghan women have come about as a result of the reconstruction project which has attempted to redefine relationships in totality; these include relations of gender, periphery, center, state, and society.

The presidential and parliamentary elections in Afghanistan have produced three positive consequences. First is that the Taliban has been weakened politically, as a moderate section of it has separated from the militant wing and has decided to join the political process. This may not end the Tal-

iban insurgency but it has opened the possibility of dialogue and reconciliation.[29] A good number of former Taliban commanders did participate in
the elections and they won seats in both houses of the legislature and
provincial councils. The ballot box provides an alternative to armed struggle for groups to empower themselves and seek representation. Ethnic and
social pressures also work in changing political preferences of armed groups
from guns to ballot papers. The Pashtun population, in a climate of ethnic
feelings and fragmentation, was eager to elect a Pashtun as president and
Pashtun members for the provincial councils and the Wolesi Jirga. It is spec-
ulated that many Taliban themselves voted for Mr. Karzai to prevent Yunus
Qanooni, a Tajik, from getting elected. And building on that experience
later fielded themselves as candidates in the legislative elections.

Successful conduct of elections in a country torn apart by conflict is not
an ordinary affair. Successes like these accrue over time and help erode the
power of the groups previously engaged in conflict. The Taliban, which is
opposed to American presence and to the entire project of nation building
under international watch, would lose out to the newly emerging democratic forces. This will, however, also depend on other elements of nation
building, like reviving sustainable agriculture, rehabilitating infrastructure,
and rebuilding institutions.

The second important gain is creating and building a legitimate state and
power structure in the country. Although there are many first-time things in
Afghanistan, the chief executive of the country has been elected for the first
time ever in the history of the country. The question on what grounds a
leader occupies a public office is extremely important in the politics of any
country. But it is more important in postconflict situations to construct
power and political process on the basis of popular legitimacy. Since
Afghanistan has seen only kings, conquerors, and coup makers in top slots,
the elections are a new but not unfamiliar way of determining who would
hold lawful authority in the country. The consent of the people through an
open electoral process is a very powerful weapon itself to defeat the warlords and the Taliban. Elections take an indirect route of weaning the population away from the militants and their leaders.

Third, armed with popular support, President Karzai has done better in
ousting some of the warlords from their fiefdoms, and has positioned himself in a better position to expand the authority of his regime, which had remained mostly confined to Kabul. The writ of the Afghan state and its presence in the periphery is important to deny social and political space to its
twin enemies, the Taliban and the warlords. As the state increases its political capacity and strengthens its coercive arms—intelligence, police, and
military—it will gradually replace the warlords. For its own survival and rationale, it must succeed; otherwise Afghanistan as a country, nation, and
state may continue to hang in the balance. Elections give the postconflict

Afghan state political energy to walk in a definite direction of peace and stability. With every mile covered, the Kabul government will gain more confidence, attract more allies, and neutralize more enemies. Politics in such
situations acquire snowballing effects, one success leading to another. The
presidential and legislative elections have in many ways paved the way for
reviving and rebuilding state capacities. The political road, however, may remain bumpy and cause quite a few accidents, but the more Afghanistan
travels on this road the better it will be for internal peace and stability of
the country.

INSTITUTIONAL CAPACITY

State building is a complex enterprise, as it involves many strands of formal
and informal institutions, political and administrative systems. Functional-
ity and effectiveness of state institutions largely determine governing capacity of the state. And it is the governing capacity of the state through which
popular will is expressed and the public policy and national purposes can
be realized. Four institutions of the state—judiciary, public administration,
armed forces, and the police—are key elements that define the modern
states. Afghanistan even as a non-modern, underdeveloped state had all of
them with variable capacities in each, but lost them in the wake of civil war.
All its achievements in building state capacity in these essential sectors disintegrated as a result of the war. Since the overthrow of the Taliban regime,
the international coalition supporting Afghanistan's revival and restructuring has attempted to address state deficiency in these areas. Let us briefly
touch on the some of the initiatives and the relative progress made.

(a) Armed Forces

The international coalition has set in motion the organizing of a national
army as one of its fundamental objectives in Afghanistan. No country in an
anarchical world order can hope to survive without armed forces. It is truer
of a country like Afghanistan, which has a long history of conflict in the
country among its warlords, ethnic groups, and rival political groups, all vy-
ing to capture state power through armed struggle. It has never been easy to
create a national army in a social and political climate of ethnic rivalry and
parochialism.

The real challenge that the international community and Afghan leaders
have faced is how to demobilize and disarm regional armies funded and
controlled by the ethnic warlords and replace them with an integrated national army. The objective of establishing disciplined, professional, and ethnically balanced armed forces cannot be realized in the presence of regional

armies. The warlords have a vested interest in keeping their militias under their own command and have hence very reluctantly only demobilized some units partially. Success in disarming militias has also been limited due to lack of trust in the authority of the new Afghan state and structural limitations of the security forces. The ethnic communities continue to rely on their local arrangements for security that includes the militias. Replacing these local forces with the effective and credible national police and national army has been a tedious and slow process. But this is a priority area in the reconstruction process, and the Afghan state may not be rehabilitated without national security forces.

The size, structure, and mission of the Afghan National Army have been some of the issues that the states involved in restructuring have had to address. Afghanistan does not have the luxury of disposable national resources or income, and it has to allocate foreign resources in a judicious way as it has competing priorities in social development, infrastructure, and services. How strong should the armed forces be and what should be the realistic range of their missions, have been the subject of debate and discussion inside and outside Afghanistan.[30] Another factor determining these choices is the question of resources. Afghanistan on its own cannot afford to equip and pay for a very large armed force. For many years, the international community will have to foot the bill, as it is currently doing. The target of the Afghanistan government is to raise the armed forces to 70,000 by March 2009. Currently, it claims to have recruited half of this number.[31] Afghanistan cannot hope to devote more resources on a sustainable basis or have forces capable of effectively defending territorial threat from any of its neighbors. Therefore a realistic mission of the forces would be to maintain internal cohesion of the state by denying territorial space to warlords, drug traffickers, and to insurgent Taliban or ethnic forces.[32]

Currently Afghanistan depends heavily on the International Security Assistance Force (ISAF) created by the United Nations with the mandate to secure and stabilize the country. The United States, Britain, and NATO have played and continue to play a critical role in fighting the Taliban insurgency. In recent years, they have inducted newly trained units of the Afghan army into joint operations.[33] Adequate training, capacity, equipment, and professionalism still remain critical issues in the development of new security forces. It will take more time and resources than are currently available to make the Afghan armed forces capable of maintaining internal security and some effective presence along the borders.

(b) Public Administration

A bureaucratic structure that is impartial and neutral among competing social groups and primordial linkages is what separates the traditional power

structure from a modern one.[34] Afghanistan had a public administration system, better organized during the later part of the twentieth century but
nowhere close to the rational model of bureaucracy in modern societies.
Monarchy, Republican government, and the communists relied heavily on
the bureaucracy to implement policies but did not pay much attention to its
professional development, structured training, and building its capacity.
Decades of war have had a very adverse effect on the personnel in administrative services. The most competent and able of them fled the country and
never returned to their positions.

The post-Taliban regime found the old administration skeletal, with little
expertise and trained officials. To meet this challenge, the new regime and
the international coalition partners launched a program of ambitious Public
Administration Reforms (PAR).[35] The objective of the reforms was to develop an efficient, transparent, and accountable civil service with strong political oversight.[36] The progress toward these goals has been slow and patchy.
The most remarkable of them are the creation of civil services reform commission and the passing of the civil services law. These provide a legal and
institutional structure within which the civil services can be organized pro-
fessionally. The reform process in this vital state-building activity continues
to face challenges. The most stubborn of them are poor quality of political
leadership, weak political commitment, disregard of merit by ministers, and
many unresolved issues relating to salaries and service structure.[37]

The major states and international institutions involved in stabilizing and
rebuilding Afghanistan have gradually evolved a strategic vision about the future of Afghanistan state and society. One may see the glimpses of this vision
in the Bonn Agreement and in the documents and declarations of the Tokyo[38]
and Berlin conferences.[39] The Afghanistan Compact, signed at the end of a
similar conference in London, presents a more comprehensive framework
with a sharp focus on security, governance, and the rule of law.[40] It goes beyond giving an outline of political institutions and devising multisector development strategies with benchmarks and deadlines that would be monitored by a board of donor countries and agencies. This document is a product
of many years of collective deliberations and an evaluation of Afghanistan's
situation. In some areas it overlaps with the Afghanistan National Development Strategy.[41] The goals and targets set by the Afghanistan Compact remain
behind schedule and are threatened by growing insurgency, weak institutional capacity to deliver, endemic corruption, and lack of political will.[42]

CHALLENGES OF REBUILDING

In envisioning the reconstruction agenda for Afghanistan, the foreign agencies have in fact undertaken a gigantic task of modernizing the country, the

effects of which will appear slowly and in the long run if the national and international actors succeed in following the script of state and nation-building.[43] There is much skepticism about the relevance, adequacy, and the pace of implementation of reconstruction in Afghanistan. Afghanistan has made some progress on its way to reconstructing its state and nationhood, but it is not yet there. Let us examine in detail the real challenges that the reconstruction program has been facing, and why it has not generated the social and economic benefits that it was expected to produce. The reconstruction process continues to face enormous challenges. We would like to list these challenges below and explain why they may continue to affect the development and modernization of Afghanistan.

(a) Warlords

With the defeat of the Taliban, the warlords gradually reclaimed their lost territorial domains that were taken away by their common foe, the Taliban. They did this with the help of American guns, money, and support. But that had not really been the intention of the United States. The United States accepted the warlords, particularly with non-Pashtun ethnicity, and relied on them because they shared its objective of removing the Taliban from power. The warlords had trained militias under their command, fighting experience, intelligence, and above all, spirit to get the country rid of the Taliban. These qualities were more than enough to draw them closer to the United States, which very desperately wanted to field local forces on the frontline, while confining itself to strategic bombardment and the use of sophisticated weaponry to instill the fear of God in the hearts of the Taliban.

On purely pragmatic grounds, the warlords served a good purpose in the first phase of the war. They were rather excited about the involvement of the United States in driving their enemies out of power. The new war also offered them an opportunity to take places that the Taliban would vacate in Kabul. In many areas, the U.S. operatives subcontracted the warlords for military operations in the local areas, and provided them with the equipment that they needed and the money to pay the fighters. It is now well established that the CIA had been tasked to develop a relationship with the anti-Taliban forces well before 9/11. Washington wanted to cultivate these forces to obtain information about Al Qaeda and use them in any operations against the transnational terrorist network of OBL. It used the connections with the Northern Alliance to strike a partnership.[44] Both the United States and the Northern Alliance had a strategic need to cooperate and saw a common enemy in both the Taliban and Al Qaeda.

Just a few days before the 9/11 tragedy struck, two Al Qaeda agents disguising as journalists from Middle East, had assassinated the legendary commander Ahmed Shah Masud. The leaders of the Northern Front and the

United States had suffered humiliation, defeat, and a colossal loss of life at the hands of the same elements. The Tajik leaders in particular wasted no time in responding to the American call for cooperation in defeating the Taliban.

They facilitated entry of the American Special Forces to set up bases for operations by the Air Force and provided them with real-time intelligence about the Taliban and Al Qaeda targets. A partnership with the United States assured the Northern Front leaders of victory and eviction of their adversaries, the Taliban and Arabs fighting along with them. But the cooperation wouldn't end with the entry of their forces in Kabul; the elimination of the Taliban and Al Qaeda as a regional and global threat would require their continued support. As later events proved, they were sort of down but not completely out of the Afghan security scene; however, there was a tacit understanding or quid pro quo. The United States would allow them to keep their fiefdoms, maintain their militias, and regain control of the territories that they had lost to the Taliban. The contribution of local allies to the success of American military strategy cannot be denied, but allowing them to establish ministates within larger national states runs counter to the broader vision of political reconstruction. Maybe it was politically expedient, and even necessary, to allow the warlords freedom to exercise local control, but gradually, they will have to be integrated into the national power structure. The United States and its coalition partners have taken some measures in this regard (encouraging warlords to participate in political reconstruction, not allowing them to form parties if they kept militias). Whether the warlords will give up easily and get themselves replaced by the Afghan national army, or change their roles from warlords to politicians is the six-million-dollar question. The warlords have a political economy that runs on drugs, extortion, and import-export duties on border trade. They have a vested interest in maintaining control over their respective regions and will continue to do so until they are forced to surrender to the national sovereignty or brought into the central structure of power. For the local populations the warlords are bad news as they frequently engage in turf battles with rivals, order attacks against suspected opponents, and engage in violence. The warlords have also not been very reliable partners for the American forces beyond realizing their primary goal of defeating the Taliban. They have often provided false information against their rivals to make them targets of attack by the American forces.

The best way to end the terrible reign of the warlords could be by extending the role and area of operation of the international stabilization forces that are presently under the command of Britain—the command may soon pass on to Turkey. The United States has refused to expand this force from Kabul city to other provincial towns. In the absence of the national police and army, and limitations on the international stabilization force to remain confined to Kabul, the writ of the Afghan state cannot be expected to go beyond its immediate environs.

Much about political reconstruction of Afghanistan is being postponed to the new government that would be formed later when the *Loya Jirga* meets in the second week of June. But any government with such a tormented legacy and political fragmentation would be disadvantaged in keeping peace within its ranks or providing security to the desperate population.

Peace, deweaponization, and economic reconstruction would be three pillars on which the future stability of Afghanistan would stand. There is hardly any concrete poured into these foundations yet. The aid that the donor countries or international agencies have committed to is still stuck up in the intricate webs of their bureaucracies. It will take time before the Afghan national army takes a definite shape and develops into a neutral, coherent, and disciplined force.

Before the hopes, which are attracting the refugees in hundreds of thousands back into their country, fade and the Afghans turn to the local warlords for security, it is necessary that the American-led coalition in Afghanistan rethink its priorities. First, the financial assistance to the interim administration must be put through the fast track, with greater attention to revival of agriculture, rebuilding of health centers, and schools for children. This aspect must be an integrated part of rehabilitation of refugees. Larger projects like rebuilding roads, communication networks, extensive trade, and economic activity would depend on the security of foreigners and Afghans involved in the reconstruction work. Local warlords would be a poor substitute for providing security.

What is also needed is a fundamental change in the role of the international stabilization force from covering just the capital city to all major towns and provincial centers. It will be a gigantic task and may require a lot of resources, but leaving things to the warlords and local contenders for power would further delay, and even undermine, the objective of rebuilding the state and society in Afghanistan.

THE INSURGENCY

While the northern parts of Afghanistan seem to be relatively calm, for reasons other than the state extending its writ, the Pashtun areas in the south and east of the country have experienced a resurgence of the Taliban. We have previously discussed the issue of the Taliban in greater detail. Here we would like to discuss how the Taliban activity hinders the reconstruction process. I think there is a dialectical relationship between reconstruction and the Taliban insurgency; the success of one will lead to the defeat of the other. There is an emerging consensus, at least among the observers of

Afghanistan, that inadequate resources, poor implementation, and slower pace of development projects have failed to create a relationship of trust between the new Afghan state and the local populations in the Pashtun regions.[45] One of the major reasons for implementing and delivering development projects on time has been the presence and activities of the Taliban.[46] With every successful project with the potential of employing idle Afghan youth, the Taliban and other warlords would lose a part of their recruiting ground.[47]

The Taliban have a very clear strategic design in denying the contractors that operated under the umbrella of reconstruction and security teams the opportunity to rebuild. They know if the government succeeds in rebuilding schools, hospitals, roads, communications and in providing security to the people in the villages, it would broaden and deepen its support base. A big window of opportunity for Kabul existed, immediately after the ouster of the Taliban, to move quickly in rebuilding but it lost considerable time in obtaining international assistance. Additionally, the donors were quite slow in responding to the needs of reconstruction. A delay in reconstruction projects has dashed the hopes of ordinary citizens to rebuild their lives and livelihoods. This is a crucial factor in explaining why larger parts of the Pashtun population have reembraced the Taliban. The Taliban is from within them, has stayed close to them, has the weapons and organizational ability to enforce its own form of order and security.

Taliban activity has further diminished the ability of the central state to maintain its presence on a sustainable basis. During the last two years, the frequency and fatality of Taliban attacks has increased. Quite a few times, it has even launched larger operations and has taken over district headquarters in the southern provinces. Its ability to do so has undermined the credibility of the U.S. and NATO forces to deliver on security. Their military operations against the Taliban have produced rather adverse effects because of the collateral damage that they have caused in bombing suspected targets.[48] The death of innocent civilian men, women, and children by the U.S. and NATO forces has enraged local populations. The Taliban has effectively exploited growing anti-American sentiment, and has largely contributed to it through its propaganda. The political effects of counterinsurgency have not been to the liking of the Kabul authorities, which has disabled them in reconnecting with the local communities or undertaking the much needed reconstruction projects.

POPPY CULTIVATION AND DRUG ECONOMY

Afghanistan has a long history of poppy cultivation, but the scale of production that it has reached during the past few years is unprecedented.

Never have Afghanistan's farmers produced so much opium as they do now. In 2006, they produced more than 90 percent of the world's heroin, breaking all previous records.[49] This has flown in the face of the much hyped about efforts of the United States to eradicate poppy cultivation. Afghanistan's reemergence as the top narcotics producer of the world in the wake of an American-led war and the removal of the Taliban from power is a reversal of what the local Taliban had achieved—i.e., making Afghanistan poppy-free with very meager material resources. The Taliban leaders enforced a ban on poppy cultivation on account of a religious edict and they enforced it effectively throughout the country. How and why did the Taliban enforce the ban effectively is a matter of debate. Was it the fear of reprisals from the Taliban for violation of their decrees that made the farmers abide by the rules? Or was it the nativity and nearness of the Taliban to the local populations that was responsible for the eradication of poppy cultivation? Or, was it the moral authority that the Taliban enjoyed over the people that made its policy work? Without going into details of these reasons that partially explain the effectiveness of the Taliban regime, there was and still remains great admiration for the Taliban for making Afghanistan free of drugs in a very short period of time.

Unfortunately, poppy cultivation is now at an all-time high and a combination of strategies of disincentives and incentives has yet to show results. Why the strategy of poppy cultivation is not working, and why the eradication of poppy cultivation is a major challenge in the reconstruction of state institutions and a formal economy, needs to be explained. First, we have to bear in mind that some of the provinces of southern and eastern Afghanistan have grown poppy for centuries but at a smaller scale. The main product was raw opium, which was mainly transported to British India for medicinal use and also was used to feed a small population of addicts. Opium use until the first half of last century was not regarded as an addiction or a drug with potentially long-term effects. It used to be a household recipe for colds and body pains that was given to peoples of all ages, including infants. *Hakeems* (local doctors) in Pakistan often prescribed opium without any legal or moral restraint to their patients for different reasons, and it used to be sold openly in shops along with hashish. The sale of opium goods was banned only in the late 1970s as a part of the Islamization process in Pakistan. Even today, opium, hashish, and heroine are easily available, and a very large population of addicts on the Pakistani periphery of Afghanistan uses it. The problem of drug addiction in Afghanistan itself and in Pakistan has grown manifold and has growing numbers in almost every city and town.[50] International trafficking and its impact on Western societies overshadow the issue of local drug addiction and trafficking.

The soviet military intervention in Afghanistan turned poppy cultivation into one of the major sources of revenue for some of the resistance groups.

This happened at a time when international drug traffickers displaced by Iranian clergy introduced new technologies of refining opium into heroine in the border regions of Afghanistan and Pakistan. Another important factor was that in the wake of popular uprising and Mujahideen resistance, the poppy-growing areas were freed of whatever little governmental control had previously existed there.

The local Mujahideen commanders who fought the war against the Soviet forces in the name of Islam and Afghan nationalism did not oppose the cultivation of poppy in the areas under their control. In place of government functionaries, they taxed the middleman who purchased opium for the international drug mafia. It is widely reported that some Mujahideen leaders struck profitable deals with the narcotics traffickers and became involved in the business.[51] It is questionable whether the top leaders sanctioned such deals to finance the war efforts officially or the local militia commanders struck independent deals to earn private money. The Mujahideen groups that are alleged to have adopted this policy received most of the arms from Pakistan and had no such compulsion for getting involved in the drug trafficking. However, involvement of some commanders cannot be entirely ruled out. Some of them might have exercised the drug option after the end of the Western support in the early 1990s. Despite denials by the Mujahideen leaders, some of the Western journalists and those who have been writing on the subject have continued to level charges of drug trafficking against the Mujahideen.[52]

The collapse of the state in Afghanistan in the wake of civil war in the country has removed the already weak, governmental authority structures. The absence of state institutions to enforce controls has further encouraged both the poppy growers and drug traffickers. The dependency of the growers on the traffickers has increased as poppy has emerged as the single most important cash crop. It will be extremely difficult for the international agencies and any government to control production on the supply side by trying to induce the Afghan farmers to grow alternative crops. It is not just the cultivators, but also a large variety of stakeholders in the opium economy, from workers, traders, and speculators to small-time traffickers who depend on the drug economy to earn their living.[53] Before the Taliban enforced a ban on poppy cultivation the United Nation Drug Control Program started a crop substitution scheme in Afghanistan at a relatively smaller scale.[54] It did not prove to be effective or sustainable due to limited funds.

After the departure of the Taliban, social and political conditions that facilitated poppy cultivation during the war or resistance have reemerged. The authority of the Kabul government is weak and its functionaries in the poppy-cultivating areas have become more a part of the problem than the solution. They have become involved in drug trafficking and take a cut from the local trade and production. The United States and the Kabul government have tolerated drug-related activities of tribal chieftains as opposed to the Taliban for their support in the counterinsurgency intelligence and operations. It is true that along with terrorism, poppy cultivation and drug-trafficking have become major enemies of Afghanistan.[55] Corruption in the Karzai government is another reason for Afghanistan earning the notoriety for the world's number-one drug producer. The link between the Taliban insurgency and drug production is too visible. The Taliban, increasingly isolated, has become partly dependent on drug trade and production. There is a political reason for its support of poppy cultivation. The government's destruction of the crop though partly successful has turned the local populations against Karzai and international forces involved in this kind of operation. For this reason, their response to the growth of poppy cultivation has been slow and may remain so because it will create more opposition for the government and support for its Taliban rivals in the Pashtun regions.

Without crop substitution, integrated rural development, formal economic activity for the local youth, poppy eradication schemes will remain ineffective. The five-point program of the United States covering interdiction, eradication, alternative livelihood development, judicial reform, and public education theoretically offers a good package and takes a holistic view of the drug situation.[56] The implementation of this program has been problematic for reasons of corruption, weak capacity, and tenacity of the Taliban groups and their disruptive activities. The economics and politics of drug production and trade in Afghanistan have regional as well as global dimensions because of international trafficking networks. With the resources it makes available to the Taliban and the political fallout of the eradication strategy against the government, the problem may remain until better strategies like buying off the product and reconstruction of a formal economy with visible impact on lives of the local population are conceived and implemented.[57]

THE TWO-WAR DILEMMA

The American decision to invade Iraq has affected its role in Afghanistan in more ways than one. First is the diversion of material resources and political attention from Afghanistan to a more intensive war in Iraq. Defeating the Taliban was a first step but not the end of a complex process of state and nation building that the Bush administration had declared at the time of launching "Operation Enduring Freedom." In the early phase of building peace and stability in Afghanistan, the United States unwisely engaged itself in a second war that has proved to be enormously costly, unwinnable, and domestically divisive. The United State had spent over $400 billion on military operations by December 2006 and it continues to spend nearly $8 billion a month, thus the final cost of the Iraq war may not be less than $2 trillion.[58] Another $34 billion was appropriated for reconstruction purposes. Compared to this substantial commitment to Iraq's security and politics, attention and resources devoted to Afghanistan appears to be very small.

The Iraq war has badly hurt Afghanistan as it has diverted the United States away from this core country in the war on terror. In a moment of fury, confusion, and haste, it prematurely declared victory in Afghanistan and moved on to Iraq without any established link of Saddam Hussein with 9/11. It is widely recognized that the intelligence was faulty at best and concocted at worst. The neoconservative elements misused international sympathy and domestic support to occupy Iraq without giving any serious thought to its regional ramifications. The American commitment to rebuilding Afghanistan was affected by its war against Iraq at a time when the Taliban and Al Qaeda forces still remained active against the coalition forces, and the warlords continued to claim autonomy and authority in their respective areas, denying the Kabul government any authority. Bob Woodward, a renowned investigative journalist, who helped expose the Watergate scandal that forced President Richard Nixon out of office, in his book *Plan of Attack* has revealed that President Bush secretively approved diverting $700 million allocated for Afghanistan for preparations to invade Iraq.[59]

If the United States withdraws without assuring a sustainable political and security structure, which is increasingly becoming evident, the Taliban and Al Qaeda will be greatly encouraged by American defeat. A growing perception about weak American commitment to Afghanistan, an uncertainty about its strategic purposes in and around Afghanistan, and the opposition to the American-supported Kabul regime is likely to grow. A feeling of triumphalism among the transnational jihad networks will further destabilize Afghanistan and make the post-Taliban regime more vulnerable. The Afghans already seem to have become disenchanted with the United States and the international coalition of forces for many of their failures.[60]

There are many critics of the political process within and outside Afghanistan who argue that the United States, leading the international coalition, has imposed a regime of exiles through military force. All the major players that dominate the Afghan political scene spent most of their time in foreign countries during the war of resistance against the former Soviet Union. They might have been concerned about the situation in their country that was devastated first by the Soviet invasion and then the civil war, but did hardly anything practical to help the country. This is a general comment that the former *Mujahideen* and Taliban leaders, in a sullen and angry mood of defeat and humiliation, make.[61] The fact is that the United States and its coalition partners had limited choices. The *Mujahideen* factions that fought the war of resistance had severely damaged themselves by factional infighting. They failed to create any workable political order or ensure stability. Some of them turned their political rhetoric against the United States and the West, while their fighters at local levels had crossed over to the Taliban. Therefore, they were an unlikely ally for the United States in combating terrorism or flushing out the Al Qaeda from their bases. But ignoring them entirely in reconstructing the post-Taliban power arrangements was not politically prudent.

The fear of Taliban regrouping in guerrilla formation after making new alliances with local tribes and ethnic groups may keep the American and NATO forces engaged in combat that may in the end prove to be exhausting, expensive, and may produce uncertain results. Much would depend on the American-led coalition and its local connection to stay in power and weed out, isolate, or drive out the Taliban and its supporting allies. At the same time they need to devote more time, energy, and resources to rebuilding the economy, social development, and reconstruction of infrastructure. Security and development are two overlapping and reinforcing activities. They have become rather interdependent and are somewhat integrated. Success in one would contribute to success in the other. Parallel gains in both would secure the state and defeat the Taliban insurgency.

NOTES

1. Richard Caplan, *International Governance of War-Torn Territories: Rule and Reconstruction* (New York: Oxford University Press, 2006).

2. See some of the following works: Samuel P. Huntington, *Political Order in Changing Societies* (New Haven: Yale University Press, 1969); Gabriel A. Almond and Sydney Verba, *The Civic Culture* (Boston: Little, Brown, 1963); Lucian W. Pye, *Aspects of Political Development* (Boston: Little, Brown, 1966); Daniel Learner, *Passing of the Traditional Society* (New York: Press Press, 1958).

3. Kjetil Tronvoll, "The Process of Nation-Building in Post-War Eriteria: Created from Below or Directed from Above?" *The Journal of Modern African Studies*, Vol. 36, No. 3 (September 1989), pp. 461–82; Cynthia J. Arnson, ed., *Comparative Peace Process in Latin America* (Stanford: Stanford University Press, 1999); Michael O'Hanion, "Nation Building: Not for the Fainthearted," *Newsweek*, 12 June 2006.

4. Leon B. Poullada, *King Amanullah's Failure to Modernize a Tribal Society* (Ithaca: Cornell University press, 1973); Abdul Rehman Khan, *The Life of Abdul Rahman: Amir of Afghanistan* (Karachi: Oxford University Press, 1980).

5. Sultan Barakat and Margaret Chard, "Theories, Rhetoric and Practice: Recovering the Capacities of War-Torn Societies," *Third World Quarterly*, Vol. 23, No 5, pp. 822–23; *Rebuilding the Afghan State: The European Union's Role* (International Crisis Group, Asia Report No. 107, 30 November 2005).

6. Michael G. Burton and John Higley, "Elite Settlements," *American Sociological Review*, Vol. 52, No. 3 (June 1987), pp. 295–307.

7. United Nations Security Council, *Agreement on the Provincial Arrangements in Afghanistan Pending the Re-Establishment of Permanent Government Institutions*, 5 December 2001, S/2001/1154. The Security Council ratified the text on 7 December 2001.

8. Ibid.

9. Thomas Johnson, "Afghanistan's Post-Taliban Transitions: The State of the State-building after War," *Central Asian Survey* (March–June 2006), p. 2.

10. Pemla Constable, "Cabinet Is Sworn in, Intense Negotiations Yield Greater Ethnic, Political Balance," *Washington Post*, Foreign Service, 25 June 2002.

11. President appoints 33 percent. Another 33 percent are selected by the provincial councils, and the remaining 33 percent by the district councils.

12. "Afghanistan Votes," (editorial), *The New York Times*, 12 October 2004.

13. Eric Schmitt, "NATO Expects Rush of Taliban Attacks in Afghanistan," *The New York Times*, 6 October 2004.

14. *Dawn*, 10 October 2004.

15. Amy Waldman, "Plan for Investigation into Afghan Election Eases Dissent," *The New York Times*, 11 October 2004.

16. Ibid.

17. Dankwart A. Rustow, "Democracy: a Global Revolution?" *Foreign Affairs*, Fall 1990.

18. The local leaders and ruling class have an elitist view of ordinary people. They have argued for almost the past sixty years, since the end of colonialism, that the postcolonial Muslim states know only limited forms of authority and those are autocracy, dictatorship and monarchies. The existing conditions cannot be presented as an evidence of failure.

19. Carlotta Gall and David Rohde, "Assessing the Afghan Election," *The New York Times*, 20 October 2004.

20. During the first presidential debate on foreign policy, President Bush referred to Afghanistan's elections as a success of his policy. http://www.thegreenpapers .com/PCom/?2004001–0 (accessed on 11 May 2007).

21. Pakistan has faced constant pressure from Afghanistan and international coalition forces in that country to control the border areas to prevent infiltration of Taliban. See for analysis, Shahid Javed Burki, "A Difficult Neighbour," *Dawn*, 9 September 2007.

22. Shoib Najafizada, "Afghan Vote Reflects Ethnic Fault Lines," *Dawn*, 27 October 2004.

23. William Maley, "Executive, Legislative, and Electoral Options for Afghanistan," http://www.cic.nyu.edu/pdf/E9ExecLegisElectoralOptionsMaley.pdf (accessed on 15 June 2007).

24. International Crisis Group, "Afghanistan Elections: Endgame or New Beginning?," Asia Report No. 101, 21 July 2005, p. 24.

25. Barnett Rubin, "Afghanistan: The Wrong Voting System," *International Herald Tribune*, 16 March 2005.

26. Thomas H. Johnson, "Afghanistan's Post-Taliban Transition: The State of State-Building After War," op. cit. 1–2, p. 15.

27. Ibid., op.cit., pp. 20–21.

28. See an alternative view that argues that Afghan women had made many gains with relative modernization of Afghanistan. See Sultan Barakat & Gareth Wardell, "Exploited by Whom? An Alternative Perspective on Humanitarian Assistance to Afghan women," *Third World Quarterly*, Vol. 23 No. 5.

29. A general amnesty law passed by the parliament in March 2007, though controversial, is the right step to win over some Taliban leaders and their supporters.

30. Anja Manuel, "A New Model Afghan Army," *Foreign Affairs*, Jul/Aug 2002, pp. 44–59.

31. Afghanistan National Development Strategy Office, Islamic Republic of Afghanistan, *Afghanistan National Development Strategy*, Kabul. http://www.ands.gov.af/ (accessed on 20 October 2007).

32. Ibid.

33. United States and NATO included Afghan National Army troops in their operations Mountain Lion, Mountain Thrust, and Medusa.

34. Max Weber, *On Charisma and Institutional Building* (Chicago and London: The University of Chicago Press, 1968), pp. 66–80.

35. The program of reform was first spelled out in Transitional Islamic State of Afghanistan, *Public Administration Programme: Implementation Strategy*, draft 23 July 2003. The Afghanistan National Development Strategy and Afghanistan Compact were launched in 2006 redefined and expanded public administration reforms. See Sarah Lister, "Moving Forward? Assessing Public Administration Reform in Afghanistan" (AREU Briefing Paper, September 2006), p. 1.

36. Ibid., pp. 1–5.

37. Ibid., pp. 9–18.

38. Tokyo Conference on Afghanistan was attended by representatives of sixty-one countries and twenty-one international organizations to make specific commitments and pledges to the reconstruction of the country. It was held on 21–22 January 2002. www.mofa.go.jp/region/middle_e/afghanistan/min0201/- (accessed on 27 April 2007).

39. Representatives of sixty-five nations and international organizations met in Berlin on 31 March–1 April 2004. They pledged $8 billion. www.state.gove/p/sca/lls/fs/32094.htm (accessed on 27 April 2007).

40. "Building on Success: The London Conference on Afghanistan: The Afghanistan Compact, 31 January–1 February 2006," Foreign and Commonwealth Office, UK website, www.fco.gov.uk/servlet./Front?pagename=OpenMarket/xcelerate/ShowPage&c=1134650705195 (accessed on 27 April 2007).

41. Afghanistan Development Strategy was launched in December 2005 but its final shape will emerge in 2008. It is about the development priorities of the government of Afghanistan and the institutional mechanism that it is going to adopt to realize its development objectives. See www.ands.gov.af (accessed on 27 April 2007).

42. "Afghanistan's Endangered Compact," *Policy Briefing*, Asia Briefing No. 59 (Kabul/Brussels: International Crisis Group, 29 January 2007), pp. 1–5.

43. Barakat and Chard, "Theories, Rhetoric and Practice," *Third World Quarterly*, Vol. 23, No. 5, 2002, pp. 817–35.

44. Bob Woodward, *Bush at War*, op. cit, pp. 51–68.

45. See Barnett R. Rubin, "Saving Afghanistan," *Foreign Affairs*, January/February, 2007.

46. James Dobbins, *Ending Afghanistan's Civil War*, testimony presented before the Senate Foreign Relations Committee on 8 March 2007. (Santa Monica: Rand Corporation, 2007), pp. 6–8.

47. Terry Friel, "Lack of Job Hurting Afghan War on Taliban," *Daily Times*, 3 April 2007.

48. On collateral damage by the U.S. and NATO forces, see for instance, Patrick Seale, "Losing the War in Afghanistan," *Daily Times*, 19 December 2006.

49. Elizabeth Rubin, "In the Land of the Taliban," *The New York Times*, October 22, 2006.

50. On drug addiction see, United Nations Office on Drugs and Crime, *2007 World Drug Report*, pp. 55–57.

51. Lt. Gen. (Ret.) Kamal Matinuddin, *Power Struggle in the Hindu Kush (1978–1992)* (Lahore: Wajidalis, 1993), pp. 321–22.

52. Lawrence Lifschultz, "Pakistan: The Empire of Heroin," in Afred W. McCoy and Alan A. Block, eds., *War on Drugs: Studies in the Failure of U.S. Narcotics Policy* (Boulder: Westview Press, 1992), pp. 319–58.

53. *Afghanistan, Strategic Study #2: The Dynamics of the Farmgate Opium Trade and the Coping Strategies of Opium Traders* (Islamabad: UNDCP, Afghanistan Programme, October 1998).

54. *The News*, 16 May 2000.

55. President Hamid Karzai quoted in *The Washington Post*, 2 December 2006.

56. As to a means of enforcing an agreement 'not to grow poppy, the U.S. Senate and House of Representatives passed U.S. Public Law 109-469, Section 1111, early 2007 with strong bipartisan support.

57. Walton Cook, "A U.S. Model Proposal: Profit from Paying Afghanistan Farmers 'Not to Grow Poppies.'" (An unpublished document that has been sent to the Government of Afghanistan, 2007.)

58. I have taken these figures from *The Iraq Study Group Report*, http://www.USIP .org/isg_study_report/report/1206/Iraq_study_Group_report.pdf (accessed on 26 April 2007), pp. 23–24, 27.

59. Bob Woodward, *Plan of Attack, Dawn* (Lahore), 21 April 2004.

60. Ahmed Rashid, "Letter from Afghanistan: Are the Taliban Winning?" *Current History*, January 2007, pp. 18–20.

61. Author's interview with Afghans, Peshawar, 15–17 July 2006.

6

Political Economy of Drugs and Warlordism

Wars and drug production and trafficking have been fellow travelers in Afghanistan's modern political history, conversely creating conditions supportive of each other. In conflict situations, the drug economy becomes an important source of developing and maintaining war-fighting capability by the insurgent groups. And internal wars with some degree of popular support edge the state out of the populations and remote territories or make its exercise of authority difficult, thus creating a power vacuum that the insurgents, terrorists, and criminals fill up with militias and illegal economic activity. Afghanistan presents a classic case of how collapse of the state under conditions of insurgency provided greater space to a variety of actors to transform the legal agricultural economy into illegal poppy cultivation on a vast scale. The void left by the disappearance of the Afghan state, which was already weak, was filled by the warlords, local commanders allied with the Mujahideen parties fighting the war of resistance against the former Soviet Union, and transnational terrorists and crime syndicates involved in drug trafficking.

Production, trafficking, and use of narcotics constitute nonmilitary threats to national security even in relatively stable societies. Afghanistan has been through various cycles of conflicts for the past three decades where the threat of drug economy to the stability of society, health of the general population, and revival of the state is far greater than in the countries with relatively effective state institutions. Afghanistan has made encouraging progress with the support of the international community and the coalition forces that are engaged against the Taliban insurgency. But the surge in opium production during the past few years is threatening to reverse the recovery of this war-torn country.[1] The post-Taliban regime has inherited an old problem that has gotten worse during the past four years. From a nearly complete ban on poppy cultivation under the guns of Taliban religious police in 2001, Afghanistan has become the largest producer of raw opium in the world, leaving countries of Latin America and the Golden Triangle far behind.[2] The country is going through a difficult and complex phase of economic and political reconstruction and faces the prospect of becoming a narco-state.[3] Any success on the war on terror would greatly depend on how the international coalition engaged in Afghanistan effectively eliminates drug production. The two issues, drugs and insurgency, reinforce each other, which complicates the task of reviving the Afghan state.[4] The functional boundaries between terrorism, crime, and insurgency have become increasingly fuzzy in the political economy of drugs. The world community may lose the war on terror if it does not deal effectively with the political economy of drugs in Afghanistan, as part of billions of drug earnings end up in the hands of terrorists.

Unfortunately, the United States and its coalition partners in Afghanistan have been slow in comprehending the full range of implications of production of illicit drugs and their distribution within the country, in the region and beyond. The U.S. security establishment did not want to add the role of antinarcotics police to its already overstretched forces.[5] While it focused its resources and energies on fighting a growing insurgency against the Taliban, the vast areas of rural Afghanistan slipped off into the hands of transnational drug traffickers and their local collaborators, which includes a wide range of criminal elements, terrorists, and Taliban insurgents, every one of them having a finger in the drug pie. The neglect of drug production of trafficking networks has been very costly and may have long-term effects over the regional security and future prospects of peace and stability in Afghanistan. The insurgents and local warlords greatly benefit from production and trafficking of Afghan opium and heroine. They provide protection to the farmers against efforts by the Afghan government to eradicate poppy cultivation and also assure safe passage to the traffickers for a charge. Earnings from the drug economy have for decades provided resources to the Afghan warlords, Mujahideen commanders, and the Taliban to finance their private armies and buy weapons. The revival of the Taliban movement after its defeat in 2001 is partly due to the revival and expansion of the drug economy. They are just one of the players, and may be smaller than others, but they do have a political stake in the drug economy as they sustain their efforts by taxing the drug trade.[6]

During the decades of wars, the Afghan government disappeared from the lives of local communities, leaving them to the local insurgents and warlords. With the disruption of normal agricultural supplies and practices by war, the farmers turned to poppy cultivation in greater numbers because that was the only means through which they could sustain their families.

The vacuum left by the state was filled quickly by the national and international drug mafia, which worked closely with the warlords and militia. The international community after the retreat of the Soviet Union pushed Afghanistan, a state that became a battleground during the second wave of the Cold War, to isolation. The political and security climate of the country was very conducive to the drug mafia to spread its tentacles in vital elements of the Afghan society and around its insecure borderlands and beyond to central Asia and Pakistan. The drug barons have emerged as a powerful and respectable class, have acquired social significance, and use their wealth to raise and maintain armed militias. In this chapter we will focus on the following questions: What are the local, regional, and international factors that have contributed to the growth of trade in illegal drugs? What is the relationship between the Afghan war and the regional distribution of heroin and other illegal substances? What is the impact of drug trade on the Afghan state and society? How has the drug production and trade affected state- and nation-building efforts of Afghanistan? What efforts have the international coalition made to control production of drugs? How successful have international counternarcotics efforts been? What is the nature of international cooperation to control narcotics trafficking out of Afghanistan?

DRUG PRODUCTION IN AFGHANISTAN

The United Nations Office on Drugs and Crime in its Opium Winter Rapid Assessment Survey of Afghanistan presents a dismal picture of how and why poppy cultivation has reached the highest point in history. It reports that 165,000 hectares were under cultivation in 2006, which showed a 59 percent increase as compared to 2005.[7] The crop yielded approximately 6,100 metric tons of opium, which was recorded as 90 percent of the world's illicit opium. The area under cultivation has doubled from 74,000 hectares in 2002, and so has the production risen from 3,400 metric tons to its present level of 6,100 metric tons.[8] The production has progressively increased since 1986 when Afghanistan produced only 350 metric tons and the poppy cultivation was confined to only 29,000 hectares.[9]

Equally shocking is the share of the narcotics sector to Afghanistan's economy. According to the UNODC report of 2005, it adds US$2.7 billion value to the total national economy of US$5.4 billion.[10] There are too many local and foreign stakeholders in the Afghan drug economy. The chain runs vertically from the farmer at the lower end to farm laborers, small traders, wholesalers, refiners, government officials, warlords, and cross-border smugglers.[11] The gains out of the drug economy accrue larger benefits for the individual and groups at the top, leaving very little income for the local farmers. Compared to other crops, however, the Afghan farmers get ten times more income from poppy cultivation than legal crops. This keeps them within the complex drug chain of Afghanistan, as the alternative agricultural activities do not make economic sense to them.

There are more than one factor that have contributed to the emergence of Afghanistan as the leading producer of opium-based drugs. Climatic conditions stand on the top of them all. The river valleys, highlands, and slopes of mountain ranges in Afghanistan have provided ideal climatic and social conditions to cultivate poppy. The tribal farmers mostly in the Pashtun regions grew poppy for limited use, essentially to sell to the trade caravans who crossed to central Asia, Iran, and India. The physical features of the area are as important in understanding the modern day drug problem as the social and political development of the regions that now have become the center of drug trade.

Geographically, the drug-producing areas of Afghanistan and the border tribal regions adjoining Pakistan have been desolate and remote from areas where the major population centers developed. Owing to distance and difficult terrain, most of these territories were left to fend for themselves, receiving little or no attention from the central governments. The social and political organization of the tribal communities further strengthened their autonomy. In Afghanistan, a rentier state did not attempt to sink its roots in the society through extraction or any other modern means of institutional development.[12] The monarchy, which was essentially tribal in character, and had a narrow social base in the Pashtun regions negotiated legitimacy through the tribal chieftains. As an oligarchic power structure began to emerge, the tribal chief became the intermediary between the tribal population and the king. The chief was the main instrument through which the king exercised power and mobilized support when it was needed to fight his internal and external enemies. In the bargain, the king left the tribal areas to be governed by the local tribal elders according to their customs and social norms. More importantly, the tribes and subtribes of the Pashtuns straddling the vast areas around the Afghanistan-Pakistan border had, over the centuries, carved out autonomous territorial domains that they fiercely defended against any intruder, including the Kabul government.

The anarchic border regions of Afghanistan and Pakistan from where the Taliban and before them the Mujahideen staged an intervention in Afghanistan have been more or less stateless or accepted nominal authority of the respective governments. Never have Afghanistan and Pakistan paid sustained attention to the borderlands to integrate them or extend writ of the state. The neglect has created a myth of "free Pashtun tribes," meaning they do not accept any external authority except that of local elders. This myth has a colonial history about the tribes on the Pakistan side of the border who control trafficking routes and are part of the wider web of the regional drug trade. The British Indian government tried for decades to bring the

Pashtun tribal areas under its administrative control but failed. Britain sent more than 42 military expeditions of varying sizes there between 1849 and 1890 into these areas. Finally, in 1897 it sent a force of 30,000 soldiers to fight against the Afridi tribe in the Khyber area alone.[13] With each failure, the British took harsher measures.

A number of things worked against the British: the terrain, the jihad culture of tribal resistance, and the availability of relatively modern firearms that were manufactured in the tribal areas and also smuggled in from the Gulf region. Even its two invasions of Afghanistan in 1838 and 1878 for strategic reasons proved disastrous, causing enormous loss of life to the British troops. The British policy after the second Afghan war settled on accepting internal autonomy of the country and keeping control over its external affairs in order to prevent it from entering into alliance with Russia. The story of the "great game" is too familiar to repeat here.[14] The point is that the Pashtun tribes on both sides of the border, which was drawn in 1893, remained out of the reach of Afghan and British power. The British policy in the region settled on autonomy, nominal presence over the horizon, and gradual integration of the Pashtuns into the Indian armed forces. This was the political legacy that Pakistan inherited at the time of independence. Pakistani authorities have never attempted wholeheartedly to integrate the tribal areas or fully extend civil laws to the tribal agencies where most of the poppy is cultivated. The old rules and regulations from the British time and the colonial administrative system of political agents supported by the Tochi Scouts, Khyber Rifles, and similar other security outfits continue to function with a little tinkering here and there.

In the tribal regions of Afghanistan and Pakistan trade in sophisticated weapons, manufacturing of small arms, and narco-trafficking take place without any control or interference from any governmental authority. Drugs—opium, hash, and heroine—are bought and sold openly like other legal merchandize. Criminals, murderers, and international terrorists quite often take refuge in these areas and in return work for the local chiefs, which may involve illegal activities. One cannot look at the problem of poppy cultivation and other processes from refining opium to heroin and smuggling out of Afghanistan without considering the social and administrative structures of the poppy-cultivating areas.

Around half a century back, Afghanistan had limited opium output, mainly for local consumption or a little export to British India. The British did not encourage commercial cultivation of poppy in the tribal belt. Rather, it built up a network of interdiction at the periphery, particularly at the entry points, to deny the bigger Indian market to the Pashtun producers of opium. The settled areas of the Frontier province, Punjab, Sindh, and other areas that now comprise Pakistan, were kept open to the opium grown in other parts of British India. Informal opium trade through smuggling at a

smaller scale, however, continued through the porous Afghan border. Officially, Pakistan continued to import opium from India for its addicts and for
pharmaceutical uses. But gradually, when the government of Pakistan began
to open up the tribal areas through new roads and launched development
schemes, the opium from these areas and from across the Durand Line began to enter the Pakistani market in a big way. The opium-producing areas
of Afghanistan and Pakistan became gradually integrated into a larger market with horizontal price variations. Within a decade after independence, the
opium supplies from Afghanistan and the tribal regions replaced the Indian
opium except for the small quantities smuggled into the bordering regions
of Punjab. Shortfalls of production on the Pakistani side due to bad weather
conditions were met through smuggling from the opium-growing regions of
Afghanistan. Market forces played an important role in integrating the
opium-growing areas of Pakistan and Afghanistan. Because of the limited
number of consumers of opium in Afghanistan, the growers there always ser-
viced the bigger markets of Pakistan and Iran. The opium traders in the region skillfully developed transnational networks and kept the local retailers
in Iran and Pakistan well supplied.

The drug traffickers have played a critical role in the political economy of
the opium-producing areas. They have provided the growers with loans,
agricultural inputs, and protection whenever needed. The farmers obtain
advance credit on opium and other crops through informal channels,
which is usually extended by the local traders and shopkeepers,[15] who serve
middlemen for the drug-trafficking network. They lift the crop at a reasonable price. The next stage is the refining of the opium into heroine. At this
crucial stage, they supply the chemicals, machinery, and experts. The final
stage is the trafficking into Pakistan and to the heroin markets of Europe
and North America. This illegal business would require thousands of dedicated and trustworthy workers to run it smoothly. The tribal traditions of
loyalty and involvement of the entire clan in trafficking give them a greater
sense of security. They work in alliance with other similar syndicates from
central Asia, Iran, and Pakistan.

In order to understand the evolution of the drug production and trafficking in Afghanistan and around the region during the past two decades,
we have to look at four important developments in the region. First was
the Islamic revolution in Iran. The new regime totally banned the cultivation of poppy, which was done on a large scale during the reign of
Shah. The Islamic regime began executing both the addicts and the traffickers.[16] The resulting shortages in the Iranian market gave a boost to the
production of opium in Afghanistan. Many of the Iranian traffickers
sought refuge in Afghanistan and began supporting the local drug production chain to supply the addict population in their country through

smuggling. In the early 1970s, for political and climatic reasons, the production of opium significantly declined in the Far Eastern Golden Triangle, leaving a big supply gap in the Western heroin market. This shifted the focus of the international drug mafia to the poppy-growing areas of Afghanistan and Pakistan. The entry of this mafia changed the entire structure of the drug trade in the region. Two changes are important to note. First was the introduction of chemicals and technology of processing opium into heroin. This occurred in the late 1970s. Second was the linking of drug-producing areas of this region with the international trafficking networks, another critical development as it brought in more powerful and resourceful actors onto the local scene. The local traffickers had international access before but it was limited and often uncertain. The international traffickers brought with them the promise of a much bigger market and greater cash flows along with relatively secure access points and trafficking routes. With their access to the European market, they generated greater demand for the Afghan drugs.

Soviet military intervention was the third important development in the region that further strengthened the hold of international drug traffickers. In the wake of popular uprising and Mujahideen resistance, the poppy-growing areas got free of whatever governmental control was there. The local Mujahideen commanders who fought the war against the Soviet forces in the name of Islam and Afghan nationalism did not oppose cultivation of poppy in the areas under their control. In place of government functionaries, they taxed the middleman who purchased opium for the international drug mafia. It is widely reported that some Mujahideen leaders struck profitable deals with the narcotics traffickers and became involved in the business.[17] The local Mujahideen commanders and the Taliban turned a blind eye to the production of illicit drugs. Some would argue that they in fact encouraged poppy cultivation and refining of opium as a commodity for trade that earned them taxes and kept the farmers and the middlemen engaged in some economic activity.[18]

It is questionable whether the top *Mujahideen* leaders sanctioned such deals to finance the war efforts officially or the local militia commanders struck independent deals to earn private money from the beginning of the war. The *Mujahideen* received most of the arms from the United States, Saudi Arabia, and Pakistan and had no such compulsion for getting involved in the narco-business as long as they were well-supplied. As Western support to the Mujahideen came to an end in the late 1980s, a good number of them turned to drugs as a source of revenue to finance their militias. Despite denials by the *Mujahideen* leaders, some of the Western journalists and those who have been writing on the subject have continued to level charges of drug trafficking against them, which appear to be quite credible.[19]

Collapse of the state in Afghanistan in the wake of civil war in the country was the final blow to a state-based authority structure. The war removed all governmental presence, which was already nominal in the peripheral regions. The drug producers took full advantage of the state vacuum and began to establish wide and deep linkages with the poppy-cultivating farmers. The dependency of the growers on the traffickers substantially increased as poppy emerged as the single most important cash crop. It became extremely difficult for the international agencies and some foreign governments that were interested in addressing this problem to induce the Afghan farmers to grow alternative crops.[20] It was not just the cultivators, but also a large variety of stakeholders in the opium economy from workers, traders, and speculators to small-time traffickers who depended on the drug economy to earn their living in the strife-stricken country.[21]

Although wars have been a major factor in encouraging poppy cultivation, farmers in Afghanistan have grown opium for centuries both for local use and trading the surplus with the adjacent regions of south and southwest Asia. The issue of social beliefs and practices is important because they do not create an ethical barrier for the poppy farmers. The values of the society and customs of the Afghan tribes do not stand in the way of growing poppy or refining opium into heroin. The only moral or religious prohibition is against use of drugs. The Afghans do not see any conflict between producing illegal drugs or trading them and their religious obligations as Muslims. Growing poppy is an accepted agricultural practice and the processing of opium and its trade falls in the category of legal business in the popular image.

Poverty and underdevelopment are also some of the issues that we cannot ignore in discussing the growth of the political economy of drugs in Afghanistan. The country is one of the poorest in the world and the least developed. It stands at the lowest line of each of the human development indicators today.[22] Whatever development Afghanistan registered before the communist revolution in 1978 was wiped out first by the Soviet war, and then the civil war between the Taliban and the Northern Front. With the complete breakdown of the Afghan state and its writ, which was never fully respected or enforced, the poverty-stricken farmers turned to poppy cultivation in great numbers to sustain themselves, as it paid far better than the regular, legal farming.

Small land holding and lack of irrigation water have increased dependence of the Afghan farmers on the poppy crop. Opium poppy does not require regular watering and the crop can resist drought which has been a regular phenomenon in this region over the past decade. From a small plot of land a farmer can obtain enough yield to buy grain, usually smuggled out of Pakistan, and meet their other daily needs.

Table 6.1. Fact Sheet—Afghanistan Opium Survey 2006

	2005	Variation on 2005	2006
Net opium poppy cultivation	104,000 ha	+59%	165,000 ha
In percent of agricultural land	2.30%		3.65%
In percent of global cultivation	62%		82%
Number of provinces affected			
(total: 34)	26		28
Eradication	5,000 ha	+210%	15,300 ha
Weighted average opium yield	39.3 kg/ha	-6%	37.0 kg/ha
Potential production of opium	4,100 mt	+49%	6,100 mt
In percent of global production	87%		92%
Number of households involved in opium cultivation	309,000		448,000
Number of persons involved in opium cultivation	2.0 million		2.9 million
In percent of total population (23 million)	8.7%		12.6%
Average farm-gate price of dry opium at harvest time	US$138/kg	-9%	US$125/kg
Afghanistan GDP2	US$5.2 billion	+29%	US$6.7 billion
Total farm-gate value of opium production	US$0.56 billion	+36%	US$0.76 billion
In percent of GDP	11%		11%
Total export value of opium to neighbouring countries	US$2.7 billion	+15%	US$3.1 billion
In percent of GDP	52%		46%
Gross trafficking profits to Afghan traffickers	US$2.14 billion	+9%	US$2.34 billion
Household average yearly gross income from opium of opium-growing families	US$1,800	-5%	US$1,700
Per capita gross income of opium-growing farmers	US$280	-7%	US$260
Afghanistan's GDP per capita	US$226	+28%	US$290
Indicative gross income from opium per ha	US$5,400	-15%	US$4,600
Indicative gross income from wheat per ha	US$550	-4%	US$530

Source: UNODC, *2007 World Drug Report*, June 2007, p. 195.

Table 6.2.   Afghanistan, Regional Distribution of Opium Poppy Cultivation (ha), 2005 to 2006

Region	2005 (ha)	2006 (ha)	Change 2005–2006	2006 as % of Total
Southern	46,147	101,900	+121%	62%
Northern	28,282	22,574	-20%	14%
Western	16,543	16,615	0%	10%
Northeastern	8,734	15,234	+74%	9%
Eastern	4,095	8,312	+103%	5%
Central	106	337	+218%	0%
Rounded Total	104,000	165,000	+59%	100%

Source: UNODC, *2007 World Drug Report*, June 2007, p. 196.

THE TALIBAN AND THE DRUG ECONOMY

In recent years, Afghanistan has emerged as the largest producer of opium gum since the toppling of the Taliban regime as we have indicated in the first section of this chapter. The real growth in the expansion of poppy cultivation took place during the rise of the Taliban regime. The well-publicized ban by the Taliban in 2000 obscured two important facts. The Taliban reportedly had massive inventories of opium before issuing a decree against poppy cultivation, which did not affect the drug trade. There is a view that the Taliban was not serious about eradication of drugs. It issued decrees to regulate drug trade. Before banning, it is reported that the Taliban leaders stockpiled 300 tons of refined heroine to corner the heroine market in central Asia. The Taliban did not eliminate the stockpiles or the trade.[23] Two years before the famous ban, poppy cultivation registered an unprecedented increase in the country during the 1998–1999 growing season and spread to twenty-seven new districts. The area under cultivation increased by 43 percent, covering an estimated 90,983 hectares, way up from 63,674 hectares of 1997–1998 season. The crop yielded around 4,581 metric tons of opium according to a United Nation Drug Control Program (UNDCP) report, which marked an increase in opium production of 70 percent from the 1998 deflated figure of 2,692 metric tons.[24] Compared to this massive increase, Afghanistan's opium production at the time of the Saur revolution in 1978 was only 200 tons.[25]

According to 1999 estimates, the poppy crop spread to 104 districts, which showed a sharp increase from 55 districts in 1994 and 73 districts in 1998. The crop was then grown in 50 percent of the provinces.[26] The Taliban which controls 90 percent of the territory, on occasions condemned the production and distribution of opium, but made no serious effort to curtail production or prosecute those involved in the illicit drug trade.[27] According to the UNDCP, 96 percent of the area where poppy is cultivated was under the Taliban control.[28] This contradicted Taliban's public declarations on the issue. The question is why a religious movement that claimed to have enforced Islamic laws in all spheres of life was loath to controlling production of illicit drugs? There are three answers to this question. First, according to the Taliban's interpretation of Islamic law, cultivation of poppy is not prohibited, use of opium and other substances is. The warnings the Taliban leaders issued against growing poppy and trading in hashish and heroin and threats to prosecute violation of such orders according to the Islamic law were for meant to leverage for funds from the international agencies and foreign donors. They linked their practical measures against poppy cultivation to the availability of sufficient funds.[29] The chief of Taliban's State High Commission for Drug Control in an interview with *The Friday Times* said, "we can't allow thousands of farmers to starve because the world only cares about the drug addicts."[30] The Taliban regime consistently argued that crop substitution, development of the infrastructure, and creation of employment opportunities in the poppy-cultivation areas would require external funding.[31] It deflected criticism of the world community against patronizing drug production by demanding material resources for eradication and for economic and social development from the world community to prove their genuineness in the drug control at the farm level in Afghanistan. The foreign powers with tremendous interest in controlling poppy cultivation were not sure if the resources they provided the Taliban would be used for the same purpose or diverted to their war efforts.

The Taliban officials had private and collective interests as a militant movement in all the elements of the drug chain and greatly benefited from the production of illicit drugs. By allowing the farmers to grow poppy they carved out a solid constituency of support among them. They charged some sort of tax on production and connived with the drug traffickers for heavy bribes. The nexus between the drug barons and the Afghan warlords goes back to the day of anti-Soviet Mujahideen war in the country. These links survived and continued to flourish; political and military changes in the country had hardly any effect on them. The drug barons merely realigned themselves with the new rulers, the Taliban. The Taliban and Mujahideen parties had a symbiotic relationship with the drug traders, as all of them had a strong financial stake in the drug business. The Taliban used a great part of income from the drug trade to buy weapons in the international market which helped them consolidate their hold on the country.

The expansion of drug production during the Taliban regime can also be explained with reference to the ruling style and political culture of the religious militia. The Taliban as it first emerged was a military movement with religious orientation. Never did it acquire any solid institutional base to form a proper government. It also lacked sustainable administrative resources to employ against narcotics, even if it wished to. Its rule was focused on fighting the ethnic minorities of the Northern Front or ensuring compliance of the population with its religious decrees. Normal functions of the state never entered its deliberations or acquired any significance in the hierarchy of its objectives. During the Taliban rule, Afghanistan became a safe haven for international criminals of all sorts. Religious and ethnic terrorists, kidnappers, smugglers, and drug cartels and transnational terrorists established a strong base with the support of locally influential figures or with the support of the Taliban leaders. All of them traded money for hospitality, protection, or found a common ideological cause with the Taliban movement.

Isolating the Taliban pushed the movement further into the grip of Al Qaeda, drug mafia, and other criminal groups. The world faced a difficult situation as recognizing the Taliban or assisting it in any manner would have enabled it to stay firm in power, something no country except Pakistan wanted. The United States had already abandoned Afghanistan to its Taliban fate after achieving its strategy of defeating the Soviet Union and causing the fall of communism. In a vastly transformed international system, the U.S. and Western priorities changed and attention shifted to other areas of the world. Neglecting Afghanistan made the Afghan society a double victim of warlords and poverty. The UN sanctions hit the poor and dispossessed hard in Afghanistan, which confused their moral and political choices on drugs, ethnicity, and allegiance to the local warlords. Perhaps constructive engagement with the Taliban regime and not isolation, as some observers argued at that time, might have helped address the problem of drug production in that country.[32] But the character of the regime, its policies toward the religious and ethnic minorities and treatment of women invoked universal contempt for the Taliban in the Western world. Thus the narcotics problem in Afghanistan became enmeshed with power relations and the nature of regime. The efforts against production of narcotics in the country consequently suffered a great deal.

Whatever assistance to control the drug problem during the Taliban regime was provided did not succeed much in linking the programs to other goals, due to the apathy of the Taliban. For instance, the United States tied its support to projects like crop substitution through non-governmental organizations with respect to international norms of behavior on narcotics, fight against terrorism, and respect for human rights. It is not difficult to infer how the Taliban regime could qualify for American support. Therefore, the narcotics issue became more vexed and equally complex as the political settlement of the civil war in that country.

The representatives of the Taliban government set equally difficult conditions for cooperation to control production and outflow of drugs from its country. In March 1999, the Peshawar-based vice consul general of Afghanistan insisted that it was difficult for his government to ban poppy cultivation, declaring that his country would resist international efforts toward that end until sufficient funds were provided for the restoration of agriculture and irrigation networks.[33] The other demand of the Taliban for extending cooperation with the eradication of poppy was international recognition of its regime, which none of the Western countries was prepared to accept, given the widely publicized human rights abuses and its refusal to form a broad-based government.[34]

Since its ousting, the Taliban has gradually reemerged as a credible insurgency movement during the past few years, gaining more strength with each passing year. We have discussed its rise in a separate chapter. One of the reasons for the Taliban's menacing presence in the rural districts is its close link with the drug trade. It does not have the same flow of funds from Pakistan and the Middle Eastern countries as it used to in its early years when it surfaced on the Afghan political scene in the mid-1990s. It is difficult to know how much the drug economy contributes to its resources, but it is the most important means to buy food, weapons, and war supplies.[35] The southern provinces of Afghanistan, like Helmand where the Taliban insurgents are most active, have emerged as the largest producers of opium.

TRAFFICKING

Drug production and trafficking in the region and beyond to the wider world is one of the most stubborn legacies of the Afghan war, which continues to trouble all countries around Afghanistan along the trafficking routes. In 2006, about 53 percent of all the opiates of Afghanistan transited through Iran, 33 percent passed through Pakistan, and 15 percent via central Asia, mainly Tajikistan. The trafficking of morphine and heroin presents a very different picture. The major portion of heroin, about 48 percent, moved through Pakistan. Iran was the second largest route with 31 percent and central Asia third at 21 percent.[36] The countries on the trafficking routes not only have to confront criminals but also have to nurse growing populations of heroin addicts, which is straining their resources. Iran even with stricter laws has the largest drug abuse rate among the regional countries. Iran has 1.2 million addicts, which is roughly 2.8 percent of its general population. The opiate use is also relatively high among the central Asia states where the number of drug abusers has touched 300,000. Pakistan's drug use in percentage is around 0.7 percent, which is far lower than Iran, but it has to take care of 640,000 opiate users of whom the overwhelming majority are heroin addicts.[37] The drugs from across the border are cheap and easily available without any strict control of the law-enforcing agencies.[38]

Most of the opium and heroin produced in Afghanistan finds its way mostly to Europe and through old and new trafficking routes. Some 80 percent of heroin seizures in western Europe alone originate from southwest Asia, in which Afghanistan has a major share.[39] The first route runs through Pakistan, which has emerged as one of the major transit countries for the illicit drugs. It is much easier for the Afghan and Pakistani drug traffickers to push their dangerous product to Pakistan's bordering provinces of Balochistan and North-West Frontier Province (NWFP). Most of the heroin is processed in the bordering regions between Afghanistan and Pakistan and parts of the NWFP and is smuggled out of Pakistan through three routes. Karachi, which is a major seaport city of Pakistan, is the traditional outlet for international traffickers. The illicit drugs travel through the vast expanses of the Punjab and Sindh in the presence of hundreds of check-posts and under the eyes of scores of law enforcement agencies. The Karachi city located on the Arabian Sea has become the hub of drug trade for further shipments to Iran, Gulf, and then to the Balkan region.

The Mekran coast of Balochistan is the second important route out of Pakistan. The presence of the law-enforcing agencies along this coast is limited and the Arabian Sea offers vast space for the traffickers to ship drugs by small fishing boats and then on to the big vessels waiting in the open waters. The Balochistan-Iran border serves as an important route for smuggling into Turkey and from there to Europe. According to a U.S. report, approximately 17 percent of the heroin seized in the United States in 1995–1996 originated in Afghanistan and Pakistan.[40] The share of Afghan and Pakistani heroin in the North American market has significantly declined because the South American traffickers dominate that region.

Smugglers of all types of goods from and to Pakistan frequently use the border with India. Acetic anhydride, a catalyzing chemical used to convert opium into heroin, is manufactured in India and smuggled into Pakistan for onward use in Afghanistan. In recent years, the consignment of heroin and other illegal substances have started to get into India for local use and further trafficking into Europe.[41] A large of group of traffickers from different countries operates in the Afghanistan, central Asian, and Pakistan triangle. The record of Anti-Narcotics Force (ANF) of Pakistan showed that in 1997 among the 5,555 defendants arrested for drug trafficking, 206 were foreigners from 38 countries. With seventy-one defendants, Afghanistan topped the list, followed by Tanzania (31) and Nigeria (25). There were nine from Britain and seven from South Africa.[42] In terms of region, Africa ranked number one with seventy-nine persons from twelve countries.[43] This trend has continued over the past ten years. Among the Africans, the Nigerian traffickers form the largest group now, leaving Tanzanians to the second position.[44] Many of those arrested are carriers that take the contraband to international market for relatively small payments. Poverty in the African countries drives lot of men and women into the risky business of drug trafficking. Most of the drug trafficking is done by the more powerful and well-connected members of the international mafia in connivance with influential drug lords of Pakistan and Afghanistan. Pakistanis perhaps carry the largest quantities of drugs into the Gulf States, Saudi Arabia, and the Western countries.

Iran constitutes an equally important element of the triangle along with Afghanistan, central Asia, and Pakistan. The Islamic government in Iran has applied the harshest of the punishments to the drug traffickers, frequently executing them. Through different measures, it brought down the addict population from 1.2 million in 1993 to half a million in 1997. After a decade, its addict population has grown back to 1.2 million. Compared to other regional countries as indicated earlier, Iran has the largest number of drug users, that is 2.8 percent of its population. It is widely reported that the Iranian borders with Afghanistan have become a safe haven for the drug traffickers. In most of the cases, Turkey is the next destination from where heroin and other opiates enter European countries. Quite often, the Afghan traffickers have fought with the Iranian security forces. Tehran has deployed some 30,000 troops on drug patrol along the borders with Afghanistan and Pakistan and spends around $400 million a year combating smuggling, some of which is offset by assets confiscated from convicted traffickers.[45] In 1999 Iran claimed that the drug traffickers had killed 2,635 of its personnel from law-enforcing agencies since 1983.[46] In recent years, the death toll of the Iranian security forces has gone much higher due to its active interdiction policy. In 2005, Iran emerged as a world leader in drug seizures with the confiscation of 29 percent of the opiates followed by Pakistan with 20 percent seizure.[47] For what Iran is doing to interdict trafficking through its territory, it gets very little international assistance or recognition for combating drug trafficking, which has mostly European destinations. A few years back, it received only $2.5 million from Britain through UNDCP, which it used among other things to buy 1,000 bullet-proof vests and 170 sets of night-vision goggles. France for its part donated five drug-sniffing dogs for detection.[48] The United States has only taken Iran out of the list of the countries that fail to meet the international standards of drug control, but because of estrangement has offered no tangible help.

In order to lessen some burden of the border security forces, the Iranian Parliament in May 2000 decided to fence larger parts of its border with Afghanistan. In addition to strict border patrols, Iran has tried to address the problem at the source, that is drug production in Afghanistan, by extending cooperation for rebuilding the country. Iran was so concerned about the flow of drugs from Afghanistan that despite serious problems with the Taliban regime, it held talks with its leaders on the drug control issue. It even promised economic assistance to poppy growers in the Afghan province of Helmand, which continues to be the largest producer of opiates.[49]

Since the disintegration of the Soviet Union, the drug traffickers have found the new routes of central Asia safer as they face fewer restrictions on their movement.[50] They have taken benefit of political transitions in the newly independent states in the region. This route has seen a 12 percent increase in trafficking in 2006.[51] The international drug mafia has asserted control over its countries and works as a part of invisible networks passing the contraband from one group to another. The central Asian drug mafia, mainly the Tajiks and Uzbeks, have taken command of drug operations, pushing the Russian gangs to their territories. The Russian crime syndicates are a vital link of the drug chain to the Nordic countries, eastern and western Europe. With investment and financing from international drug cartels, new areas of production and processing are emerging in some of the central Asian states. According to a report of International Narcotics Control Board, there is a rapid spread of illicit cultivation and abuse of drugs in the central Asian States and the Caucasus.[52]

The drug trafficking problem has international dimensions and therefore it requires international cooperation. Only recently the countries in the region have begun to cooperate. India and Pakistan have held frequent meetings at secretary level to evolve a common strategy against the traffickers. India and Pakistan have agreed to the exchange of information in identifying major operators, hold periodic border meetings between the Border Security Force of India and Pakistan Rangers, and establish direct contact between the custom officials of the two countries.[53] Pakistan has similar cooperative arrangements with Iran to interdict drug traffickers at various points along the common border. Islamabad, Tehran, and UNDCP have been cooperating on drug smuggling on the Pakistan-Iran borders under a tripartite agreement since 1994.[54] Afghanistan, Iran, and Pakistan have agreed on broad measures that include constructing physical barriers along their borders, improving law enforcement capacity, conducting joint counter-narcotic sweeps, and increasing intelligence-sharing about trafficking routes and traffickers.[55] Better coordination among the regional countries may help in interdicting trafficking but as long as cultivation of opium poppy at the present scale continues in Afghanistan, it will have only marginal effects.

THE POLITICAL ECONOMY OF DRUG TRADE

Afghanistan's opium economy generated about $3.1 billion in 2006, which was shared by the farmers, refiners, and Afghan traffickers. The size of the drug economy is roughly half of the licit Gross Domestic Product of $6.7 billion of the country or 32 percent of the entire economy. The farm-gate value that accrued to the primary producers was only $0.76 billion, about one quarter of the drug trade, the rest being skimmed off by refiners and traffickers at the top of the pyramidal chain.[56] Another shocking fact about Afghanistan's drug economy is the number of families and persons involved in its various cycles from cultivating to trafficking. *The World Drug Report 2007* estimates that 2.9 million persons were engaged in poppy cultivation in 2006. This number is equal to 12.6 percent of the country's population. The nationwide percentage obscures the fact that a greater number of peoples and households are participating in the drug economy in provinces like Helmand where poppy cultivation is more concentrated.

The social, political, and security effects of the political economy of drugs are visible all over Afghanistan in the failure of the reconstituted Afghan state to expand its authority, persistence of the warlords, and growing insurgency, mainly in the poppy-cultivating areas. What are the possible linkages between the drug economy and the worsening security situation of the country? First let us look at the massive amount of money, an estimated two billion U.S. dollars each year ending up in the hands of around twenty major drug barons of Afghanistan. They have enough resources to buy security from the warlords or assume that position by maintaining their own militias, as some of them do, bribe low-paid security officials, and share part of their illicit earnings with influential government officials. A strong parallel economy in Afghanistan has created an invisible parallel power structure run by the warlords that promotes criminality in the society.

The drug economy has devastating effects on the security climate of the country. The nexus between crime, drug trafficking, and insurgency is well-established. The actors involved in these three activities have a rational interest to cooperate, help each other, and thus impede the progress of the Afghan state. Rapid growth of the drug economy during the past four years has undermined the political process through a creeping influence in the centers of political power in Kabul and vital state institutions from law-enforcing agencies to judiciary. This has happened at a critical stage while the Afghan state was reviving itself while international support. It is not therefore surprising that the increase in poppy production and the rise in the scale of the drug economy have been parallel to the rise of the Taliban insurgency. The massive revenues that the drug trade has brought to the Afghan traffickers over the past four years has made them the most powerful economic group in the country with the capacity to influence the security environment. This is the class of actors that develops and flourishes with a weak state. They have used the drug money to further strengthen their links with insurgents as well as the government officials with rampant corruption and also extended the patronage and spoil system far and wide in the country. The relative failure of the Afghan government lies both in the corruption in the administrative machinery of the state and the economic power of the drug syndicates to buy off the law enforcement officials.

The reports published in the international press suggest that drug trafficking is not confined to the criminal gangs or some figures of the underworld of Afghanistan. The promise of getting richer, weak laws and prosecution process, and influence peddling have encouraged some members of the Afghan parliament to join the drug cartels or extend protection to their activities. According to a report in the *Newsweek* of January 2006, a large number of governors in the provinces are drug lords, and the foreign diplomats believed "that up to a quarter of the new Parliament's 249 elected members are linked to narcotics production and trafficking."[57] In the same report, Andrew Wilder, who worked for the independent Afghanistan Research and Evaluation Unit, revealed that "at least 17 newly elected M.P.s are drug traffickers themselves, twenty-four others are connected to criminal gangs, forty are commanders of armed groups, and nineteen face serious allegations of war crimes and human-rights abuses."[58]

It is difficult to estimate how much drug money remains in Afghanistan as it has a limited formal banking system, and how much of it is stashed away in the foreign banks close to the country or in the Gulf region. Money laundering is a global phenomenon. The Afghan and regional drug syndicates have international business connections, which they use to transfer proceeds from drug trafficking to the regular economy and from one country to another. Money laundering is much easier in neighboring Pakistan than many other countries.[59] Bad governance in the financial institutions, a culture of corruption, and some governmental policies are responsible for this. Some of the Afghan drug lords might have acquired Pakistani citizenship and have used the following schemes for money laundering:

1. The drug producers and traffickers have greatly benefited from investing in real estate in Kabul and other cities where they put their money in multistory plazas, houses, and shopping centers.
2. Foreign currency accounts in Pakistani banks have provided another secure means for money laundering for two reasons. First, the U.S. dollar is relatively more stable and second, hardly a question is asked regarding the source of income.
3. There is a private *hundi* or *hawala* custodial system, which is akin to financial transfers from banks from one country to another. The agents of the traffickers have established their business in the Middle Eastern countries and have operated from Europe and North America until the tightening of polices on money transfers after the 9/11 terrorist attacks. They offer a higher rate on foreign exchange than banks can to the overseas workers who send remittances to their relatives. They collect the foreign currency abroad and pay the benefiting families in Afghan or Pakistani currency. They make payments in less than twenty-four hours, and even travel long distances to reach the benefiting families in the rural areas of Afghanistan.
4. The drug barons are involved in the regional trade, both legal, and illegal with their center in the Gulf countries. Pakistan's transit facility is misused by the drug traffickers in investing drug proceeds in the third-party goods that are first imported into Afghanistan and then smuggled out to a larger market to Pakistan.

NATIONAL AND INTERNATIONAL INITIATIVES

In recent years, Afghanistan's national initiatives in controlling production and distribution of illegal drugs have largely been influenced by an emerging global consensus against the proliferation of drugs and how they undermine international efforts to stabilize the country. While the Western counternarcotics policies have neither been consistent or effective enough to stem the rising tide of poppy cultivation in Afghanistan, which has reached at an alarming point, there is a debate on what would work and what would not in the political and social conditions of Afghanistan.

One central dilemma the world community faces is how to isolate the drug producers and traffickers from the evolving power structure of the country. As indicated above, some of the drug barons have acquired representative status through elections and they are influential power brokers in the provinces and at the center. A weak government led by President Karzai is more of a hostage than a free agent to manage political affairs impartially. By pressuring Karzai to purge his government of drug lords, some of whom he depends on, his foreign backers do not want to risk further instability. The policies of the United States in the initial phase of the war against the Taliban in seeking support of the warlords and aligning with them have been counterproductive as they have become firmly established. Washington thought that the warlords were the lesser evil and could deliver on fighting against the Taliban, which they did. The warlords, empowered by the Western coalition, turned to investment in poppy to fund their private armies. But their price of this engagement with the criminal elements has been too high as they continue to defy the state and its writ. Fighting against the Taliban and Al Qaeda had greater priority than the antinarcotics policy, which made sense in the political climate of the post-9/11 tragedy. President Hamid Karzai has his own political compulsion for garnering political support. According to Paula Newberg, "desperate for unity, he cultivated warlords to avoid cultivating conflict. Poppy was outlawed, but took over the economy."[60]

A similar doctrine of necessity worked behind American policy toward the Afghan *Mujahideen* when it ignored, or even encouraged, drug production and trafficking by them to finance the resistance against the former Soviet Union. Defeating communism was a higher goal to which everything else was subordinated than keeping Afghanistan drug free. This was in view of the fact that about 70 percent of the Afghan heroin ended up in the streets of Washington's close European allies and some even filtered into its own market.[61] In the present situation of Afghanistan, reconstruction efforts have been undermined by the expansion of drug production and trafficking that has strengthened the warlords with interest in the weak governmental authority. Therefore the first task before the international community is how to strengthen institutions of police, national army, and justice to apprehend and prosecute the drug lords. Their presence in the corridors of power complicates this task as they take ownership of managing institutions from Parliament to the police department. The entire project of postconflict recovery is threatened by the emerging nexus between drug lords and the Taliban insurgency that benefit from the political economy of drugs at two different ends of the production and trafficking chain.

The development of infrastructure, revival of formal agricultural practices, and livelihood of the rural areas is another alternative. Before the series of wars visited upon Afghanistan, the country was more or less self-sufficient in food and it even exported its fruits to the neighboring countries, which it continues to do though at smaller scale. The Afghan farmers turned to poppy cultivation during the Soviet war when the entire system of agricultural credit and supplies through private and governments sources was disrupted. The drug traffickers filled the economic vacuum by providing cash advances and guaranteed buy offs but it was only for poppy cultivation. In conditions of national disorder, the Afghan farmers had a limited choice between starving their families and cultivating poppy to survive. While feeding into war, poppy cultivation played a very important role in filling the vacuum of formal economy and preventing the rural economy for total collapse. Similar considerations are behind tolerance of poppy cultivation that inhibits stricter, harsher measures like large-scale crop eradication, because the farmers who are on the edge of the drug economy will suffer the most.

The real alternative is in greater investment in rural economy, social sector development, and creating job opportunities that would wean away the farmer from poppy cultivation.[62] The success of these initiatives would depend on stability, a secure environment, and an understanding on the part of the farmers that they would not lose much by shifting to legal crops. In other words security and education of the farmers are two primary conditions through which progress can be made on shifting the crop patterns back to a traditional economy.

The poppy cultivation provinces are the hardest hit by the Taliban insurgency and the links among the criminals, traffickers, and the insurgents are the strongest. All three of them are the primary beneficiary of the political economy of illicit drugs. Their stake is more in the absence of the state, anarchy, and disorder than in stability and security. In such conditions, internationally supported development and reconstruction programs have not materialized; several projects have been delayed as the contractors and NGOs have retreated out of the region because of fear of kidnapping and murders. Paradoxically, the Afghan state and international community can establish some degree of influence and regain trust only through reconstruction, development activities, and revival of agricultural infrastructure, which the Taliban insurgents have subverted. There is an interesting finding in the *Afghanistan Opium Winter Rapid Assessment Survey 2007*, which suggests that the 42 percent of the villages that received external assistance cultivated poppy, compared to 50 percent of those that did not get any funding.[63] Development and reconstruction are slow processes in making an impact on the society and still slower in conditions of low-level, unconventional conflict that Afghanistan is experiencing currently. But there is no other viable and long-term alternative than substituting poppy with wheat, vegetables, fruits, and other crops through farm credit, subsidies, development of roads, and irrigation channels and rural industry to generate employment.

The production and distribution networks in and around Afghanistan are integrated and linked with the international drug trafficking networks. The porous borders and graft make it easy for the drug traffickers to smuggle in and out of Afghanistan to other destinations. The problem of drug trafficking is essentially international in character, which requires greater cooperation among regional states and major international players to address this problem at different levels from farms in Afghanistan to the streets of European countries where the only major Afghan product finds its way and is sold.

The growing power of the drug syndicates poses a serious threat to the society, state institutions, and formal economy. Their influence in the corridors of power and open opportunities to invest drug money in business and industry may remove the distinction between legal and illegal economy. The governance and rule of law that are already weak in Afghanistan may further suffer if criminals continue to enter politics and use political offices and patronage to protect their crimes against the Afghan society and humanity at large.

NOTES

1. "Opium vs. Democracy in Afghanistan," (editorial), *The New York Times* (www.nytimes.com), 5 April 2005.

2. See press release of United Nations Office of Drugs and Crime, "Afghan Opium Production up 50 Percent: UN," *Daily Times*, 27 June 2007.

3. President Hamid Karzai has said "We are dealing with narco-terrorism in Afghanistan." See, United States, Congress, House of Representative, Committee on International Relations, *Afghanistan Drugs and Terrorism and U.S. Security Policy*, Hearings, One Hundred and Eighth Congress, 2nd Session (Washington, D.C.: U.S. Government Printing Office, 2004), p. 4.

4. Ibid., p. 1.

5. Ibid., p. 2.

6. Tamara Makarenko argues that the Taliban and Al Qaeda are minor players in the Afghan drug trade, which the transnational criminal groups and international drug mafia dominates. See Tamara Makarenko, "Crime, Terror and the Central Asian Drug Trade," *Harvard Asia Quarterly*, Vol. 6, No. 3, Summer 2002, p. 12.

7. United Nations, Office on Drugs and Crime, *Afghanistan Opium Winter Rapid Assessment Survey 2007* (Vienna: UNODC, February, 2007), p. 6.

8. United Nations, Office on Drugs and Crime, *Afghanistan Opium Winter Rapid Assessment Survey 2005* (Vienna: UNODC, November, 2005), pp. 1–6.

9. Edouard Martin and Steven Symansky, "Macroeconomic Impact of the Drug Economy and Counter-Narcotics Efforts," in eds., Boris Buddenberg and William A. Byrd, *Afghanistan's Drug Industry: Structure, Functionaing and Implications for Counter-Narcotics Policy* (Vienna: United Nations Office on Drugs and Crime and the World Bank, Year N.A.), pp. 26–30.

10. UNDOC, op. cit., November 2005.

11. William A. Byrd and Olivier Jonglez, "Prices and Market Interactions in the Opium Economy," in eds., Boris Buddenberg and William A. Byrd, *Afghanistan's Drug Industry: Structure, Functioning and Implications for Counter-Narcotics Policy*, op. cit., p. 130.

12. Barnett R. Rubin, *The Fragment of Afghanistan: State Formation & Collapse in the International System* (Lahore: Vanguard, 1996), p. 62–73.

13. C. Colin Davies, *The Problem of the North-West Frontier, 1890–1908* (London: Curzon Press, 1932), pp. 26–28.

14. See for instance, a fascinating account, Peter Hopkirk, *The Great Game: The Struggle for Empire in Central Asia* (New York: Kodansha International, 1992).

15. *Afghanistan, Strategic Study #3: The Role of Opium as a Source of Informal Credit* (Islamabad: UNDCP, Afghanistan Programme, January 1999).

16. Anyone arrested with 11 pounds of opium or 30 grams of heroine can be given the death sentence under the Iranian law. *The News*, 18 May 2000.

17. Lt. Gen. (Ret.) Kamal Matinuddin, *Power Struggle in the Hindu Kush (1978–1992)* (Lahore: Wajidalis, 1993), pp. 321–22.

18. K. K. Katyal, "Taliban Encouraging Drugs Production," *Hindu*, 19 October 1996.

19. Lawrence Lifschultz, "Pakistan: The Empire of Heroin," in Afred W. McCoy and Alan A Block, eds., *War on Drugs: Studies in the Failure of U.S. Narcotics Policy* (Boulder: Westview Press, 1992), pp. 319–58.

20. "The Roots of Poppy Problem in Afghanistan," *The News*, 16 May 2000.

21. *Afghanistan, Strategic Study #2: The Dynamics of the Farmgate Opium Trade and the Coping Strategies of Opium Traders* (Islamabad: UNDCP, Afghanistan Programme, October 1998).

22. United Nations Development Programme, *Afghanistan: National Human Development Report 2004: Security with a Human Face: Challenges and Responsibilities* (Islamabad: UNDP, 2004).

23. Hearings, op. cit., pp. 3, 9.

24. United Nations International Drug Control Programme, *Afghanistan: Annual Opium Poppy Survey 1999* (Islamabad: UNDCP, Afghanistan Country Office, date n/a), p. ii.

25. *UNDCP Update* Vol. 01, No. 01 (Vienna: United Nations International Drug Control Programme, 2 January 1997).

26. Ibid., p. v.

27. See, "Taliban Conniving with Drug Traffickers," *The Nation* (Islamabad), 2 March 1999.

28. Ibid.

29. *Afghanistan Annual Poppy Survey 1999*, op. cit., p. 6.

30. *The Friday Times* (Lahore), 21–27 April 2000, p. 5.

31. Imtiaz Gul, "Poppy Cultivation in Afghanistan: An Overview," *The Friday Times*, 27 November–3 December 1998, p. 6.

32. "Drug Danger," *The News* (editorial), 3 March 2000.

33. *The Nation*, 1 March 1999.

34. Ahmed Rashid, "Afghanistan: Drugs for the Infidels: Ruling Militia Encourages Poppy Cultivation for Export," *Far Eastern Economic Review*, 1 May 1997, pp. 25–26.

35. Gretchen Peters, "Taliban Drug Trade: Echoes of Colombia," *Christian Science Monitor*, (on the Web), 1 November 2006.

36. We have taken these figures from UNODC, *Afghanistan Opium Survey 2006*, October 2006.

37. UNODC, *Global Assessment Programme on Drug Abuse (GA), National Assessment of Problem Drug Use in Pakistan 2007*, preliminary results, May 2007.

38. Author visited Habib Nallah, a rainwater drain that runs through the center of Quetta city; found tens of drug addicts injecting, smoking, and sniffing heroin and other drugs openly. 12 June 2006.

39. *UNDCP update* vol. 01, no. 01 (Vienna: United Nations International Drug Control Programme, 2 January 1997).

40. "Pakistan Major Transit Country for Drugs, Says US Report," *The Nation*, 8 March 1997.

41. Sanjiv Sinha, "Indian Chemical Feeding Heroin Boom in Pakistan," *Statesman*, 21 January 1995.

42. *Anti-Narcotic Force Yearly Digest–1997* (Rawalpindi: Directorate General Anti Narcotics Force, June 24, 1998), pp. 5–6.

43. Ibid.

44. Unpublished ANF documents, Rawalpindi, 6 June 2000.

45. *Christian Science Monitor*, 10 March 1999.

46. See a report by Shamim Shahid, "Iran Has Taken Concrete Steps to Stop Drug Trafficking," *The Nation*, 5 May 1999.

47. UNODC, World Drug Report 2007, op. cit., p. 47.

48. *Christian Science Monitor*, 29 February 2000.

49. *The News*, 18 May 2000.

50. MAK Lodhi, "Drug Trade Through New Routes Thriving in Golden Crescent States," *Dawn*, 10 March 1997.

51. UNODC, World Drug Report 2007, p. 47.

52. *The News*, 14 March 2000.

53. "Pact with Pak to Control Drug Trafficking" *The Hindu*, 26 April 1997.

54. *Dawn*, 30 March 1998.

55. "Afghanistan, Iran and Pakistan Agree on Drug Fight Plan," *Daily Times*, 13 June 2007.

56. UNODC, World Drug Report 2007, p. 197.

57. Ron Moreau and Sami Yousafzai, "Afghanistan's Drug Trade is Threatening the Stability of a Nation America Went to War to Stabilize," *Newsweek*, January 2006, pp. 28–31.

58. Ibid., p. 31.

59. Mohammad Saeed Alrai, director Assets Investigation, ANF, "Country Report: Pakistan," an unpublished paper presented at Regional Conference on Money Laundering for South Asia, New Delhi, India, 3–5 March 1998.

60. Paula R. Newberg, "A Drug-Free Afghanistan Not So Easy," *Yale Global Online*, http://yaleglobal.yale.edu/display.article?id=5385, accessed on 11 June 2007.

61. See John K. Cooley, *Unholy Wars: Afghanistan, America and International Terrorism*, op. cit., pp. 126–60.

62. Newberg, "A Drug-Free Afghanistan Not So Easy," op. cit.

63. UNODC, *Afghanistan Opium Winter Rapid Assessment Survey 2007*, pp. 10–11.

7

Afghanistan and the Neighboring States

The reconstruction of fractured states and societies or combating insurgencies effectively always requires goodwill, support, and constructive engagement of neighboring states. If the insurgents find sanctuaries and support bases across the borders with or without the connivance of governments, the postconflict societies find it extremely difficult to revive themselves. This is a lesson that one can easily draw from a number of cases of postconflict reconstruction efforts around the world. There are also many examples that show that internal conflicts never remain domestic affairs; they become externalized with destabilization strategies of antagonistic neighbors.[1] Afghanistan presents a more complex situation because of it geopolitical position, transethnic populations, and a history of rivalry among its neighbors. An even more important factor is three decades of war in Afghanistan, which has an active involvement of the neighboring states in supporting rival groups, locked in a fierce power struggle at one point or another.

Therefore, for explaining what role Afghanistan's neighbors have, or will have, in stabilizing or destabilizing Afghanistan, one must understand the linkages between Afghanistan's internal political dynamics and its geopolitical environment. In recent decades, Afghanistan's geopolitical environment has been shaped by distrust, ambitions, and power politics of the neighboring states. The conflict in Afghanistan, from the revolution and revolt in 1978, to the Soviet war and American-led international action against the Taliban regime, has had a region-wide political and security impact. The events that took place during the three decades of war in Afghanistan also severely affected the security, politics, and internal harmony of Iran, Pakistan, and some of the central Asian states. Adversity and hard times in this region did not respect territorial jurisdictions or state boundaries; there was massive proliferation of arms, inflow, of millions of refugees, and flow of armed insurgents, supported by major international players, in the neighboring states.

Nonstate transnational Islamic militant groups in particular have troubled the security of all neighboring states in varying degrees. Consequently, fear and insecurity were as responsible in shaping the responses neighboring states had to the Afghan conflict, as did their latent and manifest desires to influence the political outcomes of the civil war in their favor. In order to understand the relations of neighboring countries with Afghanistan we need to examine three sets of factors. The first factor is that the Afghan groups, which were interlocked in the civil war, depended on external sources for material and political support. The post-Taliban Afghan regime has not been able to entirely replace those factional linkages. One finds convergence of political and strategic interests between the Afghan groups and their foreign supporters, which they use to influence the weak Afghan state and retain the option of doing business out of the state's control. The second factor is the establishment of independent support networks between Afghan groups and transnational religious, ideological, and ethnic groups from within the region. Afghanistan and other states are finding it hard to challenge the influence of nonstate actors that threaten the traditional order and stability of the nation state. Thirdly, Afghanistan's neighbors have followed predatory policies toward Afghanistan and have exploited many of its vulnerabilities to their advantage. Fears and ambitions of neighboring states have, in the past, fomented rivalry that has worked to the disadvantage of Afghanistan. The intervention by foreign powers in Afghanistan has been both a cause and effect of the conflict among the Afghan groups. The internal confrontation in Afghanistan somewhat mirrored the disagreement among the regional states on the question of organizing political power in Afghanistan, and its future role in the region.

With the removal of the Taliban and the end of civil war, the situation has begun to change. Afghanistan has new major players—the United States, NATO, and a larger international coalition on the scene that has a United Nations mandate to reconstruct the Afghan state. The international presence and interest in reviving Afghanistan has pushed its neighbors out of the power struggle, but since they are a permanent part of Afghanistan's geopolitical system, they are waiting to see how Afghanistan rebuilds itself and what kind of role Afghanistan will play in the region. In the following sections, we will look at the interests, strategies, and policy framework of some of the important neighbors of Afghanistan. We will devote a little more space to Pakistan, since it has played a key role in the politics of Afghanistan.

IRAN

Among the regional states, Iran and Pakistan have been most affected by the Afghan conflict, and in return, have influenced the politics of the Afghan groups in varying degrees. During the Soviet war, their approach toward the Afghan problem was more or less similar. But now they widely differ on almost all aspects of the Afghan problem.

Iran had a lingering fear that once the Soviets were driven out of Afghanistan, the more powerful Pashtun groups would be better placed to reorder the political landscape of the country to their advantage. Iran, hence, made all efforts to ensure a greater representation for the Shia groups in any future political institutions of the Mujahideen resistance. Pakistan did recognize Iran's interest in Afghanistan and regularly consulted Iran on all political and diplomatic initiatives. Curiously, Iran absented itself from the Geneva negotiations that aimed to settle the Afghan problem, insisting that the *Mujahideen* parties should be represented at the negotiating table instead of neighboring states. Since the Geneva parleys were primarily between the Soviet-supported Kabul regime and Pakistan, the Mujahideen groups were kept out. However, Iran did not raise any serious objections to the Geneva talks and fully trusted Pakistan's endeavors to seek Soviet withdrawal. Once it became clear that Moscow would be pulling out its troops from Afghanistan, Iran began to pay more attention to the issue of representation for the Shia groups. The kind and degree of representation given to the Hazara Shia community in political power has been a serious point of contention for Iran. It has supported the demand of the Shia groups that they should be given 25 percent representation in all echelons of political power, a demand that was fiercely contested by all other parties because the Shia population is estimated around 15 percent or below.[2]

After the Soviet defeat in Afghanistan, Iran became more actively involved in the internal conflict of Afghanistan. By that time, its eight-year war with Iraq had also ended, freeing its foreign security policy resources, which were, hence, increasingly focused on building alliances with substate social, ethnic, and ideological forces in the larger Middle East and its non-Arab periphery. Iran has opposed Pakistan on issues, like the composition of a broad-based government, distribution of power among the various parties, and the direction of political change in Afghanistan. Iran extended full support to the Rabbani regime, although it had no mandate to stay in power beyond the eighteen months period during which it was supposed to make preparations for elections and transfer power to the elected government.[3] After the eviction of the Rabbani government in Kabul by the Taliban in September 1996, Iran substantially increased its support to the anti-Taliban coalition, which is comprised the Tajiks, Uzbeks, and the Hazara Shia groups. Gradually, Iran has become one of the major players in the power game of Afghanistan.[4] Iran's policy has been generally influenced by three sets of interests. The first and foremost objective of Tehran's policy is to seek protection of the political interests of the Hazaras. These are a higher representation in any future government, regional autonomy, and the implementation of separate Islamic laws for the Shiite community. Secondly, Iran wants to counterbalance Pakistan's influence in the internal affairs of Afghanistan. It has accused Pakistan of helping the Pashtuns regain their traditional dominance, which Tehran thinks will work against the interests of the ethnic minorities. Iran has carefully cultivated and materially supported the Northern Alliance to defeat the Taliban movement.[5] The third interest is that of geopolitical regional strategy. Iran considers Afghanistan an important element in her regional strategy, through which it seeks to build closer associations with ethnic communities and states that have a Persian lingual and cultural heritage. Such an association also provides economic and political benefits for Tehran.

Iran had troubled relations with the Taliban from the outset. The Taliban was regarded by Iranian clergy as rivals, both politically and on account of conflicting sectarian Sunni and Shiite doctrines that they respectively represent in the Islamic world. The Taliban challenged the regime of Burhanuddin Rabbani, which was supported and sponsored by Iran, which had many foes inside Afghanistan and across the border in Pakistan for not complying with the terms and conditions of the power-sharing agreement that Islamabad and Saudi Arabia had brokered among the Afghan Mujahideen factions. The Taliban was generally perceived to have the backing of Pakistan, which directly threatened Iranian influence in Afghanistan. The Taliban leaders contested and condemned Iranian intervention in supporting various factions of the Northern Front as much as Iran detested the ideology and religious interpretations of the Taliban. Consequently, Afghanistan became yet another battleground of religious schism during the Taliban regime in which Tehran, Riyadh, and many other private groups played a supportive role to their client Afghan factions.

Fueled by anger and conventional hate and inspired by conflicting views about questions of Islam, stability, governance, and peace, the Taliban and Iran-supported groups in the north of the country committed some of the most horrific atrocities against each other.[6] The victims of violence included a large group of Iranians in Mazar-i-Sharif that Iran claimed as diplomats while the Taliban accused them of supervising and assisting commanders and fighters of the Northern Front.[7]

Iran has the aspirations, credentials, and a policy framework to act and project itself as a regional power, but it cannot do so without radically altering the existing power structure of its neighborhood. After a deadly eight years war with Iraq, it changed its geopolitical outlook to transforming the Islamic countries in the adjacent regions according to its vision of revolutionary Islam. Iran's policy toward Afghanistan has reflected a secular interest in political stability of the country, along with the empowering of the Shia community. Iran's response to the American war against the Taliban has been shaped by two factors. Firstly, it is guided by Iran's hostility toward the Taliban regime, which Iran was unable to remove and or directly confront. The policy of indirect confrontation that Iran had followed backfired as the Taliban turned its guns on the beleaguered Shia groups in Afghanistan. Shia groups in Afghanistan were subjected to violence, displacement, and ouster from power. The American war in Afghanistan and the removal of the Taliban regime in a long-term perspective has an unintended positive gain for Tehran. The same has been the case with the later removal of Saddam Hussein and his regime. Iran therefore did not oppose American action against the Taliban and did nothing politically and militarily that would create trouble for the international coalition forces.

The second important reason for Iran's guarded neutrality, which makes it indirectly supportive of the American-led war, was the question of stability and unity of Afghanistan. Iran has for the past five years helped in creating a regional environment that would promote reconstruction and stability of Afghanistan and has not made the foreignness of the forces or occupation an issue yet.[8] Iran has apparently no interest in assisting the Taliban insurgency that has been on the rise during the past few years. The return of the Taliban, with whom Iran nearly went to war when they were in power, is the last thing that Iran would like to see in Afghanistan.

There are wider regional security issues, beyond Afghanistan, that may force Tehran to rethink its neutral stance. With the growing insurgency in Afghanistan, and the presence of the multinational security forces under the umbrella of NATO, the question of confrontation or cooperation between the United States and Iran in stabilizing Iraq and the Gulf region will have an impact on Iran's policy toward Afghanistan. Therefore, an aggressive and hostile attitude of the United States toward Iran on the nuclear issue or influence of the anti-West hardliners in the Iranian foreign policy establishment will change Iran's neutrality and parallel assistance program for reconstruction in Afghanistan into a spoiler.

This is no longer a remote possibility and seems to be happening in Iraq and Afghanistan. Interestingly, Iran quietly supported the removal of the regimes in these countries by the United States–led international coalitions, and the hardliners rejoiced the moment, which they saw as an opportunity to expand their influence. But the challenge faced by Iran and the United States is that they do not have any strategic understanding of the future political and security landscape because of conflicting interests. Iran is a rival and a competitor of the United States in Iraq and Afghanistan, and Iran has the political capacity, on account of its complex webs of religious and political alliances, to create trouble for the Western countries.

Facing increasing threats from the United States, in 2007 Iran began to shift its policy toward Afghanistan with a purpose to raise the costs of American presence in three significant areas. First it began to force tens of thousands of Afghan refugees to leave the country. This increased the pressure and burden on the American-supported Afghan government. Second, although Iran maintained good relations with the new Afghan government, there are reports that Iran has been providing assistance to a new political coalition, the United Front, comprised of the former *Mujahideen* leaders. Thirdly, NATO and other sources have accused Tehran of providing similar types of weapons to the Taliban insurgents that it has been giving to the Shia militants in Iraq.[9] Tehran has no political or security interest in the revival of the Taliban movement or in its recapturing of political power in Afghanistan. This however, does show how Iran can widen its conflict with the United States and hit its adversary at its weakest points.

PAKISTAN

For the past quarter of a century, successive bouts of war in Afghanistan that have devastated its economy, society, and state institutions have further deepened linkages, contacts, and a sense of common stakes between Afghanistan and Pakistan. However, parallel to this feeling of common stakes is the issue of a conflicting definition of what is common between the two countries. This has been the most fundamental and critical problem in Pakistan's relations with Afghanistan primarily for two reasons. First, and foremost, Afghanistan as a nation and country has remained fragmented along regional, sectarian, and ethnic lines, and no group in Afghanistan can authoritatively claim to be a representative of national interests. Afghan groups have been politically polarized and divided into at least two camps; and the choices made by these camps are guided by their material and political need to seek foreign support and involvement of regional and other powers. As a result of the internal confrontation among the Afghan groups, the issue of commonality of interest became a function of the nature of ties between Pakistan and a particular Afghan group or set of groups. It is therefore not only the ethnic definition of what is good for Afghanistan, which cannot in any way be separated from groups' interests in political power, but also the choices that Pakistan made in the Afghan game. Pakistan's image as a friend or enemy of Afghanistan has therefore largely been determined by the degree of closeness to any specific group and the degree of material assistance that Pakistan has provided it to fight its rivals.

PAKISTAN'S KEY ROLE

Pakistan has played a key role in the Afghan conflict both during the Soviet war and after the collapse of the Marxist regime in Kabul. On a broader level, therefore, Pakistan's Afghan policy may be analyzed in two phases: the war of resistance against the Soviet occupation and the subsequent intergroup Afghan civil war, and the post-Taliban politics and security in Afghanistan. The first phase, which started with the Soviet invasion in December 1979 to the Geneva Accords, which were signed in April 1988, Pakistan's goals were centered around vacating the Soviet occupation and helping the *Mujahideen* replace the Marxist government in Kabul. The sudden collapse of the Najibullah regime in April 1992 was a turning point in both the political history of Afghanistan as well as in Pakistan's policy toward that country. A unified and friendly Afghanistan under a broad-based government has been the main concern for Pakistan since 1992. In understanding Pakistan's role one has to look at a wide array of domestic, regional, and international factors that have shaped Pakistan's responses to the political and military situation in Afghanistan.

Pakistan staged a counterintervention in Afghanistan under two considerations. The first one was domestic and the other one was related to the security situation created by the Soviet intervention. Domestically, the military regime of General Zia ul-Haq was isolated and under tremendous stress from the political forces in Pakistan, which wanted him to hold elections and transfer power to the elected government. Internationally, Zia-ul-Haq's regime was seen as brutal and illegitimate. But the Soviet intervention next door in Afghanistan changed all perceptions about Zia-ul-Haq's regime. The military regime in Pakistan exploited the Afghan situation very effectively and used it to gain domestic and foreign support. The foreign support came mainly from the United States and her regional and European allies. Internally, Zia was able to structure an alliance of right-wing religious political parties that shared his views on the Afghan situation and supported his drive for Islamization in the Pakistani society.

On the other hand, Pakistan's security concerns about the Soviet military engagement in Afghanistan were genuine. What would have been Moscow's next move if it succeeded in stabilizing the political situation in Afghanistan? How far would the Soviet Union have gone in encouraging and supporting an allied Afghanistan to raise its historical claim over the Pakistani territories in the Northwest Frontier Province (NWFP)? Would the Soviet Union have used Afghanistan as a base to incite and aid ethnonational movements in Pakistan? These were some of the troubling questions that Pakistan faced and Pakistan had sufficient reasons to fear the Soviet motives. Moscow had been quite hostile toward Islamabad for joining the

American security alliances during the Cold War. It supported Pakistan's rival India, in the war of 1971, and emerged as India's major source of modern weapons and defense technology. Two assumptions defined Pakistan's decision to stand up to the Soviet superpower. First, the scale of the national uprising in Afghanistan was such that no amount of Soviet atrocities fashioned on the pattern of eastern Europe could succeed in suppressing the resistance in Afghanistan. Second, the Soviet Union could be forced out of Afghanistan by raising the economic and military costs of occupation and counterinsurgency campaigns. At the same time, Pakistan responded favorably to any suggestion of a negotiated settlement on two conditions. First, it would not recognize the Soviet-backed regime, nor would it hold any peace talks directly with its representatives. Second, the Soviet Union would unconditionally withdraw its forces from Afghanistan. After tremendous costs and destroying much of Afghanistan, the Soviet Union made virtue out of necessity in agreeing to quit Afghanistan by February 1989 under the Geneva Accords. Pakistan greatly succeeded in achieving its objectives in the first phase of the Afghan conflict.

Pakistan's interest in Afghanistan and its involvement with the *Mujahideen* groups did not end with the departure of the Soviet forces because its objectives were not confined to getting the Soviets out of Afghanistan alone. The Soviet-backed government headed by Najibullah was still in power, to which Pakistan was unwilling to concede legitimacy or enter into any deal for settling the political future of Afghanistan. Not only had the Soviets dumped a large quantity of arms while leaving the country but they also continued assisting their Afghan clients. Pakistan's next move was to install a *Mujahideen* government in Kabul. Pakistan combined military attacks against the border towns like Jalalabad and secretively supported coup plans to get Najibullah out. Under the negative symmetry, meaning that the United States and the Soviet Union would cease giving any assistance to their respective Afghan clients, the Najibullah regime began to crumble from within. The political changes within the Soviet Union sealed the fate of the Afghan communists. Pakistan assembled all the Afghan groups to agree on power-sharing arrangements and form an interim government in April 1992. The meeting produced the Peshawar Accords under which first Sibghatullah Mojeddadi and then Rabbani were installed as interim presidents.

A new phase of civil war began in Afghanistan when Rabbani refused to step down from his office at the end of his tenure toward the end of 1993. In fact, Rabbani's faction and that of Hikmatyar had been at war from the very beginning when Rabbani had refused to share power with Hikmatyar. Rabbani also used force to eject other groups from Kabul, which included *Hizb-i-Wahdat* and *Jumbesh-i-Milli* led by Uzbek warlord Abdul Rashid Dostum. Pakistan kept shifting its support from one Pashtun group to another in order to put pressure on Rabbani to honor the Peshawar Accord and to stop his transitional government from tilting toward India and other regional powers. Ahmed Shah Masud and Rabbani were unhappy with Pakistan for supporting their rival, the Hizb and its leader, during and after the war of resistance and wanted to use Iran, Russia, and India as new levers to contest Pakistan's influence in Afghan politics. Pakistan repeatedly reminded Afghanistan of the sacrifices it had made for liberating Afghanistan and supporting it by giving shelter to refugees and providing arms and money to their forces. It seems these leaders were not punctilious about expressing gratitude to a former benefactor in the midst of being locked in a bitter struggle for power. In a fit of anger over the killing of four Afghan hijackers on a school bus in Islamabad, they organized an attack on the Pakistan Embassy in Kabul, set it on fire, killing one employee and injuring many others, including the ambassador, in the summer of 1994. Afghan relations with Pakistan became frosty thereafter and Pakistan began to explore other possibilities, along with supporting Hikmatyar. Pakistan was more concerned about Rabbani and Masud inviting Indian technicians and intelligence operatives in the Afghan air force and other military installations. The creeping back of Russian and Indian influence in an Afghanistan, which had been liberated after a massive loss of money and blood at the hands of the Afghan communist and the Soviet intelligence agencies, was the last thing Pakistan could expect would happen.

COURTING THE TALIBAN

Pakistan was very eager to open up the Afghan route to central Asian states, and see the return of the three million Afghan refugees that were housed on its land, but without peace among the warring Afghan factions and stability in Afghanistan it could gain neither of the two. The pressures that it exerted on the Rabbani government, through Hikmatyar, pushed the transitional government further toward Iran, Russia, and India, which were eager to support Rabbani against his Pashtun rivals who had close links with Pakistan. With a new bout of civil war, fragmentation of the country, and different regions being controlled by rival warlords, the internal conditions in Afghanistan further worsened. The *Mujahideen* commanders who were loosely affiliated with the major resistance parties became autonomous actors. Without the lever of arms and money funneled through Pakistan, they turned to arms-trafficking, drug-trafficking, taxing transport, and extorting businessmen as new sources of revenue. The central authority of the Rabbani government became confined to a few sections of Kabul city, which itself was under constant rocket attack. However, Kabul suffered complete devastation only after the fall of the Najibullah government in April 1992.[10] The ordinary Afghans, who saw some sign of hope with the departure of the

Soviet forces and the fall of communist regime, were utterly frustrated to see their country go through another phase of destructive war. Frustration with the former resistance parties, their leaders, and former commanders who had by then turned into warlords, was widespread and genuine among the Afghan population inside the country and living in exile. This frustration was perhaps higher in the vast and greatly fragmented Pashtun areas than in other regions, since the Pashtuns had suffered greater destruction and physical dislocation than any other group in the country. While the former *Mujahideen* parties kept fighting turf wars in and around Kabul, the ethnic and local warlords divided the country into fiefdoms and kept the restive population under control at gunpoint.

The excesses of the local warlords in the south of the country in the Kandhar region attracted the attention of the local clergy members who had gone back to teaching Islam to their old and new Taliban (students) after waging a war against the communists. The leading clergy or *ulema* of Afghanistan were part of the resistance movement and were at the forefront of mobilizing support for the war and recruiting young fighters from their *madrasa* (Islamic school) networks. During the Soviet-Afghan war, they had closed down their religious institutions, arguing that fighting in the holy war against the Soviets who had invaded the country, was more urgent—both in the religious as well practical terms, than mere imparting of education. The ulema in Afghanistan have had a strong social base, more perhaps in the Pashtun areas than other regions, and *sufi* (mystic) and madrasa associations have existed with the local population showing tremendous reverence to them. It is a contentious issue whether the local chieftain or the religious scholars enjoyed more respect, loyalty, and following in the Pashtun territory than other regions.[11] But the fact is that the ulema in Pashtun society have emerged as an integral part of the power arrangements, and their sphere of influence has expanded with the spread of Deobandi and Wahabbi religious beliefs and practices.

The war against the Soviet Union forced the leading Afghan ulema and their students to fight part time and to relocate their madrasa institutions in and around the refugee population in Pakistan. They concentrated their efforts mainly in the Pashtun areas of Balochistan and the NWFP where they not only had similar ethnic groups but also had former teachers, colleagues, and peers as their main support base. The finances for the maintenance and expansion of the madrasa networks came from the local communities, the Islamic Nongovernmental Organizations (NGOs) and charities from the Middle Eastern countries, and from the refugees despite their difficult economic conditions. The madrasa networks were the only large-scale educational institutions that gave shelter, food, and education to hundreds of thousands of orphans who did not have anybody to take care of them. Most of the latter-day Taliban were graduates of these madrasa who grew up and socialized in a purely religious and conservative environment. Their world outlook, ideology, attitude toward other religions, and sects of Islam, views about the West, and political culture were shaped at a very impressionable age. They had never been exposed to any alternative view of religious, or world affairs. Their mental and intellectual conditioning was quite firm, after which they took up arms against their political foes in Afghanistan.

The tradition of settling the question of power through armed struggle is as old as the formation of the Afghan state itself; but such armed incursions were always led by the tribal chiefs, members of the oligarchy, or the Afghan kings themselves. In some cases, they enlisted the support of the clergy to gain religious sanction to their quest for power, but always kept the ulema in a secondary position. The ulema were seldom involved directly or in a leading position in waging a war to capture political power in the country. Why did the Taliban, which included the top clergy and its students, take up arms and how did they succeed in capturing Kabul, defeating the *Mujahideen* rivals and bottling up the forces of the Northern Front in a narrow corner of the country? This question is at the center of all studies done on the rise of the Taliban movement in Afghanistan. But they usually have different explanations for the phenomenon. The most convenient explanation of the emergence of the Taliban and its quick victories is that Pakistan equipped, financed, and guided the Taliban's struggle for advancing its own interests. Although we cannot dismiss the Pakistani factor in the growth and military success of the Taliban movement, we should also look at the internal and regional environment in Afghanistan. Pakistan's political and strategic interests and the situation in and around Afghanistan pushed it toward the Taliban and Pakistan emerged as the most vital source of support for them. This support included diplomatic recognition, allowing the Taliban to use Pakistani madrasa and mosque networks to raise funds and recruit fighters. Whether the Arab and Pakistani contingents in the Taliban militia made any difference is a controversial matter. Their presence alone suggests that foreign actors in Afghanistan were deliberately allowed to come in due to political considerations. There was hardly any check from the Pakistani side on the cross-border movement of war-fighting materials, equipment, vital life-supporting resources, or movement of men in either direction. What type of financial or military assistance was provided and at what scale the government of Pakistan extended support to the Taliban is not publicly known, but no serious student of Pakistan's Afghan policy would rule it out. In the absence of public scrutiny and lack of transparency in the dealing of the governments in such matters, the information remains the prerogative of a few. While concealing facts helps the policy, it also hurts the policy by creating an exaggerated and inflated assessment of a country's involvement. Pakistan is no exception to this. Pakistan's contribution to the

Taliban both official as well private, political, or economic, in the way of hard material assistance or in the shape of soft social support, evidenced by the constant flow of Pakistani and Arab fighters was perhaps substantial. But our contention is that the foreign support Pakistan extended to the Taliban movement should not obscure us from the internal and regional environments that shaped the Taliban movement. Almost every analyst of the Taliban phenomenon has focused on the religious and ideological aspects, ignoring the ethnic considerations behind the popularity of the Taliban movement. Why was it that the Taliban militia expanded like a whirlwind in the Pashtun parts of Afghanistan, and were able to capture them without a single fight, after which they rolled on to capture Kabul? Where did the Pashtun warlords, the former *Mujahideen* fighters, and the local chieftains go and why did they not pose any challenge to the Taliban?

There was a strong resentment among the Pashtun that power in Afghanistan had passed on to the Tajiks and there was no leader or party that could deliver power back to the Pashtuns. The decade-long war against the Soviet Union had transformed ethnic relations, and this change could be viewed as more significant than either the defeat of communism or the communists in Afghanistan.[12] The Taliban was the only organized force to do exactly what the Pashtuns had wanted, i.e., change the power-sharing arrangements in Afghanistan. It was for this reason that the Pashtuns threw their weight behind the Taliban. Some would also argue that the Afghans were exhausted by the war and they hardly had any will to fight the new force (the Taliban) that had emerged. Also, the Pashtuns did not really have any affiliations or love left for the Masud-Rabbani combination in Kabul to do anything that would stop the Taliban. The political and military vacuum in the country, the loss of hope in the *Mujahideen* parties, political fragmentation, and the chaotic economic and security conditions played a significant part in the popularity of the Taliban.

Pakistan was an important regional player in the Afghan power game, and as indicated previously, it supported the Taliban movement to checkmate its regional rivals and keep itself in a position of greater influence than others. Pakistan's public posturing regarding Afghanistan asserted that Pakistan sought a unified, peaceful, and friendly Afghanistan. This three-in-one strategy has defined Pakistan's Afghan policy for more than two decades. Pakistan has argued that politically fragmented, anarchical, and unfriendly Afghanistan would menace Pakistan's security environment. Even during the reign of the Taliban, Pakistan tried to promote the idea of a negotiated settlement that would bring about a broad-based government and would enable the sharing of power among all Afghan groups. It sought the involvement of the United Nations in brokering peace among the Afghan groups.[13] Pakistani diplomats kept shuttling between Mazar-i-Sharif, the power center of the northern coalition, and Kandhar, the political base of the Taliban movement, to bring the two sides to a negotiating table.[14] Also, Pakistan made several efforts to convene a conference of regional countries to promote a consensus on the political future of Afghanistan. In all these efforts, Pakistan faced tremendous difficulties from its Islamic neighbors and the Afghan opposition to the Taliban rule. Iran, Tajikistan, Uzbekistan, and Turkmenistan all accused Pakistan of supporting the Taliban movement. Iran, another player with a long history of involvement and regional ambitions, was quite vehement in peddling the theory that Saudi Arabia and the United States financed the Taliban movement and Pakistan played the role of an intermediary between the Taliban and these countries.[15]

But why did Pakistan move away from the traditional *Mujahideen* parties that it supported for fifteen long years and began to support their rivals in the Taliban movement? Pakistan's disappointment with the Rabbani government was quite obvious as it failed to maintain a good degree of influence in Kabul. Professor Rabbani and Ahmed Shah Masud, the two prominent and most powerful leaders of the Mujahideen government, had serious complaints against Pakistan's Afghan policy. They were irked by Islamabad's continued assistance to their political rival Gulbedin Hikmatyar, who had established his headquarters in Charasiab, which placed Kabul under constant threat of his rocket attacks. Hikmatyar never spared any opportunity to attack and weaken the Rabbani government. Rabbani and Masud blamed Pakistan for whatever Gulbedin Hikmatyar did to them. There is enough evidence to suggest that Pakistan wanted to get the Rabbani government replaced by Gulbedin Hikmatyar since he had proved to be the most reliable and closest ally of Pakistan during the anti-Soviet war of resistance. There are two other reasons that explain Pakistan's preference for Hikmatyar. Rabbani and Masud had been pushed by Pakistan's constant support to Hikmatyar who had joined the Iranian camp. Russia and the two adjacent central Asian states, Uzbekistan and Tajikistan, also formed an alliance with the Rabbani government. India, which had been very eager to enter the Afghan political scene, sensed greater opportunity with the growing alienation of the Rabbani government with Pakistan. New Delhi used its influence in Tehran to build bridges with the Mujahideen government in Kabul and began to extend technical, and in some areas, intelligence support. Loss of influence with the Mujahideen government and its slipping away to the group of rival powers further raised the stakes of Gulbedin Hikmatyar among the managers of Pakistan's Afghan policy. The second and more important reason was ethnic, as Gulbedin Hikmatyar with all the pretensions of leading an all-Afghan party, *Hizb-i-Islami*, was largely Pashtun in character having deeper ties to the Pashtun religious groups across the border in Pakistan. The Pashtuns, being the largest ethnic group that had historically controlled Kabul and its various dynasties that had ruled Afghanistan, had a feeling that power had shifted away from them to the non-Pashtun minorities who were dominant in the Mujahideen government led by Rabbani and Masud. Both of them were Tajiks, the second largest ethnic group in the country that the Pashtun culturally looked down upon. Hikmatyar led the strongest, better organized and equipped fighting force which had the ability to topple the regime in Kabul. His political capacity to rally the Pashtun tribes around him added significance to Pakistan's betting on him as the winning horse. In an atmosphere of growing regional rivalry, the more the Kabul regime moved to the opposite powers, the more Pakistan became aligned with Gulbedin Hikmatyar, allowing him a flow of money and weapons.

At the open diplomatic level, Pakistan kept the pretensions of neutrality, trying to broker peace between Hikmatyar and Rabbani. It used the emergence of the Taliban movement (in its formative phase) to bring Hikmatyar and Rabbani together against this new force that seemed to be gaining ground in and around the volatile Kandhar region. Qazi Husain Ahmad, leader of the Jamat-i-Islami of Pakistan, with the tacit support and blessings of the government of Pakistan traveled to Kabul in 1994 to seek reconciliation among the Mujahideen parties, especially between *Jamiat* and *Hizb*, led respectively by Rabbani and Hikmatyar. Like many earlier initiatives of the Pakistanis this bid to end the feud among the Mujahideen parties ended in failure. At this point Pakistan began to reassess its relationship with Hikmatyar, as he had failed to deliver what he had promised, and was not able to recapture Kabul and return it back to the control of Pashtun-dominated groups. Due to the high emphasis on the Islamist leanings of Hikmatyar and his party, the *Hizb*, the ethnic factor of the party has been ignored almost by all writers who have published anything on that period of Afghanistan's political history. Hikmatyar was known more by his over-exaggerated character of Islamic fundamentalism than his Pashtun roots. Pashtun tribes supported Hikmatyar more than any other group because his forces were better equipped and organized; he was a better paymaster and had enjoyed greater support from Pakistan than his rivals. The Pashtun tribes and Pakistan were the twin pillars of support of Hikmatyar, but they had later began to move away from the *Mujahideen* parties toward the Taliban, who they taken not taken seriously in the early stages of its development.

Pakistan's interest in the Taliban government was pragmatic, not ideological. They were strong enough to provide stability in the Pashtun areas of Afghanistan, which was important for Pakistan's security. The Taliban also ended the Indian influence on Afghanistan, and raised Pakistan's hope for a gas pipeline from Turkmenistan and trade possibilities with central Asian states. But supporting the Taliban was not without domestic and foreign policy costs. At the domestic front, Islamic extremism and its links with the Taliban grew menacingly and raised fears of Pakistan falling under the reign of religious political parties. This has somewhat materialized with the electoral success of the MMA, a coalition of religious parties in the 2002 elections. These parties have increased their political space using the defeat of the Taliban and have consequently emerged as a dominant force in Balochistan and the NWFP. The MMA's success is partly based on sympathy for the Taliban and anti-American sentiment, but largely it is due to popular disenchantment with the nationalist and mainstream political parties in Pakistan. The pro-Taliban feelings still run deep in Pakistan and go well beyond the Pashtun territories, and this will remain an important force in the political process of Pakistan irrespective of what shape it takes in the coming years.

In the area of foreign policy, even though the strategic partnership with the Taliban placed Pakistan in a somewhat better position, the alliance gave rise to other complex problems. Rivalry with Iran and central Asian states grew more intense and became unmanageable. Since the world community saw Taliban rule as extremely harsh, medieval, and discriminatory toward women and minorities, Pakistan's association with them caused major image and policy problems for Pakistan. The Taliban rule that was essentially security oriented did not earn any international support for reconstruction of the country, as a result of which millions of refugees could not be repatriated. In the end, involvement with the Taliban proved to be a messy affair for Pakistan and Pakistan gained very little from its policy of Taliban support. Pakistan's dream of opening up trade with central Asia and building gas pipelines has remained unrealized. Additionally, there was a sentiment of passive hostility in that region against Pakistan for the support it gave to the Taliban. The United States, European countries, and even China, its closest ally, were offended by Pakistan's failure to influence policies or politics of the Taliban on any issue. Even in the face of international isolation and harsh criticism Pakistan found it extremely difficult to extricate itself from the pro-Taliban policy, changing its policies only after the Al Qaeda terrorists with links in Afghanistan struck the Pentagon in Washington, D.C., and the World Trade Center towers in New York on 11 September 2001. These tragic events changed some of the fundamentals of world politics, and Pakistan, being a backer of the Taliban, could not escape a tremendous fallout on its domestic and foreign policy orientations.

PAKISTAN'S DEFINING MOMENTS

The fast movement of events in the wake of the terrorist attacks in New York and Washington presented a difficult diplomatic terrain to negotiate for Pakistan. Essentially, it had only two options: to stay an ally and supporter of the Taliban or join the American-led international coalition against terrorism. Realistically, there was nothing in between these two alternatives, even genuine attempts to find a neutral course would not have earned any credibility with the world community and would have damaged Pakistan's national security interests. Triggered by public anger, humiliation, and the scale of human tragedy, the immediate reaction of the United States left no room to maneuver for Islamabad.

It would be redundant to overemphasize the point that statecraft, strategic decisions, and pursuit of national interests require prudence, cool reflection, and careful weight of the costs and benefits of various alternatives. This amounts to what, in policy-making jargon, is known as rational choice theory. By calculating risks and payoffs of the two options and after consulting with every section of the power structure of the government, General Pervez Musharraf made the right decision in supporting the United States' new war against terrorism—which was directed against Pakistan's former ally, the Taliban. It was a timely decision dictated by Pakistan's prudence and difficult circumstances. Any delay or margin of error would have taken the initiative away from Pakistan and perhaps might have pushed Pakistan to the brink of diplomatic and even strategic disaster. The government, understanding the gravity of the situation, the intensity of the international revulsion against terrorism, and global sympathy and support for the United States, easily read the grave dangers that wavering, hedging out, or riding on the public's emotions could pose to national interests.

A misstep would have provided India the opportunity to lead a formidable international coalition of forces against Afghanistan, placing Pakistan on the hit list. Had such a situation unfolded, Pakistan might have suffered incalculable losses that could have included destruction of its nuclear assets. In Pakistan's immediate interests, turning its back on the Taliban and going along with the United States meant the collapse of India's attempt to categorize Pakistan with the Taliban, and as a source of international terrorism, and to declare Pakistan as a rogue state. Pakistan's decision to fight a common war against terrorism brought it back to the center stage, and, for the second time in twenty years, it is a frontline state, this time, against international terrorism. The nature of war against the faceless enemy, who may be living next door and may have the ability to cause colossal damage, required strategic partnership with countries like Pakistan that are close to the sources of trouble.

Therefore, Pakistan was a natural choice as a strategic partner in the war against terrorism. Pakistan has assisted the United States and other allies in a variety of ways, offering its bases for reconnaissance and rescue operations, extending logistic support to the American troops operating in Afghanistan, providing intelligence resources and airspace for strikes against the Taliban and Al Qaeda targets. There are two other important areas of cooperation that also need to be mentioned. First, the denial of Pakistani territory to the retreating Taliban and Al Qaeda fighters was a crucial step in preventing them from claiming sanctuary with their comrades in Pakistan. For this purpose, the United States and Pakistan set up joint patrolling of the borders, and Islamabad deployed troops in some areas of the tribal belt bordering Afghanistan for the first time in history. Pakistani concentration on the Afghan border swelled to 100,000 troops along its border around Tora Bora in March 2002, when the United States was conducting its largest military operation against the Taliban and Al Qaeda forces in eastern Afghanistan.[16] The substantial numbers of Pakistani troops that remain there are assisted by the technical means provided by the United States in checking infiltration. In such a difficult, long mountainous terrain, it was a difficult operation that succeeded in netting hundreds of Al Qaeda members. All the same, quite a few members of Al Qaeda did succeed in crossing over the border to take shelter in Karachi and other densely populated towns. The second important and perhaps most long-term impact of Pakistani cooperation with the United States relates to the hunt for terrorists hiding in Pakistan. Through joint operations the Pakistani authorities and the FBI have arrested several leading Al Qaeda members. Many Al Qaeda members are on the run and now there is evidence that Pakistani religious extremists have organized terrorist networks of their own to carry out attacks against foreigners and Western interests in the country. The joint Pakistan–United States operations against them may continue for some time.[17] The fight against terrorism in central Asia is going to be of a long duration, and Pakistan will remain a critical participant until the situation in Afghanistan stabilizes and the region around it, including Pakistan itself, makes a peaceful transition to stable political order.

SEEKING NEW PARTNERSHIP WITH AFGHANISTAN

It has been a difficult task for Pakistan to forge new ties with the new rulers of Afghanistan for a number of reasons. Pakistan has an image of being a strong supporter of the Taliban and there is considerable evidence that Pakistan allowed supplies of material and its men to assist the religious militia to defeat their ethnic and sectarian rivals in Afghanistan. This has proved to be a psychological barrier for the international coalition in the way of accepting Islamabad as a partner. The leaders of the Northern Front in particular have been very hostile, since they attribute a large amount of their territorial loss, human suffering, and misery indirectly to Pakistan.[18] The late Ahmed Shah Masud and his followers from the Panjsher valley, who hold major positions in the Karzai administration, consider Pakistan responsible for the unending civil war in Afghanistan. Their animosity against Pakistan runs very deep. In June to July 2002, there were a number of stories, confirmed by central Asian diplomats, circulating in the national and international press that the Northern Front warlords sold out thirty or more Pakistani prisoners to India, who were allegedly flown out from Dushanbe, the capital of Tajikistan.[19] This caused outrage in Pakistan and has further strengthened the view that the Northern Front leaders hold a prejudice against Pakistan and its citizens. The Northern Front leaders have kept thousands of Pakistani Taliban in their private prisons, tortured them severely and later released them on receipt of payment of huge ransom by their family members.[20] The released prisoners have told unthinkable stories of torture and reported how thousands of them died in containers without a single hole to breathe from, while being transported. Every Pakistani Taliban, irrespective of his motivation to go and fight against the Northern Front, has violated Afghan sovereignty; but the view in Pakistan and among the government circles is that the Taliban should have been treated as prisoners of war with all the protection of rights and punishments under the international law. There are still Pakistani prisoners in the captivity of the warlords and even the intervention of the Karzai government has not succeeded in getting them released. Karzai and many of his advisers and cabinet ministers from the Pashtun areas have been eager to mend fences with Pakistan and start a new chapter. Karzai chose Pakistan as his first foreign destination after assuming the chairmanship of the Afghan interim administration. While visiting he asserted that "we, Afghan, have nothing but goodwill for Pakistan, and it is from the heart. We don't have to put it into writing or express it in any other form."[21]

Pakistan for its part has tried to reassure all factions in Afghanistan that it has a new outlook and that it would not side with any faction nor would it allow the use of its territory for any hostile action against the new government in Kabul. During the period from the launching of the military strikes to the Bonn Agreement among the Afghan groups in December 2001, Pakistan has tried to seek assurances from the United States and other partners in the war against terrorism that Pakistan's interests in Afghanistan would not be neglected. While political stability, political and economic reconstruction, and peace are old concerns of Pakistan, it wanted better understanding and accommodation of interests of the Pashtun majority in the post-Taliban political arrangements. Islamabad used its influence indirectly by pushing the idea that the neglect or alienation of the Pashtun majority would bring about instability and insecurity. A feeling of alienation among the Pashtuns does exist but with Hamid Karzai as the head of the transitional government and the cooptation of other Pashtuns into decision-making and power-sharing arrangements, the Pashtuns are better off now than at any other time during the past twenty years.

The Northern Front leaders who hold key positions in the new government have slowly reassessed the need to forge relations with Pakistan on pragmatic grounds. It was the combined influence of Karzai, and a gesture of goodwill to Pakistan on the part of Abdul Rashid Dostam, the Uzbek warlord, that he released 400 Pakistani prisoners in May 2002 in addition to the 500 that he released earlier.[22] The Afghans understand better than they did in the early 1990s that the economy of the eastern and southern parts of Afghanistan is integrated with that of Pakistan. Pakistan offers the most economical, shortest, and safest transit route and is a major source of supplies for reconstruction of physical infrastructure. However, there are still 1.8 million refugees on Pakistani soil waiting to be repatriated. The existing problems, including the fight against terrorism and the prospects of Afghanistan's economic revival and stability, are tied up with Pakistan more than any other neighbor. Pakistan has made conscious efforts on a sustained basis to cultivate relations with the new leaders of Afghanistan. It has been a strong advocate in assisting Afghanistan's recovery in world forums and has pledged $100 million in assistance over a period of five years.[23] It has already disbursed $18 million to this end. It has also allowed liberal donations and sale of wheat from its surplus stocks and other supplies on a regular basis, coupled with access to ports, roads, and railways, which are being used for reconstruction activities.[24]

Relations between the two countries have improved substantially. The government leaders of the two countries have been regularly visiting each other and they are engaged in high-level consultation. Some of the mistrust and bitterness that they felt toward each other is gone, but there is still more work to be done. For this they have taken the route of economic cooperation in furthering mutual interest. There are good signs that they are succeeding in this respect. The bilateral trade has gone up. In July to November, 2002, Pakistan exported goods worth $165 million to Afghanistan compared to $185 million in the entire fiscal years of 2001 to 2002.[25] Imports from Afghanistan also registered an increase during this period from $55 million for the previous year to $27 million in the first four months.[26] The two countries have revived the Turkmenistan, Afghanistan, and Pakistan gas pipeline project, which was thrown into cold storage after UNOCOL, a United States–based consortium of companies withdrew from the project. They also announced the signing of a landmark tripartite agreement on 27 December 2002, to construct a 1,400-kilometer pipeline from Daulatabad gas fields in Turkmenistan to Multan in Pakistan. The $2.7 billion project would immensely contribute to the economy of Afghanistan and integrate the economies of south and central Asian regions. The pipeline is planned to be extended in the future to the central areas of India.

There are a number of problems that the two countries have yet to resolve. Repatriation of refugees, release of Pakistani prisoners from Afghan jails, and transit trade facilities will be on the top of the coming years' agenda. Pakistani prisoners are being released, though at a slow pace, and Pakistan is not averse to punishing those involved in crimes against Afghan citizens. They have reached an understanding to expedite a process that will include the release of Afghans from Pakistan prisons. The issue of refugees is troublesome; Pakistan has hosted more than 3 million refugees in the past, and there are an estimated 1.8 million in the country. Most of the refugees wish to return home with or without assistance from the United Nations High Commission for Refugees, which has been funding their return. Over 1.2 million have gone back voluntarily during the past year. But the flood of returning refugees has already caused economic and social problems, since the interim government lacks the resources to rehabilitate more of them. Recently, Afghanistan and Pakistan reached an agreement to facilitate refugee repatriation in phases over the next three years. Conditions of war, peace, and economic opportunity will determine whether the refugees return home to Afghanistan or stay in Pakistan or whether more reenter Pakistan or not. Therefore, Pakistan's vital interest lies in the stability and peace of Afghanistan, which would remove the burden of the refugees on Pakistan's labor market, utilities, and services.

The transit trade issue between Afghanistan and Pakistan is as old as the independence of Pakistan. Landlocked Afghanistan has right of transit through Pakistan, which was recognized through a bilateral agreement of 1965. However, Pakistan has terminated this facility or tried to control the list of items that Afghanistan can import through Pakistan on occasion to use as political and economic leverage. In recent decades and years, the issue has been of the reexportation of third-party goods back to Pakistan—which has been causing massive damage to its local industry and revenue—revenue that it could otherwise collect in customs duties. The volume of this informal trade is very large, estimated to be about $3 billon, and it involves Pakistani traders and the connivance of Pakistani custom officials as well. Afghanistan wants an unfettered transit trade, and Pakistan wants to ensure that whatever is imported through Pakistan stays in Afghanistan and is consumed there. There is a running dispute on the list of items that Afghanistan can import. This will continue to be a problem until Pakistan puts itself in order, as most of the Afghan transit goods are sold openly in its markets.[27]

For the past few years, there has been a lot of debate in the Western and domestic media about how serious Pakistan's President Pervez Musharraf has been about defeating the Taliban insurgency. This debate has taken two strands. The first line of argument is that Musharraf is either not in control of the intelligence agencies or he is being kept in the dark about the involvement of some persons within the Inter Services Intelligence (ISI) with the transborder movement of Pakistani and Afghan Taliban or directly extending support to the Taliban.[28] Musharraf on different occasions has vigorously rejected this view, saying that anybody who blames the ISI of involvement in Afghanistan is casting aspersions on his integrity, and that the agency would not do a thing or hide anything without his knowledge.[29] In our view, Pakistan has one of the best organized, tightly controlled, and commanded intelligence networks in the world. The talk of intelligence agents on the loose, freely operating or advancing any agenda other than that of the government, doesn't fit the history and the profile of the agencies.

The second strand of accusations is more serious, that Pervez Musharraf has changed his tracks on Afghanistan, and that Pakistan is no longer interested in the stability of the Karzai regime. Since the reemergence of the Taliban as a coherent guerrilla force, Afghanistan and the international coalition fighting against the Taliban have repeatedly pointed their fingers at Pakistan. Why would Pakistan change its policy after catching and handing over hundreds of Taliban and Al Qaeda suspects to the United States and having lost more 700 security personnel in the fights with the pro-Taliban tribes in the Waziristan region bordering with Afghanistan? The accusation of change of priorities and the charge of not doing enough doesn't look plausible prima facie. But there has been some deep rethinking in Pakistan about the political and security costs of being the frontline state in the war on terror. In a first reversal, Pakistan decided to end its military campaign against the pro-Taliban tribes in September 2006 by singing a peace accord with them. The accord has been the subject of controversy for withdrawal of the security forces to their fixed positions, leaving the lawless region to tribal chiefs, clergy, and the Taliban fighters.

Pakistan justified its Waziristan deal on grounds of pragmatism and on account of assurances that the tribes would not provide sanctuary to the Taliban or to foreigners hiding in the mountains. Fierce fighting broke out in April 2007 between the tribes and the Uzbek militants that were residing in the region since the end of the Taliban regime. Hundreds of fighters lost their lives on both sides in some of the worst clashes.[30] This fight may give a different interpretation to the Waziristan deal, and supports the notion that the deal was more about ousting the Uzbeks and Arabs, who are affiliated with Al Qaeda, from the region than hampering the movement of the Taliban.

The shift in Pakistan's policy from stopping the Taliban from crossing the border in either direction to neglecting their links with the private Pakistani groups or giving them support cannot be entirely ruled out in the changing circumstances of Afghanistan and the dimming prospects of any victory for the United States in Iraq. The Iraq debacle has badly exposed the weakness of the United States both in terms of sustainable domestic support for war or the ability of the U.S. forces to engage in asymmetrical warfare in Afghanistan.[31] The growing perception in the region among the governments and the insurgents fighting against foreign military forces in Afghanistan is that the United States and its allies may not stay for too long. The Taliban insurgents have time, territory, and supportive populations, which they believe would be assets to raise American costs of war and force it to rethink its nation- and state-building enterprise. This thought might have forced the

Pakistani policy makers to rethink their long-term interests and consider which social groups in Afghanistan would be their allies in the regional rivalry, which will most probably be exacerbated with the withdrawal of U.S. and NATO forces. The Pashtuns have emerged as the focal point of Pakistan's strategy to secure its interests in Afghanistan.

CENTRAL ASIAN STATES

The independence of central Asian republics after the breakup of the Soviet Union in 1991 has added three more countries to the list of Afghanistan's neighbors and consequently to its troubles. The central Asian societies have evolved on a different pattern than Afghanistan, which remains essentially feudal and tribal in character. Under the Soviet rule central Asia went through a process of modernization and political change that has produced new patterns of political leadership. However the institutional thinking of the state in central Asia is patterned on the old Soviet regime that is not willing to accept political pluralism and views dissent as a security threat.

The new leaders belong to the class of individuals who benefited from the Russification of education and the patronage of the Communist Party. After independence, they have retained links with the Russian Federation, and in the field of national security, they have entered into wide-ranging agreements. In this difficult process of state formation and promotion of separate national identities, they have relied heavily on Russian protection, while exploring alternative external linkages to balance Russian dominance. Russian forces remain in all central Asian states allegedly under mutual arrangements.

The Russian military presence in central Asia serves two important objectives. One, it provides internal security and an assurance that no state in the region would exploit internal political vulnerabilities of these states. Second, it signals the Russian interest in retaining central Asia as a sphere of influence. Given the density of past interactions with Russia and the continuing dependence on the Russian market and outlets to the rest of the world, the central Asian states may not be able to delink themselves from Moscow. Although state and nation building would require them to diversify sources of support and lessen their dependence on Russia, it would be a slow and calculated process based on tangible benefits. Afghanistan presents to them both a barrier and a bridge to the outside world away from the Russian metropolis. A peaceful, friendly and noninterventionist Afghanistan may be the bridge to south and southwest Asian regions, while the civil war there may block their access to alternative routes for the export of energy resources that they have in abundance. If they cross the Afghan bridge, there is a one-billion-people-strong market in south Asia starved of energy resources at a stage of economic takeoff. Therefore, central Asian states have a natural interest in the political developments and power transitions in Afghanistan.

The ethnic polarization in Afghanistan and the emerging divide between the Pashtun majority and ethnic minorities of the north seem to have dragged the central Asian states into the civil war. Three of them, Turkmenistan, Uzbekistan, and Tajikistan, share a common border with Afghanistan. Tajiks form the second largest ethnic group in Afghanistan, while the Uzbeks rank fourth. The central Asian leaders are apprehensive about the return of the Taliban, who are Pashtuns, for two reasons. First, they fear that an Islamic state in Afghanistan under the control of conservative and militant elements would destabilize their societies, and perhaps incite similar elements across the border. Second, they echo the concerns of their ethnic cousins in Afghanistan who believe that the Taliban would reestablish Pashtun dominance and deny the ethnic minorities autonomy in their affairs.[32] Since the ouster of Rabbani government, which was dominated by the Tajiks, Tajikistan and Uzbekistan have increased their political and material support to the forces of northern coalition. Tajikistan has offered sanctuaries to the anti-Taliban forces and has even allowed them to move their aircraft from Afghanistan to its own airfields and operate from there.

INDIA

Afghanistan is not a distant country in the larger geopolitical vision of India, but rather falls in a region where India would like to establish its influence. India's self-perception of being a regional power and ambitions to play a vital role in the security of the adjacent regions has been a major factor in shaping its policy toward Afghanistan since its independence.[33] Traditionally, the Indian leaders have cultivated closer ties with the Afghan ruling dynasty and other influential sectors of the Afghan society; India has showed generosity in providing assistance in different areas of social development in Afghanistan. Since the early years, India has appeared to be very keen to win over Afghanistan to its side in its multiple disputes with Pakistan. This was never a one-sided feeling of goodwill and cooperation. Afghan leaders, with the exception of the Mujahideen and Taliban regimes that were closely linked to Pakistan, gave tremendous importance to their relationship with India and reciprocated with warmth and understanding on regional issues.

Let us consider the motivations, interests, fears, and ambitions of India and Afghanistan and how have they determined the nature of ties between these two countries. The Afghan leaders understood the importance of the geopolitical space they occupied; located on the periphery of the subcontinent, it served as a vital land bridge to central Asia, but we are not sure if they had a very clear idea about their vulnerabilities as being an essentially landlocked country with transit routes through Pakistan. They were also cognizant of the strategic landscape that evolved in the wake of the Cold War rivalry between the former Soviet Union and the United States, and the pressures this placed on Afghanistan.

Afghanistan had three primary interests that it wanted to pursue in its immediate neighborhood through links with the larger world community. These were: national autonomy, security, and development. Perhaps these interests could better be pursued by maintaining neutrality as a historical buffer. But Afghanistan felt that it was no longer compelled by the same consideration that made the country a buffer on the edge of empires. National ambitions in the age of the postcolonial nation-building process moved Afghan leaders away from their traditional policies. The creation of Pakistan between Afghanistan and India included a vast majority of the Pashtuns and their border regions; this was a factor in rethinking their role in the region and world affairs.

Afghanistan's foreign policy formation is a classical case of how elite orientations shape perceptions of threats, opportunities, challenges, and a national role in underdeveloped states. In the absence of participatory politics and an unequal distribution of power in the state institutions, individual leaders in many of the developing countries have left a deep imprint on domestic and foreign policy directions; the same is true of the Afghan leaders. The Afghan leaders began to reassess their position in the region after the departure of the British from the subcontinent and developments in Cold War politics. They were not enthused about the creation of Pakistan, and in their view the newly formed state unfairly included Pashtun regions that they considered unfair. Also, prominent Pakistani Pashtun leaders like Abdul Ghaffar Khan echoed similar concerns about the future of the Pashtuns after the departure of the British. They wanted the Pashtun regions to stay out of the new state of Pakistan and pressed for a referendum on this issue.[34] They got the referendum demand accepted but boycotted it themselves at the last moment.

In the early years of Pakistan's independence, the Pashtun ruling oligarchy of Afghanistan followed a parallel line on Pashtun rights by raising questions about the Durand Line and demanding that the Pashtun tribal regions be made into a separate state of Pashtunistan or be joined to Afghanistan on the basis of their right to self-determination.[35] They found sympathy and support in India and the Soviet Union against Pakistan. Moscow and Delhi were estranged from Pakistan for their own reasons.

Afghanistan's policy framework was quite rational in seeking cooperation with as many countries in the region and beyond as possible, in order to obtain assistance for development of their state and avoid too much dependence on Pakistan. India was keen to court Kabul due to India's rivalry with Pakistan. India saw a leverage of influence in Kabul that it could use against Pakistan. Afghanistan, however, was very careful in not becoming openly aligned with India for domestic political reasons as well as for the costs of open confrontation with Pakistan.

All the neighbors of Afghanistan have a direct interest in the reconstruction of Afghanistan as a normal state, country, society, and nation. The war in Afghanistan has adversely affected the economies, societies, and security environment of the region. Building a safe society, functional state institutions, and reviving the economy of Afghanistan would benefit all its neighbors; but perhaps Pakistan is most likely to gain the most because there is a greater integration of economies, of the bordering provinces, and there is an extensive transit trade network. While thinking about reconstruction one must remember that the reconstruction in Afghanistan is a multilateral project that needs the positive involvement of all state actors that have the capacity to influence its internal politics and security.

Afghanistan's neighbors, including Pakistan, have exploited the internal fragmentation and intergroup rivalry in Afghanistan to advance their own strategic interests. The situation of Afghanistan with the international community's focus on economic and political reconstruction after the departure of the Taliban is radically different. At the moment, Afghanistan's neighbors are somewhat neutralized by the presence of American forces and other partners of the coalition against terrorism. But they retain an intrusive capacity because of their proximity; and their entangled geopolitical and economic considerations both benefit and harm Afghanistan's rebuilding process. The policy choices of Afghanistan' neighbors determine their future stability, peace, and reconciliation, as much as the choices of the Afghan factions and Afghanistan's ability to resolve divisive issues within its own borders. Judging from past history, neighbor involvement in war and peace would greatly impact the future stability and economic growth in Afghanistan.

Pakistan has been involved in Afghanistan for more than two decades, and now it has a frontline position in the war against terrorism that has targeted Taliban. Pakistan policy had been pro-Taliban, and now it is supporting the war against its former allies in Afghanistan; this raises serious questions about the efficacy of Pakistan's foreign policy which today stands in stark contrast to what it was before 11 September 2001. 9–11 gave Pakistan a good excuse to change the direction of its Afghan policy. But its involvement with the Afghan groups locked in internal struggle for power has left Pakistan with fewer friends and more enemies in Afghanistan, particularly among the literate urban middle class and non-Pashtuns. Other countries around Afghanistan have equally antagonized Pashtuns for supporting their ethnic rivals in the past. Afghanistan is itself on the course of national recovery; simultaneously it is trying to recover its relations with its neighbors. However, since the new state is trying to bring various social groups and warlords that had conducted parallel foreign policies, under its control, the direction of its foreign policy remains undetermined. Afghanistan as a state is on the margins of its neighbors and, hence, is inextricably linked to each of them in a number of important ways. Let us hope that the forces of history, ethnicity, markets, and logic of profit would bring the countries around Afghanistan closer, as all of them would benefit from peace and stability. Among the many lessons that neighbors can draw from their Afghan experience, one stands out very clearly: The free-spirited Afghans want friends, not masters.

NOTES

1. Kingseley de Silva, ed. *Internationalization of Ethnic Conflict* (Kaudy: ICES, 1991); Also see Hasan Askari Rizvi, *Internal Strife and External Intervention* (Lahore: Progressive Publishers, 1981).

2. Rasul Bakhsh Rais, *War Without Winner: Afghanistan's Uncertain Transition after the Cold War*, op. cit., p. 195.

3. See the text of the Peshwar Accord that was brokered by Pakistan to shape the interim Mujahideen government. *Dawn*, 25 April 1992.

4. Mariana Babar, "Tehran-Kabul Pact to Secure Rabbani's Rule" *The News*, 3 March 1996.

5. Author's interviews with the Pakistani diplomats in Islamabad in June, 1997.

6. Human Rights Watch, *Afghanistan: The Massacre at Mazar-i-Sharif*, Vol. 10, No. 7, November 1998.

7. "Iran Hold Taliban Responsible for 9 Diplomats' Death," *New York Times*, 11 September 1998.

8. Vali Nasr and Ray Takeyh, "What We Can Learn from Britain About Iran," *The New York Times*, 5 April 2007.

9. "Iranian Arms to Taliban Bother NATO," *Daily Times*, 31 May 2007.

10. The Najibullah regime collapsed on 16 April 1992 when he agreed to step down under a UN peace plan brokered by Benon Sevan. See, Diego Cordovez and Selig Harrison, *Out of Afghanistan: The Inside Story of Soviet Withdrawal* (New York: Oxford University Press, 1995).

11. Akbar S. Ahmed, *Pakistan Society: Islam, Ethnicity and Leadership in South Asia* (Karachi: Oxford University Press, 1993), pp. 71–99.

12. Anwar-ul-Haq Ahady, "The Decline of the Pashtuns in Afghanistan," *Asian Survey*, op. cit., p. 621.

13. Rashid Ahmad Khan, "Prospects for Peace in Afghanistan," *The Nation*, 15 July 1997.

14. *The News*, 14 July 1997.

15. See John-Thor Dahlburg, "Washington Supporting Taliban?" *Dawn*, 6 October 1996.

16. "Pakistan deployed 100,00 troops: US," *Dawn*, 2 August 2002.

17. See story, "Plot to Kill U.S. Diplomats Foiled," *The News*, 16 December 2002.

18. A. Siddique, "Anti-Pakistan Gambit in Afghanistan," *The Nation*, 12 October 2001.

19. "A Heinous Deal," (editorial) *The Nation*, 3 July 2002.

20. Rahimullah Yusfzai, "The Stir of Echoes," *The News*, 8 August 2002.

21. *The Nation*, 9 February 2002.

22. *The News*, 6 May 2002.

23. *Dawn*, 9 December 2001.

24. In August 2002, Pakistan announced donating 50,000 metric tons of wheat in installments and immediately sent 900 metric tons. *The News*, 6 August 2002.

25. Pakistan's financial year runs from July 1 to June 30.

26. *The News*, 17 December 2002.

27. Khaleeq Kiani, "Islamabad, Kabul Fail to Remove Trade Differences," *Dawn* 17 May 2002.

28. "Musharraf 'betting' on Taliban," *Daily Times*, 5 April 2007.

29. "Musharraf Urges Karzai to Stop Finger-pointing," *Daily Times* 25 April 2007: "Claims of Mullah Omar, Al Qaeda Hideouts Rubbish," *Dawn*, 19 January 2007.

30. Since 2004, tribal areas of Pakistan, particularly Waziristan, have been in turmoil. There are reports that Al Qaeda and the local Taliban have been using these regions as a sanctuary to plan attacks in Afghanistan and Pakistan. After negotiating an accord with the tribes (Taliban) in September 2006, which ended active hostilities, Pakistani forces went back to the region a year later in 2007. The region has remained in a state of conflict and a source of much of the suicide bombings in Afghanistan and Pakistan. See one of the reports, Rahimullah Yusufzai, "Putting out the Fire in Waziristan," *The News*, 9 January 2007; John Kifner, "Sorting Out Pakistan's Many Struggles," *The New York Times*, 21 October 2007.

31. See for instance, HY S. Rothstein, *Afghanistan & The Troubled Future of Unconventional Warfare* (Annapolis, Maryland: Naval Institute Press, 2006).

32. See a report by Ahmed Rashid, "550 Pak Students Captured by Afghan Opposition," *The Nation*, 14 July 1997.

33. George K. Tanham, *Indian Strategic Thought: An Interpretive Essay* (Santa Monica: Rand Corporations).

34. Rajmohan Gandhi, *Ghaffar Khan: Nonviolent Badsha of the Pakhtuns* (New Delhi: Penguin/Viking, 2004), pp. 147–200.

35. S. M. M. Qureshi, "Pakhtunistan: The Frontier Dispute Between Afghanistan and Pakistan," *Pacific Affairs*, Vol. 39, No. 1–2 (Spring–Summer, 1966), pp. 99–114.

8

Conclusion

Afghanistan and the international community face a gigantic task of restructuring a fractured state, normalizing a society that has seen nothing except violence over the past thirty years, and rebuilding the shattered economy and infrastructure in order to create and sustain livelihoods for the people. The real challenge is how to reintegrate microsocial communities and microstates, which are run by numerous warlords who emerged with the collapse of the Afghan state. After seven years of international assistance to the country toward achieving stability and peace, successes are few and far between. This is understandable because nation and state building is a historical process and many of its essential elements cannot be superficially implanted. Luckily Afghans have a common sentiment of nationalism and have subjective allegiance to the country that they have lived in and owned for centuries. While this is a necessary condition for nationhood, it is, however, not enough by itself; it requires institutional means for its realization, which has to be brought about through the agency of the state. The complex web of social, political, and economic relationships that make the nation and state grow and get strengthened are in place with the support of international community.

The international community, with a wide range of reconstruction programs in different areas of national life, has been trying to balance the need for modernization with the culture and values of an underdeveloped, Muslim society that has lived on the margins of the world system. Afghanistan is not the first postconflict reconstruction project for the donor agencies or great powers. Their experience of rebuilding in other societies may provide good learning points to avoid costly mistakes. But the modeling of postconflict reconstruction in Afghanistan on positive experiences of state rebuilding by the world community in other countries may or may not work. In many respects, each conflict's situation is different and requires contextualization of perspective while applying lessons learned in other social and regional contexts. What makes the difference is the character of the combatants, the nature of their social support base, the regional environment, longevity of conflicts, and their cumulative effect on the state and society. Judging on these counts, Afghanistan presents itself as a more complex case of stubborn internal feuds and external intervention than both its neighbors and great powers.

The international community and the post-Taliban regime found Afghanistan devoid of a state, institutions, legal order, formal economy, and any sense of a security order. They entered into this emptiness through a collaborative war that bombed the Taliban out of power. The war that was ostensibly waged to get the Taliban out of power for providing a safe haven to Osama bin Laden, Al Qaeda, and other transnational Islamic militants had a strange mix of motives. Retribution for the tragedy of 9/11 was the most dominant and immediate one. But fighting what the American conservative sections of the society regarded as new enemies of the West require measures beyond the removal of an unwanted regime. The United States and its allies were perhaps more sanguine about the permanent departure of the Taliban from the Afghan scene, and for that reason, they did not anticipate their revival of war-fighting capability. The military operations to destroy or capture the Taliban and fleeing Al Qaeda operatives did not end with the removal of the regime.

The demands of fighting insurgency from largely Pashtun areas conflicted with the aim of the international community to reconstruct the country. Afghanistan and its foreign allies found themselves in a fix as how best to reconstruct the infrastructure, economy, and state institutions in a climate of insurgency. Therefore, nation and state building became enmeshed with securing Afghanistan from the attacks of the Taliban and transnational or nonstate actors opposed to the United States. The dual tasks of fighting the insurgency and rebuilding have strained material and political resources, while achieving only modest success.

THE TALIBAN THREAT

The resurgence of the Taliban, mainly in the Pashtun regions from where it emerged as a military force nearly twelve years back, poses a serious challenge to the stability of Afghanistan. The Taliban has regrouped and reorganized as a viable guerrilla force by reestablishing links with Al Qaeda's transnational networks. During the past three years it has regularly attacked outposts of the Afghan government and NATO forces. Occasionally, it has launched conventional attacks by occupying districts; these have, however, been only for short periods. They do not have the military strength to establish their rule over fixed territory or to defend themselves against the dislodging campaigns of NATO or against the U.S. air power. Nor do they have any credible plan or strategy to reconquer Afghanistan as long as American and NATO forces are in the country.

They seem to be pursuing two objectives by transforming themselves into a guerrilla force. The first objective is to raise the human and material cost for the U.S. and NATO forces. The Taliban is aware of the damage Americans have suffered in stabilizing Iraq, which has made American presence there unpopular and controversial in the United States. The lessons from the Iraqi resistance in this regard or those of its own experience against the former Soviet Union are not lost to them. The Taliban know that time is never on the side of foreign forces, as they lose domestic support when they suffer too many casualties. The NATO countries except Britain have placed too many conditions on the deployment of their troops in combat zones because of the negative reaction they face when soldiers get killed or are injured by the Taliban. Compared to what Americans and the British have suffered in Iraq, their casualties and material cost in Afghanistan remains within the limits of tolerance. There is also a difference in the combat environment of the two countries. Afghanistan is largely rural and Taliban, unlike the Iraqi militants, usually operates in the countryside. However, the Taliban has demonstrated its capacity to penetrate the major towns, as it has caused major deadly explosions in Kabul, Kandhar, and other provincial towns.[1] The second objective of the Taliban is to prevent Afghan security forces and other state institutions from maintaining an effective presence in the Pashtun areas. Enlarging the writ of the Afghan state would defeat their objective of running a parallel authority system through the use of the gun.

The Afghan government and the international community have faced tremendous difficulties in launching and completing reconstruction projects because of attacks from the Taliban insurgents. Security problems and frequent attacks against the workers and contractors have slowed down the pace of reconstruction in the Pashtun provinces; this has worked to the political advantage of the Taliban. The Taliban has exploited poverty, anger, and powerlessness among the Pashtuns to create a political space for its ideology and political vision.

Although some Afghans might be looking toward the Taliban as the true deliverers, closer to the Pashtun cultural and religious ethos, and better enforcers of a security order, the majority accepts them as a necessary evil in the absence of an effective Afghan state with enough authority to protect them. The Taliban are close by, have guns, and are willing to engage in battles with anybody who challenges their parallel rule in the Pashtun countryside.

There is a dialectical relationship between the Taliban warlords and the Afghan state, which is supported by the American and NATO forces. The stronger the Afghan state and its security forces grow, the weaker the Taliban and other warlords would become. The Afghan state is gradually encroaching upon the undefined fiefdoms and self-proclaimed territorial domains of the Taliban and similar militant outfits through building roads, putting schools and health centers back in service, and increasing the presence of police and other departments of the government. But the march of the Afghan state into the Taliban territories has been slow. Too much time was wasted in the first few years, during which the military effort to destroy the fighting capability of the Taliban could have been complemented with political alliances with influential tribes and by putting enough money into the reconstruction program.

We do understand that military means are necessary to fight an insurgency, but are not sufficient by themselves in conditions like those prevalent in conflict-ridden societies like Afghanistan and, hence, need to be complemented with political means of negotiation and reconciliation with all groups. The Afghan government has occasionally demonstrated its willingness to grant qualified amnesty to moderate elements in the Taliban movement, but its efforts have been half-hearted, and it has failed to convince the international coalition about the effectiveness of political means to weaken the Taliban insurgency.

ILLUSIVE PEACE AND STABILITY

Peace and stability have been, and continue to be, defining concepts in this enterprise, but have been elusive in terms of their realization. There are questions about who has the real responsibility in establishing peace and stability in Afghanistan, how it can be done, and what should be a realistic time frame to reconstruct the war-torn country. There are no easy answers to these questions because of the complex legacies of the long war, the nature of the ongoing conflict, and the involvement of multiple diverse actors at both ends of the stability and confrontation spectrum.

The first question is easy to comment on; if the task is left to Afghanistan, it will not be able to rebuild itself. Afghanistan has very limited resources, and has too many internal divisions. Afghanistan therefore needs sustained international support and participation to reorganize its political institutions, rehabilitate its infrastructure, and restart its economic activities. Afghan peoples and the country genuinely need the positive engagement of great powers, particularly of the United States, NATO, and European countries with continued flow of economic assistance and active involvement in rebuilding national security institutions. At this point, the withdrawal of the international coalition would push Afghanistan back to civil war, and expose the entire geopolitical region around the country to the rivalry of insecure and ambitious neighbors. The presence of coalition forces has, to some extent, neutralized the predation of neighbors, but it might be a temporary affair. Iran and Pakistan, for very different reasons, are reported to have been providing assistance to the Taliban, though this has been officially denied by both of them.[2] The premature departure of international forces from Afghanistan without the presence of a strong national army to keep internal cohesion will most likely cause Afghanistan to fall back into a chaotic civil war along ethnic lines. The neighboring states will also reengage in a proxy war by supporting political groups aligned to them.

The international community has a moral responsibility as well as a genuine self-interest in rebuilding Afghanistan as a functional and secure state. The perils of letting Afghanistan lapse back to anarchy are too many and would be felt not only in Afghanistan's neighborhood but also in far-off places.

While there are no two opinions about the collective international ownership of reviving Afghanistan, there are however differences on how best this task can be accomplished. The multiple actors involved in post-Taliban Afghanistan have rightly conceived reconstruction in terms of security and development. The two themes run parallel and would conceptually reinforce each other, as security would create a peaceful environment to launch and implement development schemes, and the success of the latter would build a constituency of support for the new political arrangements. Securing Afghanistan, upon which the entire reconstruction project hinges, has proved to be a tougher mission than expected. After six years of ousting the Taliban from power, the international coalition is still fighting them in the southern and eastern provinces of the country. The Taliban insurgency in recent years has grown in numbers and lethality, denying the Kabul government sustained access to the local populations. The Taliban's conventional attacks against fixed targets in the districts and suicide missions against the NATO forces have increased manifold. The original assumptions about quick victory and rehabilitation have proved wrong, and it appears that the international forces will be in Afghanistan for a long haul.

Apparently a lot has gone wrong in the struggle for reconstructing Afghanistan. The reliance on the warlords, accommodating them in the post-Taliban power structure, tolerance of their corruption, and involvement in the drug trafficking that directly finances the Taliban insurgency is just one of the mixed-up priorities. Heavy reliance on military means in order to defeat the Taliban is yet another issue. Military means are necessary in countering insurgency but are not sufficient by themselves. They must have a parallel political track to negotiate with the insurgents. The international coalition and the Kabul authorities seem to have a strong psychological barrier against the Taliban, whom they consider to be out of the pale of civility and hence deem any efforts to negotiate with them useless. This cannot be wrong if we think of the Taliban insurgency inspired by Al Qaeda and its global Islamic outlook; however, what we may be missing is the internal character of the Taliban movement, the question of power and ethnicity, and the possibility that some sections of the Taliban movement can negotiate deals.

Military means are not without serious political consequences as they do not show sensitivity to the feelings and interests of the local populations. The use of air power, which is frequently called in to bombard suspected Taliban hideouts, has caused massive collateral damage. The civilian casualties have rather estranged the local populations and have turned them against the international coalition and the Karzai government.[3] This may be a cheaper alternative to ground forces that ISAF cannot put on the ground in Afghanistan, but its political backlash may have heavy costs for the Kabul authorities.

The time frame is another crucial variable in the reconstruction of Afghanistan. Populations need to see visible gains for their interest in reconstruction and hope of leading a normal life to be reestablished. At the same time, Afghanistan, because of its broken personality, needs a long-term commitment of international players to rebuild it. It was a big blunder to go after Iraq when the war in Afghanistan was still ongoing. The second war has hurt the cause of Afghanistan very badly, and the failure in Iraq, the specter of which looms very large, would damage it more with Al Qaeda centering on this theater. This mistake might be corrected with unwavering, resolute support to Afghanistan for as long as it takes to help Afghanistan in being able to defend itself.

ETHNIC PLURALISM

One of the major conclusions of this book is that the three-decades-long conflict has substantially changed the conventional ethnic balance of Afghanistan. It has ended the centuries-old Pashtun dominance over the state structure. The minority ethnic groups with a history of grievances, both real and imagined, against the Pashtuns have greatly empowered themselves in the multilayered and multidimensional Afghan conflict. Before the entry of American forces in Afghanistan supported by the United Nations and its European allies, the ethnic minorities were locked in a deadly conflict with the Islamist but essentially Pashtun Taliban forces. It was partly due to the ethnic dimension of the conflict that they entered into the American fold, a marriage of convenience against a common Taliban foe. The Northern Front, created out of the ethnic minorities, pooled up its resources with the international coalition against the Taliban rule, and was able to capture Kabul and the country after the U.S. and allied forces threw the Taliban out of power. They emerged as the most influential factor in negotiating and shaping the post-Taliban power structure in light of the Bonn process that the United Nations authorized. In the first few years, the representation of minorities in power at the center and their autonomy in the provinces was the most glaring feature of Afghanistan's political scene. Mr. Hamid Karzai, a Pashtun president, appeared to be helplessly powerless with too many Northern Front stars occupying positions of power and influence and dictating to him domestic and foreign policy choices that Afghanistan was to take.

The situation has changed considerably with the presidential and parliamentary elections, and the electoral system has allowed greater regional representation of every group in multimember constituencies. The electoral process, which has been one of the most important gains for Afghanistan, has only confirmed the ethnic fragmentation of the country as communities have largely voted on an ethnic basis. Afghanistan as a multiethnic society will require a democratic framework to create a sense of nationhood and national integration. The Pashtun will have to disregard the numbers of the ethnic minorities, and let go of the sense of majority and historical claim they have over the country and will have to learn lessons of political and social pluralism and cohabit with and share power with other ethnic groups. The questions of identity, empowerment, and representation are as important for the Tajiks and Uzbeks as they might be for the Pashtuns.

One remarkable thing about Afghanistan's ethnic groups is that even during the most brutal phases of the Afghan war, during the reign of the Taliban they never thought of breaking out of their historical union with Afghanistan. Long-term common interests rather than emotionalism and political rhetoric endure political bonds among the social groups. Democracy and rule of law as they evolve with other facets of state and nation building in Afghanistan would create the essential environment for negotiating power relations more than fighting over them. This will also lead all parties to begin resorting to peaceful political means as opposed to violent ones, sharing rather than dominating each other, and teach them to live in an environment of cultural diversity. It may sound more optimistic than might be the view of an average observer of Afghanistan's history. But this optimism rests on the assumption of the slow growth of democracy, and the interests of the great powers and neighboring states in rebuilding Afghanistan as a normal state. The failure to rebuild Afghanistan as a cohesive and integrated state would force the ethnic communities back to their local structure of authority, and would lead to ethnic and tribal warlordism, keeping the country fragmented as it was during the civil war.

AVOIDABLE MISTAKES

The United States, as the leading country and with a lot at stake in the war on terror, must take responsibility for what has already gone wrong in Afghanistan. It is evident from the rise of the Taliban insurgency, though largely confined to the Pashtun regions, that there is growing frustration over the lack of economic opportunities and the climate of fear and insecurity that they continue to live in. Seven years down the line, the United States supported by regional and international partners is nowhere close to achieving its avowed objectives in Afghanistan. It is partly due to some major miscalculations of its capacity to fix complex issues of war and stability in remote areas of the world and partly due to the underestimation of the adversaries it faces in Afghanistan. It could perhaps have done a better job in stabilizing Afghanistan if it had set its priorities right and applied appropriate means.

Washington planned its invasion of Afghanistan in haste, out of political compulsions, and with a sentiment of retribution against the Taliban and their Al Qaeda allies. Changing the Taliban regime by bombing its army and functionaries to dust became its war cry. In this effort, Washington relied heavily on the local adversaries of the Taliban, the Northern Front leaders who belonged to minority ethnic communities. The Afghan civil war before the entry of the American and allied forces had a very strong ethnic dimension. The United States in its fury did not ponder over the long-term consequences of courting the minority groups against the majority community, the Pashtuns. It had some Pashtuns on its side, like Commander Abdul Haq and Hamid Karzai, who stirred up trouble around Jalalabad and Kandhar in the wake of the American invasion, but their effort was cosmetic-aimed to give the impression that Pashtuns also supported removal of the Taliban. Perhaps the United States was frustrated with the Taliban leaders who appeared to be as rigid and inflexible as ever in acceding to the demands of handing over the Al Qaeda leaders, and therefore did not see any reason in further engaging with them. The American war and post-Taliban power arrangements created a lopsided ethnic balance, lending credence to the feeling that power had shifted to the Tajiks and Uzbeks. The Pashtuns in the first few years considered Karzai more as a symbolic head of the state than a real chief executive. The political process following the adoption of the new constitution and elections of the president and the *Loya Jirga* have begun to erase that impression, but the residual grievances about marginalization among the Pashtun do exist, which the Taliban continues to exploit.

With initial success of dislodging the Taliban, the United States appeared very optimistic about stability, peace, and reconstruction of the Afghan state. Declaring quick victory of its "Operation Enduring Freedom," it decided to dislodge another dictator in Iraq, perhaps too soon. The Iraq invasion has cost the United States dearly in terms of image and credibility to defeat its new adversaries, and has overstretched its resources and strategic assets. The diversion of war resources to a new theater in Iraq greatly undermined the United States' overall capacity to bring peace and stability to Afghanistan. Washington's two-war strategy has failed and has left a negative impact on the situation in Afghanistan. Its probable retreat from Iraq would send a wrong message to the Taliban and Al Qaeda in Afghanistan, and would lead them to believe that the United States does not have staying power, and that it can be forced to withdraw by raising the costs of its occupation. Its Iraqi debacle will have negative demonstrative effects on its counterinsurgency operations; this is somewhat already visible in the suicide bombings that are carried out on more or less the same pattern as that of the Middle Eastern conflict.

Yet another failure of American strategy in Afghanistan is not persistently exploring the option of negotiations with the Taliban. Aside from a few feelers from President Karzai, there has hardly been any serious initiative to enter into negotiations with the Pashtun Taliban. War in the form of counterinsurgency operations is no permanent solution of the Afghan problem. It has rather hardened attitudes on both sides of the conflict, created greater sympathy for the Taliban guerrillas, and has denied political and social space to the Afghan government in the Pashtun provinces.

NEUTRALIZING NEIGHBORS

All the neighbors of Afghanistan have a direct interest in the reconstruction of Afghanistan as a normal state, country, society, and nation. War in Afghanistan has adversely affected the economies, societies, and security environment of the region. Building a safe society, functional state institutions and reviving the economy of Afghanistan would benefit all its neighbors; but perhaps Pakistan is likely to gain the most because of greater integration of economies in the bordering provinces and because of the extensive transit trade network. While thinking about reconstruction, one must remember that Afghanistan is a multilateral project that needs positive involvement of all state actors who have the capacity to influence its internal politics and security.

Afghanistan's neighbors, including Pakistan, have for long exploited the internal fragmentation and inter-group rivalry to advance their own strategic interests. The situation of Afghanistan after the departure of the Taliban with the international community's focus on economic and political reconstruction is radically different. At the moment, Afghanistan's neighbors are somewhat neutralized by the presence of American forces and those of other partners of the coalition against terrorism. However, the neighboring states retain intrusive capacity because of their proximity and entangled geopolitical and economic considerations. This is both a benefit and harm in Afghanistan's rebuilding process. Judging from the past history of neighbor's involvement, the conditions prevalent in Afghanistan would greatly impact the future stability and economic growth in the region. Also the choices of Afghan factions and the nation's ability to resolve divisive issues within its own borders would determine future stability, peace, and reconciliation.

AFGHANISTAN HAS TO STAND ON ITS FEET

Never has Afghanistan seen so much positive involvement of the international community in its reconstruction as it has since the ouster of the Taliban regime. It is important for the Afghans to ponder what brought so much assistance to them, and how long it will last. It was not their poverty, mass dislocation of population inside and outside the country, or the civil war that turned the attention of the West and its regional allies toward their country. It was the negative side of Afghanistan in being a safe haven for transnational terrorist networks and a source of terrorism and insecurity for the region that made the world finally change its attitude from benign neglect to active participation in Afghanistan's economic and political reconstruction. Although the international interest in reviving Afghanistan as a functional and effective state is borne out of fear and anxiety about a failed state in the crossroads of three strategic regions, it is nevertheless genuine, well meaning, and constructive.

It is also true that without international assistance Afghanistan cannot hope to develop itself into an effective state and nation. Its material resource base, including land, water, and natural resources are either too poor or unexplored and underdeveloped to sustain its revival. Its human resources in education, bureaucracy, and other state institutions withered away with the destructive war. Sustainable international assistance is vital for Afghanistan to recover its lost social and economic energies. While recognizing the significance of international involvement in Afghanistan, we need to be aware of two caveats. First, the reconstruction program should be aimed at helping Afghans to help themselves. Some of the programs, like the ring road connecting all outlying provinces, rehabilitation of irrigation channels, plans for hydroelectric plants the and investment in social sector are geared toward that end. The objective should be to tap local Afghan resources and reduce dependence of the country on external assistance, which at the moment seems unrealistic given the massive cost of rebuilding the country.

Another caution is about the neoliberal framework underlying economic reconstruction. Uncritical application of market-based economic models to poverty-stricken Afghanistan may cause inequality of incomes, concentration of legal and illegal wealth in sectors of the society that dominate its political life and create a large rent-seeking class. There is a clear bias in the reconstruction in favor of private groups and companies that limits the sphere of the state. This is not entirely due to the weak capacity of the state to provide effective and transparent governance in managing reconstruction programs; what really shapes the policy of the donors is ideological skepticism about the ability of the modern state to provide services efficiently. The market-oriented reconstruction may spur growth, which is necessary, but may leave the vast majority of poor without social safety nets. In conditions of social anarchy that exist on the periphery of the Afghan state, old and new enemies may exploit popular anger and turn it against the state and its emerging rapacious elites. This may prove counterproductive to the objective of establishing positive and deep linkages between the state and the society that have historically been week.

The Afghan have to be urged to stand on their own feet, as Hamid Karzai in one of his speeches to an assembly of elders said in June 2007.[4] International support and sympathy for their country has come about in unusual circumstances that may not last forever. Donors get fatigued or turn to new causes when they are drawn toward more demanding events. Countries like Afghanistan slide down on their ladder of the hierarchy of interests and priorities. How can the Afghans best take advantage of international support to be stable, peaceful, and unified would largely depend on their own vision and social capacity to reconcile differences among them. For too many years, and too often with repetitive boredom, they have accused others, particularly intervention by their neighbors, for their woes. Their narrative of victimization by external enemies is only partially credible. They must take responsibility for their own follies and admit their own hand in taking the Afghan tragedy from a self-destructive socialist revolution to civil war. Their perpetual infighting at every turn of events earned them an unfortunate image that Afghans know only one thing, how to fight and nothing else. Afghans have to bury the hatchet and turn a new leaf in their relationships. Perhaps they need to evolve a new social contract that outlaws war as a means of settling disputes. There are peaceful alternatives, and one can find a lot in the traditional institutions and norms of Afghanistan to reconcile differences. After the overthrow of the Taliban, they have a better constitutional framework, having elected legislature and provincial councils that they can use as forums to pursue reconciliation as a political objective and settle differences over power sharing.

Afghanistan's neighbors have frequently fished into the muddy waters of Afghanistan and transferred their own conflicts and rivalries to Afghanistan.[5] The fragmentation among the Afghan groups and their violent struggle for power pushed them to seek patronage of the external powers. The presence of the United States and NATO forces has severed horizontal linkages of the Afghan groups to some degree, far from completely eliminating them. As the Afghans create greater consensus among themselves and resolve their problems over power sharing and other issues, the menacing role of the neighbors may get diffused over time. One important way the Afghans can better handle their neighbors is by rethinking their place and role in the complex geopolitical system of their region. They may recast their foreign policy in a framework that would alleviate the fears of one neighbor using Afghanistan for hostile purposes against another and contain their ambitions by denying the use of Afghanistan as an arena of any fresh "great game."

This framework must rest on two pillars: neutrality and cooperation with all neighbors. It would be prudent for the Afghans to redefine Afghanistan as a neutral state. Neutrality will not lessen Afghanistan's statehood; it will rather remove apprehensions of countries like Pakistan and contain ambitions of all other neighbors.[6] It will also restore the historic personality of Afghanistan as a buffer, but with a different definition and value than was required by the strategic need of the old European empires that were fearful of touching each other's colonial boundaries. Afghanistan's revival and its future progress would largely depend on regional cooperation that the Afghans may consider as the core principle of their foreign policy.[7] This would transform Afghanistan from an area of geopolitical contestation to a zone of opportunity. Afghanistan occupies a central position to emerge as a transit commercial state that would give positive meanings to its buffer status. It can be a meeting point for regional trade, serve as a corridor for energy resources, and provide an opportunity to all for investment in its infrastructure and exploration of mineral resources.

NOTES

1. "Attack on Police Bus in Kabul Kills 35," *Daily Times*, 20 June 2007.
2. "Iran Baring Its Teeth to U.S. in Afghanistan," *Daily Times*, 2 July 2007.
3. "NATO Air Raid Kills 65 Civilians in Afghanistan," *Daily Times*, 1 July 2007.
4. "Karzai Urges Afghans to Stand on Their Own Feet," *Daily Times*, 19 June 2007.
5. Barnett R. Rubin and Andrea Armstrong, "Regional Issues in the Reconstruction of Afghanistan," *World Policy Journal*, Vol. 20, No. 1, Spring 2003, p. 32.
6. Peter Tomsen, "Untying the Afghan Knot," *Fletcher Forum of World Affairs*, Vol. 25 (Winter 2001), p. 17.
7. Rubin and Armstrong, "Regional Issues in the Reconstruction of Afghanistan," op. cit., p. 40.

Bibliography

BOOKS

Abou, Zahabi, Marriam. *Islamic Networks: the Pakistan-Afghanistan Connection*. London: C. Hurst, 2004.

Adamec, L. W. *Historical Dictionary of Afghanistan*. Metuchen and London: Scarecrow Press, 1991.

Adamec, L. W. *Afghanistan, 1900–1923*. Berkeley and Los Angeles: University of California Press, 1967.

Albinati, Edoardo. *Coming Back: Diary of a Mission to Afghanistan*. London: Hesperus Press, 2003.

Ali, Mehrunnisa. *Pak-Afghan Discord—A Historical Perspective (Documents 1855–1979)*. Pakistan Study Centre: University of Karachi, 1990.

Ahmed, A. S. *Pashtun Economy and Society*. London: Rutledge & Kegan Paul, 1980.

Ahmed, Rashid. *The Turkmenistan–Afghanistan–Pakistan Pipeline: Company–Government Relations and Regional Politics*. Washington, D.C: Focus on Current Issues, The Petroleum Finance Company, October 1997.

Amin, T. *Afghanistan Crisis: Implications and Options for Muslim World, Iran, and Pakistan*. Islamabad: Institute of Policy Studies, 1982.

Anonymous. *Through Our Enemies' Eyes: Osama bin Laden, Radical Islam, and the Future of America*. Washington, D.C.: Brassey's NC, 2003.

Anwar, Raja. *The Tragedy of Afghanistan: A First-hand Account*. London and New York: Verso, 1989.

Arney, G. *Afghanistan*. London: Mandarin, 1990.

Arnold, Anthony. *Afghanistan's Two-Party Communism: Parcham and Khalq*. Stanford, California: Hoover Institute Press, Stanford University, 1983.

Art, Robert J. and Patrick M. Cronin. *The United States and Coercive Diplomacy*. Washington, D.C.: United States Institutes of Peace Press, 2003.

Bakshi, G. D. *Afghanistan: The First Fault Line War*. New Delhi: Lancer, 1999.

Bergen, Peter L. *The Osama bin Laden I Know: An Oral History of Al Qaeda's Leader*, New York: Free Press, 2006.

Benjamin, Daniel and Simon Steven. *The Age of Sacred Terror: Radical Islam's War Against America*. New York: Random House, 2005.

Bodansky, Yossef. *Bin Laden: The Man Who Declared War on America*. Rocklin, California: Forum, 1999.

Borer, D.A. *Superpowers Defeated: Vietnam and Afghanistan Compared*. London: Frank Cass, 1999.

Brentjes, Burchard and Helga Brentjes, Taliban: *A Shadow over Afghanistan*. Varanasi: Rishi, 2000.

Byrd, W. A. and Gildestad, B. *The Socio-Economic Impact of Mine Action in Afghanistan: A Cost-Benefit Analysis*. Islamabad: World Bank, 2001.

Caroe, O. *The Pathans*. Karachi: Oxford University Press, 1958.

Chakravarty, Suhash. *Afghanistan and the Great Game*. Delhi: New Century Publications, 2002.

Chishti, Mehroze Nighat. *Constitutional Development in Afghanistan*. Karachi: Royal Book Company, 1998.

Chopra, V. D. (ed.). *Afghanistan and Asian Stability*. New Delhi: Gyan, 1998.

Christensen, A. *Aiding Afghanistan: The Background and Prospects for Reconstruction in a Fragmented Society*. Copenhagen: NIAS Books, 1995.

Cooley, John K. *Unholy Wars: Afghanistan, America, and International Terrorism*, London: Pluto Press, 2001.

Cordesman, Anthony H. *The Lessons of Afghanistan: War Fighting, Intelligence, and Force Transformation*. Lahore: Vanguard, 2003.

Cordovez, D. and Selig S. Harrison. *Out of Afghanistan: The Inside Story of the Soviet Withdrawal*. New York: Oxford University Press, 1995.

Davidson and P. Hjukstrom (eds.), *Afghan, Aid and the Taliban: Challenges on the Eve of the 21st Century*. Stockholm: The Swedish Committee for Afghanistan, 1999.

Dixit, J. N. *An Afghanistan Diary: Zahir Shah to Taliban*. New Delhi: Konark Publishers Pvt. Ltd., 2000.

Dupree, L. and L. Albert, (eds.), *Afghanistan in the 1970s*. New York: Praeger Publishers, 1974.

Eaton, R., Horwood, C., and Niland, N. *Afghanistan: The Developments of Indigenous Mine Action Capacities*. Washington, D.C.: UN Department Humanitarian Affairs, 1997.

Edwards, David. *Heroes of the Age: Moral Fault Lines on the Afghan Frontier*. Berkeley: University of California Press, 1996.

Edwards, David B. *Before Taliban: Genealogies of the Afghan Jihad*. Berkeley, University of California Press, 2002.

Edwards, Michael. *Playing the Great Game: A Victorian Cold War*. London: Hamilton, 1975.

Ekanayake, S. B. *Afghan Tragedy*. Islamabad: Al-Noor Publishers, 2000.

Emadi, Hafizullah. *State, Revolution and Superpowers in Afghanistan*. Karachi: Royal Book Company, 1997.

Embree, A. B. (ed.). *Pakistan's Western Borderlands: The Transformation of a Political Order*. New Delhi: Vikas Publishing House, 1977.

Ewans, Martin. *Afghan—A New History*. Richmond, Surrey: Curzon, 2001.

Ferrier, J. P. *A History of Afghanistan*. Lahore: Sang-e-Meel, 2002.

Fraser-Tytler, W. K. *Afghanistan: Study of Political Development in Central Asia and Southern Asia*. London: Oxford University Press, 1967.

Frederick, Forsyth. *The Afghan*. London: Bantam Press, 2006.

Friedman, Norman. *Terrorism, Afghanistan, and America's New Way of War*. U.S.A.: U.S. Naval Institute Press, 2003.

Fry, M. J. *The Afghan Economy*. Leiden: E. J. Brill, 1974.

Fujimura, Manabu. *Post-Conflict Reconstruction: The Afghan Economy*. Tokyo: Asian Development Bank Institute, 2004.

Fullerton, J. *The Soviet Occupation of Afghanistan*. Hong Kong: Far Eastern Economic Review, 1983.

Gandhi, Rajmohan, *Ghaffar Khan: Nonviolent Badsha of the Pakhtuns*. New Delhi: Penguin Viking, 2004.

Gankovsky, Y. *The Durrani Empire in Afghanistan: Past and Present*. Moscow: USSR Academy of Sciences, 1982.

Gellner, E. *Postmodernism, Reason and Religion*. London and New York: Routledge, 1993.

Ghaus, A. S. *The Afghanistan: An Insider's Account*. Washington: Pergamon-Brassey's International Defence Publishers, 1998.

Grare, Frederic. *Pakistan and the Afghan Conflict, 1979–1985: With an Afterward Covering Events from 1985–2001*. Karachi: Oxford University Press, 2003.

Grasselli, G. *British and American Response to the Soviet Invasion of Afghanistan*. Aldershot: Dartmouth Publishing Company, 1996.

Gregorian, V. *The Emergence of Modern Afghanistan: Politics of Reform and Modernization, 1880–1946*. Stanford: Stanford University Press, 1969.

Griffin, Michael. *Reaping the Whirlwind: The Taliban Movement in Afghanistan*. London: Pluto Press, 2001.

Griffiths, J. C. *Afghans: History of Conflict*. London: Andre Deutsch, 2001.

———. *Afghanistan: Key to a Continent*. Boulder: Westview Press, 1981.

Grover, Verinder (ed.). *Afghanistan: Government and Politics*. New Delhi: Deep & Deep, 2000.

Gul, Imtiaz. *The Unholy Nexus: Pak-Afghan Relations under the Taliban*. Lahore: Vanguard, 2002.

Gupta, G. S. *Afghanistan: Politics, Economy, and Society*. London: Frances Pinter, 1986.

Hobsbawm, E. J. *Nation and Nationalism Since 1780: Programme, Myth, Reality*. Cambridge: Cambridge University Press, 1990.

Hopkirk, P. *The Great Game: The Struggle for Empire in Central Asia*. New York: Kodansha International, 1992.

Jafri, H. A. *Indo-Afghan Relations (1947–1967)*. New Delhi: Sterling Publishers, 1976.

Jalalzai, Musa Khan. *Taliban and the Great Game in Afghanistan*. Lahore: Vanguard, 1999.

———. *The Politics of Religion and Violence in Afghanistan*, Lahore: Dua Publications, 2002.

———. *Afghanistan's Internal Security Threats: The Dynamics of Ethnic and Sectarian Violence*. Lahore: Dua Publications, 2002.

Jawad, N. *Afghanistan: A Nation of Minorities*. London: Minority Rights Group, 1990.

Kaplan, Robert D. *Soldiers of God: With Islamic Warriors in Afghanistan and Pakistan*. New York: Vintage, 2001.

Kaye, William John, *History of the War in Afghanistan*. Vol.1, Delhi: Shubhi Publications, 1999.

Khan, Hayat Azmat. *The Durand Line: It's Geo-Strategic Importance*. Islamabad: Pan-Graphics (Pvt.), 2000.

Klaits, Alex and Gulchin Gulmamadova–Klaits. *Love and War in Afghanistan*. New York: Seven Stories Press, 2006.

Kulwant, Kaur. *Pak-Afghanistan Relations*. New Delhi: Deep & Deep Publications, 1985.

Ma'aroof, Mohammad Khalid. *Afghanistan in World Politics—A Study of Afghan-U.S. Relations*. New Delhi: Gyan, 1987.

Ma'aroof, Mohammad Khalid. *United Nations and Afghanistan Crisis*. New Delhi: Commonwealth, 1990.

Ma'aroof, Mohammad Khalid. *Afghanistan and Super Powers*. New Delhi: Commonwealth, 1999.

Mackey, Chris and Miller Greg. *The Interogators: Inside The Secret War Against Al Qaeda*. New York: Little, Brown and Company, 2004.

MacMunn, George Fletcher. *Afghanistan: From Darius to Amanullah*. Lahore: Sang-e-Meel Publications, 2002.

Mahmood, Mamdani. *Good Muslim, Bad Muslim: America, the Cold War, and the Roots of Terror*. New York: Pantheon Books, 2004.

Male, B. *Revolutionary Afghanistan: A Reappraisal*. London and Canberra: Croom Helm, 1982.

Maley, W. *The Afghanistan Wars*. London: Palgrave Macmillan, 2002.

Maley, W. and F. H. Saikal. *Political Order in Post-Communist Afghanistan*. Boulder: Lynne Rienner Publishers, 1992.

Maley, W. (ed.) *Fundamentalism Reborn? Afghanistan and the Taliban*. New York: New York University Press, 1998.

Malik, Murtza. *The Curtain Rises: Uncovered Conspiracies in Pakistan, Afghanistan*. Karachi: Royal Book Co., 2002.

Margolis, Eric S. *War at the Top of the World: The Struggle for Afghanistan, Kashmir, and Tibet*. New York: Routledge, 2000.

Marsden, Peter. *The Taliban: War, Religion, and the New Order in Afghanistan*. London: Zed Books Ltd., 1998.

Mousavi, Syed Askar. *The Hazaras of Afghanistan: An Historical, Cultural, Economic and Political Study*. Surrey: Curzon, 1998.

Musharraf, Pervez. *In the Line of Fire: A Memoir*. New York: Simon & Schuster, 2006.

Noelle, Christine. *State and Tribe in Nineteenth-Century Afghanistan: The Reign of Amir Dost Muhammad Khan (1826–1863)*. Richmond Surrey: Curzon, 1997.

Nojumi, Neamatollah. *The Rise of the Taliban in Afghanistan: Mass Mobilization, Civil War, and the Future of the Region*. New York: Palgrave, 2002.

Norris, J. A. *The First Afghan War, 1838–1842*. Cambridge: Cambridge University Press, 1967.

Olesen, A. *Islam and Politics in Afghanistan*. Richmond: Curzon Press, 1995.

Overby, P. *Holy Blood: An Inside View of the Afghan War*. Westport: Praeger, 1993.

Pennel, T.L., *Among the Wild Tribes of the Afghan Frontier*. London: Seely, 1909.

Pillar, Paul R. *Terrorism and U.S. Foreign Policy*. Washington, D.C.: Brookings Institution Press, 2002.

Poullada, L. B. *The Road to Crisis 1919–1980—American Failures, Afghan Errors and Soviet Success,* in R. Klass (ed.), *Afghanistan: The Great Game Revisited*. New York: Freedom House, 1987.

Quddus, S. A. *Afghanistan and Pakistan: A Geopolitical Study*. Lahore: Ferozsons Ltd., 1982.

———. *The Pathans*. Lahore: Ferozsons, 1987.

Rais, Rasul Bakhsh. *War without Winners: Afghanistan's Uncertain Transition after the Cold War*. Karachi: Oxford University Press, 1994.

Rall, Ted. *Gas War: The Truth behind the American Occupation of Afghanistan*. New York: Writers Club Press, 2002.

Randel, Jonathan C. *Osama: The Making of a Terrorist*. London. New York: I. B. Tauris, 2005.

Rao, Vinayak, *International Negotiations: The United Nations in Afghanistan and Cambodia*. New Delhi: Manak, 2001.

Rashid, Ahmed. *Taliban: The Story of the Afghan Warlords*. London: Pan Books, 2001.

Rashid, Ahmed. *Taliban, Islam, Oil and the New Great Game in Central Asia*. London: I. B. Tauris, 2000.

Rezun, M. *Intrigue and War in South West Asia: The Struggle for Supremacy from Central Asia to Iraq*. New York: Praeger, 1992.

Rose, L. E. and K . Matinuddin, (eds.). *Beyond Afghanistan: The Emerging U.S.-Pakistan Relations*. Berkeley: Institute of East Asian Studies, University of California, 1989.

Rothstein, H. S. *Afghanistan and the Troubled Future of Unconventional Warfare*. Annapolis, Md.: Naval Institute Press, 2006.

Roy, Oliver. *Islam and Resistance in Afghanistan*. Cambridge: Cambridge University Press, 1986.

Rubin, Barnett R. *The Search for Peace in Afghanistan: From Buffer State to Failed State*. New Haven and London: Yale University Press, 1995.

Rubin, Barnett R. *The Fragmentation of Afghanistan: State Formation and Collapse in the International System*. New Haven and London: Yale University Press, 1995.

Saikal, Amin. *Modern Afghanistan: A History of Struggle and Survival*. New York: I. B. Tauris, 2004.

Saikal, Amin & William Maley. *Regime Change in Afghanistan*. Boulder: Westview Press, 1991.

Schofield, Victoria. *Afghanistan Frontier: Feuding and Fighting in Central Asia*. New York: Tauris Parke, 2003.

Selig, S. Harrison. *In Afghanistan's Shadow: Baloch Nationalism and Soviet Temptation*. New York: Carnegie Endowment for International Peace, 1981.

Sen Gupta, Bhabani. *Afghanistan Politics, Economics and Society*. Oxford: Oxford University Press, 1985.

Shah, Ali Ikbal. *Afghanistan of the Afghans*. Lahore: Vanguard, 1998.

Shah, I. A. *Modern Afghanistan*. London: Low, 1939.

Sinclair, Gordon. *Khyber Caravan: Through Kashmir, Waziristan, Afghanistan, Balochistan, and Northern India*, Lahore: Sang-e-Meel Publications, 2003.

Smith, A. D. *The Ethnic Revival*. Cambridge: Cambridge University Press, 1981.

Smith, Harvey H. et al. *Area Handbook for Afghanistan*. Washington, D.C.: U.S. Government Printing Office, 1969.

Sreedhar, Sinha Rakesh, Nilesh Bhagat, and O. N. Mehrotra. *Taliban and the Afghan Turmoil: The Role of USA, Pakistan, Iran and China*. Mumbai: Himalaya, 1997.

Stephen Coll. *Ghost Wars: The Secret History of the CIA, Afghanistan, bin Laden, from the Soviet Invasion to September 10, 2001*. New York: Penguin Press, 2004.

Stobdan, P. *Afghan Conflict and India*. New Delhi: Institute for Defence Studies and Analysis, 1998.

Strand, A. *Bombs and Butter: Compensation Issues in Protracted Conflicts: The Case of Afghanistan*. Denmark: Human Rights in Development, 2002.

Strand, A., K. B. Harpviken, and K. Ask, *Humanitarian Challenges in Afghanistan: Administrative Structures and Gender and Assistance*. Bergen: Chr. Michelsen Institute, 2001.

Tanner, Stephen. *Afghanistan: A Military History from Alexander the Great to the Fall of the Taliban*. Karachi: Oxford University Press, 2003.

Tapper, R. (ed.), *The Conflict of Tribe and State in Iran and Afghanistan*. New York: St. Martin's Press, 1983.

Teresita C. Schaffer, *Pakistan's Future and U.S. Policy Options*. Washington, D.C.: CSIS Press, 2004.

Umarzai, General. *Nights in Kabul: Actions behind the Curtain during the Last Two Decades in Afghanistan*. Peshawar: Area Study Centre, Peshawar University, 2004.

Urban, Mark. *War in Afghanistan*. 2nd ed. New York: St. Martin's Press, 1990.

Van Dyk, Jere. *In Afghanistan: An American Odyssey*. New York: Coward, McCann & Geoghegan, 1983.

Warikoom K., Singh Uma, and A. K. Ray. *Afghanistan Factor in Central and South Asian Politics*. New Delhi: Trans Asia Informatics, 1994.

Weaver, Mary Anne. *Pakistan: In the Shadow of Jihad and Afghanistan*. New York: Farra Straus and Giroux, 2002.

Wilber, Donald Newton. *Afghanistan: Its People, Its Society, Its Culture*. New Haven: HRAF, 1962.

Woodward, Bob. *Plan of Attack*. New York: Simon & Schuster, 2004.

———. *Bush at War*. New York: Simon & Schuster, 2002.

Yapp, Malcolm. *Strategies of British India: Britain, Iran, and Afghanistan, 1798–1850*. Oxford: Clarendon Press; Publisher, N. A., 1980.

Yousaf, Muhammad and Mark Adkin. *The Bear Trap: Afghanistan's Untold Story*. Lahore: Jang Publishers Press, 1992.

Yunas, S. Fida. *Afghanistan: A Political History*. Peshawar: 2003.

———. *Afghanistan: Organization of the Peoples Democratic Party of Afghanistan/Watan Party, Government and Biographical Sketches 1982–1998*. Peshawar: Publisher, N. A. 1999.

PERIODICALS

Ahady, Anwar-ul-Haq. "The Changing Interests of Regional Powers and the Resolution of Afghan Conflict." *Asian Affairs* (Summer 1994): 80–93.

Ahady, Anwar-ul-Haq. "The Decline of the Pashtun in Afghanistan." *Asian Survey*, Vol. 35, No. 7 (July, 1995): 621–34.

Ahmed, Rashid. "Letter from Afghanistan: Are the Taliban Winning?" *Current History, Journal of Contemporary World Affairs*, Vol. 106, No. 696 (Jan, 2007): 17–20.

Ahmed, Samina. "Warlords, Drugs, and Democracy." *World Today*, Vol. 60, No. 5 (May, 2004): 15–17.

Ahrari, Ehan M. "China, Pakistan, and the Taliban Syndrome." *Asian Survey*, Vol. 40, No. 4 (July, 2000): 658–67.

Alan J. Kuperman. "The Stinger Missile and U.S. Intervention in Afghanistan." *Political Science Quarterly*, Vol. 114, No. 2 (Summer, 1999): 219–63.

Ali, M. "The Attitudes of the New Afghan Regime Towards its Neighbors." *Pakistan Horizon*, Vol. 27, No. 3 (1974).

Allan, Nigel. "Rethinking Governance in Afghanistan." *Journal of International Affairs*, Vol. 56, No. 2, (March, 2003): 193–202.

Alvi, Hamza. "Pakistan between Afghanistan and India." *Middle East Report*, No. 222 (Spring, 2002): 24–31.

Anatol, Lieven. "Don't Forget Afghanistan." *Foreign Policy*, No. 137 (July, 2003): 54.

Anderson, N., da Sousa, C.P. and Paredes, S., "Social Cost of Land Mines in Four Countries: Afghanistan, Bosnia, Cambodia, and Mozambique." *British Medical Journal*, Vol. 311 (1995): 781–821.

Andres, Richard B., Craig Wills, and Thomas Griffith Jr. "Winning with Allies: The Strategic Values of the Afghan Model." *International Security*, Vol. 30. No. 3 (Winter, 2005): 124–60.

Arya, L. S., Qureshi, M. A., Jabor, A. and Singh. "Lathyrism in Afghanistan." *Indian Journal of Pediatrics*, Vol. 55. (1988): 440–42.

Barakat, Sultan. "Setting the Scene for Afghanistan's Reconstruction: The Challenges and Critical Dilemmas." *Third World Quarterly*, Vol. 23. No. 5 (October, 2002): 801–16.

Batricia, Gossman. "Afghanistan in the Balance." *Middle East Report*, No. 221 (Winter, 2001): 8–15.

Bearden, Milton. "Afghanistan: Graveyard of Empires." *Foreign Affairs*, Vol. 80, No. 6 (Nov./Dec. 2001): 13–30.

Benini, Aldo A. and Lawrence H. Moulton. "Civilian Victims in an Asymmetrical Conflict: Operation Enduring Freedom, Afghanistan." *Journal of Peace Research*, Vol. 41, No. 4 (July, 2004): 403–22.

Benjamin E. Goldsmith, Yasaku Horiuchi, and Takasashi Inoguchi. "American Foreign Policy and Global Opinion: Who Supported the War in Afghanistan?" *Journal of Conflict Resolution*, Vol. 49, No. 3 (June, 2005): 408–29.

Biddle, D. Stephen. "Allies, Airpower, and Modern Warfare: The Afghan Model in Afghanistan and Iraq." *International Security*, Vol. 30, No. 3 (Winter, 2005): 161–76.

Boot, Max. "The American Way of War." *Foreign Affairs*, Vol. 82, No. 4 (July/August, 2003): 41–58.

Brown-Felbab, Vanda. "Afghanistan: When Counternarcotics Undermines Counterterrorism." *The Washington Quarterly*, Vol. 28. No. 4 (Autumn, 2005): 55–72.

Chard, Margaret and Sultan Barakat. "Theories, Rhetoric and Practice: Recovering the Capacities of War-Worn Societies." *Third World Quarterly*, Vol. 23, No. 5 (October, 2002): 817–35.

Chopra, Jarta and Alexander Thier. "The Road Ahead: Political and Institutional Reconstruction in Afghanistan." *Third World Quarterly*, Vol. 23. No. 5 (October, 2002): 893–907.

Cohen, Craig and Derek Chollet. "When $10 Billion Is Not Enough: Rethinking U.S. Strategy Toward Pakistan." *The Washington Quarterly*, Vol. 30, No. 2 (Spring, 2007): 7–19.

Constable, Pameela. "A Wake-Up Call in Afghanistan." *Journal of Democracy*, Vol. 18, No. 2 (April, 2007).

Cullather, Nick. "Damming Afghanistan: Modernization in a Buffer State." *Journal of American History*, Vol. 89. No. 2 (September, 2002): 512–37.

Dai Yu, Shen "China and Afghanistan." *The China Quarterly*, No. 25, (January/March, 1966): 213–21.

Drumbl, A. Mark "The Taliban's 'Other' Crimes." *Third World Quarterly*, Vol. 23, No. 6 (December, 2002): 1121–43.

Dupree, L. "A New Decade of Daoud? AUFS Reports Service." *South Asian Series*, Vol. 18, No. 8 (1974).

Dupree, L. "Afghanistan and the Unpaved Road to Democracy." *Journal of the Royal Central Asian Society*, Vol. 56, No. 3 (1971).

Edwards, David B. "Afghanistan, Ethnography, and the New World Order." *Cultural Anthropology*, Vol. 9, No. 3 (August, 1994): 345–60.

Edwards, David B. "Summoning Muslims: Print, Politics, and Religious Ideology in Afghanistan." *The Journal of Asian Studies*, Vol. 52, No. 3 (August, 1993): 609–28.

Fielden, M. B. "The Geopolitics of Aid: the Provision and Termination of Aid to Afghan Refugees in North West Frontier Province, Pakistan." *Political Geography*, Vol. 17, No. 4 (1998): 87–95.

Frank, Peter G. "Economic Planner in Afghanistan." *Economic Development and Cultural Change*, Vol. 1, No. 5 (Feb. 1953): 323–40.

Fuller, Graham E. "The Emergence of Central Asia." *Foreign Policy*, No. 78 (Spring, 1990): 49–67.

Ganguly, Sumit. "India and Pakistan in the Shadow of Afghanistan." *Current History*, Vol. 55, No. 2 (Spring, 2002): 245–74.

Ghufran, Nasreen. "The Taliban and the Civil War Entanglement in Afghanistan." *Asian Survey*, Vol. 41, No. 3 (May, 2001): 462–87.

Goodhand, Jonathan. "Aiding Violence and Building Peace: The Role of International Aid in Afghanistan." *Third World Quarterly*, Vol. 23, No. 5 (October, 2002): 817–35.

Goodhand, Jonathan, Christopher Cramer. "Try Again, Fail Again, Fail Better? War, the State and the 'Post-Conflict' Challenge in Afghanistan." *Development and Change*, Vol. 33, Issue 5 (November, 2002): 885–909.

Goodson, Larry P. "Afghanistan in 2004: Electoral Progress and an Opium Boom." *Asian Survey*, Vol. 45, No. 1 (January/February, 2005): 88–97.

Goodson, Larry P. "Afghanistan's Long Road Reconstruction." *Journal of Democracy*, Vol. 14, No. 1 (January, 2003): 82–99.

Gossman, Patricia. "Afghanistan in the Balance." *Middle East Report*, No. 221 (Winter, 2001): 3–26.

Grinter, Lawrence E. "The United States and South Asia: New Challenges, New Opportunities." *Asian Affairs* (Summer, 1993): 101–19.

Guha, A. "The Economy of Afghanistan During Amanullah's Reign, 1910–1929." *International Studies*, Vol. 9, No. 2 (1967).

Halliday, F. and Z. Tanin, "The Communist Regime in Afghanistan 1978–1992: Institutions and Conflicts." *Europe–Asia Studies*, Vol. 50, No. 8 (1998).

Haq, Ikram. "Pak-Afghan Drug Trade in Historical Perspective." *Asian Survey*, Vol. 36, No. 10 (October, 1996): 945–63.

Harpviken, Berg Kristian. "Breaking New Ground: Afghanistan's Response to Landmine and Unexploded Ordnance." *Third World Quarterly*, Vol. 23. No. 5 (October, 2002): 931–43.

Hasan, K. "Pakistan-Afghanistan Relations." *Asian Survey*, Vol. 2, No. 7 (1962).

Hastert, Paul L. "Operation Anaconda: Perception Meets Reality in the Hills of Afghanistan." *Studies in Conflict & Terrorism*, Vol. 28, No. 1 (January 2005): 11–22.

Horn, Robert C. "Afghanistan and the Soviet-Indian Influence Relationship." *Asian Survey*, Vol. 23, No. 3 (March, 1983): 244–60.

Horsman, S. "Uzbekistan's Involvement in the Tajik Civil War 1992–1997: Domestic Consideration." *Central Asian Survey*, Vol. 18, No. 1 (1999).

Hupe-Robert Strausz. "Politics of the Afghan Resistance Movement: Cleavages, Disunity, and Fragmentation." *Asian Survey*, Vol. 31. No. 6 (June, 1991): 479–95.

Jalali, Ali A. "Afghanistan in 2002: The Struggle to Win the Peace." *Asian Survey*, Vol. 43, No. 1 (January, 2003): 174–85.

Khalilzad, Zalmay. "Afghanistan in 1994: Civil War and Disintegration." *Asian Survey*, Vol. 35, No. 2, Survey of Asia in 1994: Part 1.

Khanna, Ranjana. "Taking a Stand for Afghanistan: Women and the Left." Vol. 28, No. 1, *Gender and Cultural Memory* (Autumn, 2002).

Khurshid, Hassan. "Pakistan-Afghanistan Relations." *Asian Survey*, Vol. 2, No. 7 (September, 1962): 14–24.

Kuperman, Alan J. "The Stinger Missile and U.S. Intervention in Afghanistan." *Political Science Quarterly*, Vol. 114, No. 2 (Summer, 1999): 219–63.

Laporte, Robert, Jr. "Pakistan in 1996: Starting Over Again." *Asian Survey*, Vol. 37, No. 2, *A Survey of Asia in 1996: Part II* (Feb. 1997): 118–25.

Leslie, Jolyon and Johnson, Chris. "Afghans Have Their Memories: A Reflection on the Recent Experience of Assistance in Afghanistan." *Third World Quarterly*, Vol. 23. No. 5 (October, 2002): 661–874.

Maass, C.D. "The Afghanistan Conflict: External Involvement." *Central Asian Survey*, Vol. 18, No. 1 (1999).

Magnus, Ralph H. "Afghanistan in 1996: Year of the Taliban." *Asian Survey*, Vol. 37, No. 2, *A Survey of Asia in 1996: Part 1*.

Maley, W. "Afghanistan Observed." *Australian Journal of International Affairs*, Vol. 51, No. 2 (1997).

———. "The Dynamics of Regime Transition in Afghanistan." *Central Asian Survey*, Vol. 16, No. 2 (1997).

———. "Mine Action in Afghanistan." *Refuge*, Vol. 17, No. 4 (October 1998).

Maley, William. "The Future of Islamic Afghanistan." *Security Dialogue*, Vol. 24 (December 1993): 383–96.

———. "Political Legitimization in Contemporary Afghanistan." *Asian Survey*, Vol. 27, No. 6 (June, 1987): 705–25.

Malik, Iftkhar H. "Pakistan in 2001: The Afghan Crisis and the Rediscovery of the Frontline State." *Asian Survey*, Vol. 42, No. 1, *A Survey of Asia in 2001* (January/February 2002): 204–12.

Mangnus, Ralph H. "Afghanistan in 1997: The War Moves North." *Asian Survey*, Vol. 38, No. 2, *A Survey of Asia in 1997: Part II*, (February, 1998): 109–15.

Matinuddin, Kamal. "Post-9/11 Afghanistan." *South Asian Journal*, Issue 3 (January/March, 2004): 107–19.

Miles, M. "Disability and Afghan Reconstruction: Some Policy Issues." *Disability, Handicap & Society*, Vol. 5. (1990): 257–67.

Miles, M. "Formal and Informal Disability Resources for Afghan Reconstruction." *Third World Quarterly*, Vol. 23, No. 5 (October, 2002): 945–59.

Mukherjee, Dilip. "Afghanistan under Daud: Relations with Neighboring States." *Asian Surevy*, Vol. 15, No. 4 (April, 1975): 301–12.

Naby, Eden, Ralph, Magnus H. "Afghanistan and Central Asia: Mirrors and Models." *Asian Survey*, Vol. 35, No. 7 (July, 1995): 621–34.

Newman, Joseph, Jr. "The Future of Northern Afghanistan." *Asian Survey*, Vol. 28, No. 7 (July, 1988): 729–39.

Ottaway, Marina. "Nation Building." *Foreign Policy*, No.132 (Sep./Oct. 2002): 16–24.

Ozerdem, Alpaslan. "Disarmament, Demoblisation and Reintegration of Former Combatants in Afghan: Lessons Learned from a Cross-Cultural Perspective." *Third World Quarterely*, Vol. 23, No. 5 (October, 2002): 961–89.

Payind, Alam. "Evolving Alternative Views on the Future of Afghanistan: An Afghan Perspective." *Asian Survey*, Vol. 33, No. 9 (September, 1993): 923–31.

Prados, John. "Notes on the CIA's Secret War in Afghanistan." *Journal of American History*, Vol. 89, No. 2 (September, 2002): 466–71.

Qurashi, S. M. M. "Pakhtunistan: The Frontier Dispute between Afghanistan and Pakistan." *Pacific Affairs*, Vol. 39, No. ? (Spring, 1966): 99–114.

Rais, Rasul Bakhsh. "Afghanistan and the Regional Powers." *Asian Survey*, Vol. 33, No. 9 (Sep. 1993): 905–22.

Reiter, Dan, and Stam Allan. "Democracy, War Initiation and Victory." *American Political Science Review*, Vol. 92, No. 2, (June, 1998): 377–89.

Rohall, David E. Marten G. Ender, and Michael D. Matthew. "The Effects of Military Affiliation, Gender, and Political Ideology on Attitudes toward the Wars in Afghanistan and Iraq." *Armed Forces & Society*, Vol. 33, No. 1 (October 2006): 59–77.

Rubin, Barnett. "Women and Pipelines: Afghanistan's Proxy Wars." *International Affairs*, Vol. 73, No. 2 (1997): 283–96.

———. "Political Elites in Afghanistan: Rentier State Building, Rentire State Wrecking." *International Journal of Middle East Studies* (Feb. 1992): 77–99.

———. "Post-Cold War State Disintegration: The Failure of International Conflict Resolution in Afghanistan." *Journal of International Affairs* (Winter 1993): 486–87.

———. "Lineages of the State in Afghanistan." *Asian Survey*, Vol. 28, No. 11 (November, 1988): 1188–1209.

———. "Afghanistan in 1993: Abandoned but Surviving." *Asian Survey*, Vol. 34, No. 2, *A Survey of Asia in 1993: Part 1*.

———. "The Political Economy of War and Peace in Afghanistan." *World Development*, Vol. 28, No. 10 (2000): 1789–1830.

———. "Rebuilding Afghanistan: The Folly of Stateless Democracy." *Current History*, Vol. 103. No. 672 (April, 2004): 165–70.

———. "Saving Afghanistan." *Foreign Affairs*, Vol. 86, No.1 (Jan/Feb 2007): 57–57.

Rubin, Barnett R. and Armstrong, Andrea. "Regional Issues in the Reconstruction of Afghanistan." *World Policy Journal*, Vol. 20, No. 1 (Spring, 2003): 31–30.

Saikal, A. "Afghanistan: Culture and Ideology under Pre-1978 Governments." *Central Asian Surevy*, Vol. 11, No. 1 (1992).

———. "The UN and Afghanistan: A Case of Failed Peacemaking Intervention." *International Peacekeeping*, Vol. 3, No. 1 (Spring, 1996).

———. "Afghanistan's Ethnic Conflicts." *Survival*, Vol. 40, No. 2 (Summer 1998).

———. "The Role of Outside Actors in Afghanistan." *Middle East Policy*, Vol. 7, No. 4. (October 2000).

Segal, Gerald. "China and Afghanistan." *Asian Survey*, Vol. 21, No. 11 (November, 1981): 1158–74.

Shadid, Anthony. "The Shape of Afghanistan to Come." *Middle East Report*, No. 2 (Spring, 2002): 14–15.

Shahrani, Nazif. "Resisting the Taliban and Talibanism in Afghanistan: Legacies of a Century of Internal Colonialism and Cold War Politics in a Buffer State." *Perceptions: Journal of International Affairs*, Vol. 4 (2002): 121–40.

Shahrani, Nazif M. "War, Factionalism, and State in Afghanistan." *American Anthropologist*, Vol. 104, No. 3 (Sep. 2002): 715–22.

Siakal, Amin. "Afghanistan, Terrorism and American Australian Responses." *Journal of International Affairs*, Vol. 56, No. 1 (April, 2003): 23–30.

———. "Securing Afghanistan's Border." *Survival*, Vol. 48, No. 1 (Spring, 2006): 129–42.

Stork, Joe. "U.S. Involvement in Afghanistan." *MERIP Reporters*, No. 89, *Afghanistan* (July, 1980): 2–26.

Suhrke, Astri. "Afghanistan: Retribalization of the War." *Journal of Peace Research*, Vol. 27, No. 3 (August, 1990): 241–46.

Suhrke, Astri, Berg, Harpviken, Kristian and Arne Stran. "After Bonn: Conflict Peace Building." *Third World Quarterly*, Vol. 23, No. 5 (October, 2002): 875–91.

Sullivan, Daniel. "Tinder, Spark, Oxygen, and Fuel: The Mysterious Rise of the Taliban." *Journal of Peace Research*, Vol. 44, No. 1 (January, 2007): 93–108.

Talal, Hassan Bin. "Afghanistan: Parallels and Anti-Parallels." *Perceptions: Journal of International Affairs*, Vol. 8, No. 1 (March–May, 2002): 5–20.

Tapper, Richard. "Tribal Societies and Its Enemies." *RAIN*, No. 34 (Oct. 1979): 6–7.

Thesiger, Wilfred. "The Hazaras of Central Afghanistan." *The Geographical Journal*, Vol. 121, No. 3 (September, 1955): 312–19.

Tier, Alexander and Chopra, Jarat. "The Road Ahead: Political and Institutional Reconstrution in Afghanistan." *Third World Quarterly*, Vol. 23, No. 5 (October, 2002): 893–907.

Vayrynen, Raimo. "Afghanistan." *Journal of Peace Research*, Vol. 17, No. 2, Special Issue on Imperialism and Militarization (1980): 93–102.

Wardell, Gareth and Sultan, Barakat. "Exploited by Whom? An Alternative Perspective on Humanitarian Assistance to Afghan Women." *Third World Quarterly*, Vol. 23. No. 5 (October 2002): 909–30.

Weinbaum, Marvin G. "Pakistan and Afghanistan: The Strategic Relationship." *Asian Survey*, Vol. 31, No. 6 (June, 1991): 496–511.

Weinberger, Naomi. "Civil Military Coordination in Peace Building: The Challenge in Afghanistan." *Journal of International Affairs*, Vol. 55, No. 2 (Spring, 2002): 245–74.

Zelier, Barbie. "Death in Wartime: Photographs and the 'Other War' in Afghanistan." *Harvard International Journal of Press/Politics*, Vol. 10, No. 3 (July, 2005): 26–55.

Index

About the Author

Rasul Bakhsh Rais is professor of political science in the Department of Social Sciences, Lahore University of Management Sciences. Dr. Rais has a Ph.D. in political science from University of California–Santa Barbara. Before joining LUMS, he served as professor/director of the Area Study Centre and prior to that was associate professor in the Department of International Relations, Quaid-i-Azam University, Islamabad, for nearly twenty-two years. He was professor of Pakistan Studies at Columbia University, New York, for three years, from 1991–1994. He took a Fulbright fellowship at Wake Forest University, 1997–1998, Social Science Research Council fellowship at Harvard, 1989–1990, and a Rockefeller Foundation fellowship in International Relations at the University of California–Berkeley, 1985–1985. He is author of *War Without Winners: Afghanistan's Uncertain Transition after the Cold War* (Oxford University Press, 1996); *Indian Ocean and the Superpowers: Economic, Political and Strategic Perspectives* (Croom Helm, London, 1986), and editor of *State, Society and Democratic Change in Pakistan* (Oxford University Press, 1997). He has published widely in professional journals on political and security issues pertaining to South Asia, the Indian Ocean, and Afghanistan.